(01466) 805516.

Writing
Under Control

SECOND EDITION

JUDITH GRAHAM AND ALISON KELLY

Published in association with University of Surrey Roehampton

 David Fulton Publishers

David Fulton Publishers Ltd
The Chiswick Centre, 414 Chiswick High Road W4 5TF

www.fultonpublishers.co.uk
www.onestopeducation.co.uk

David Fulton Publishers is a division of Granada Learning Limited, part of ITV plc.

First edition published in Great Britain by David Fulton Publishers 1998
Second edition published in 2003, reprinted 2004(twice), 2005
10 9 8 7 6 5 4

Note: The right of Judith Graham and Alison Kelly to be identified as the editors of this work has been asserted by them in accordance with the Copyright, Designs and Patents Act 1988.

Copyright © Judith Graham and Alison Kelly 2003

British Library Cataloguing in Publication Data
A catalogue record for this book is available from the British Library.

ISBN 1 84312 017 8

Typeset by FiSH Books, London
Printed and bound in Great Britain

Contents

Contributors

Rebecca Bunting is Pro-Rector (academic) at University College Northampton. Her research interests include teacher development, literacy and educational linguistics. She is co-editor of the journal *Education through Partnership* and author of *Teaching about Language in the Primary School* (David Fulton).

Fiona M. Collins is Principal Lecturer and coordinator of English Education at the University of Surrey Roehampton. Her research interests are in children's literature, popular culture and visual literacy. She co-edited *Historical Fiction for Children* and contributed to a QCA project looking at progression and assessment in children's writing.

Judith Graham was Principal Lecturer English Education at the University of Surrey Roehampton with interests and teaching commitments in all areas of literacy and children's literature. Her previous teaching has been in inner London schools, at the Institute of Education and at the University of Greenwich. She is the author of *Pictures on the Page, Cracking Good Books* (both NATE) and co-editor of *Reading Under Control* (David Fulton).

Alison Kelly is Senior Lecturer in English Education at the University of Surrey Roehampton. She worked for many years as a primary teacher in London as a class teacher, a peripatetic teacher for Traveller families and an advisory teacher for language. She teaches on undergraduate, postgraduate and Inset courses and her current interests include poetry. She co-edited *Reading Under Control* (David Fulton) and writes teaching materials for Scholastic Publications.

Liz Laycock has been involved in primary education for several decades as a classroom teacher, an advisory teacher and in higher education and initial teacher education. She was Programme Convener for Primary PGCE and Director of Initial Teacher Education Programmes. She is a contributor to *The Literate Classroom, Historical Fiction for Children* and *Education in the United Kingdom* (all David Fulton). She also writes literacy materials for Scholastic Publications.

Pat Pinsent was for many years Principal Lecturer in English and is now a Senior Research Fellow at University of Surrey Roehampton. She is involved in the Distance Learning mode of the MA in Children's Literature. Current research interests include children's literature, poetry and equality issues. Her publications include *The Power of the Page* and *Children's Literature and the Politics of Equality* (both David Fulton).

Cathy Svensson is a Senior Lecturer in English Education at the University of Surrey Roehampton. For many years she was a Special Needs Coordinator and classroom teacher in a Richmond beacon school. She has extensive experience in both special and mainstream primary teaching. She has been and remains involved in teaching on specialist dyslexia courses. Her particular interests are in dyslexia, whole school assessment procedures and the early years.

Anne Washtell is Senior Lecturer in English Education at the University of Surrey Roehampton where she contributes to all language and literacy courses. She is interested in many aspects of children's early literacy development including the role of names in both reading and writing. Children with literacy difficulties and the writing that children do outside school are other current areas of interest.

Preface

At the start of the twenty first century literacy and the school's role in teaching literacy are enjoying the highest profile. All but a handful of schools in the country operate a daily Literacy Hour in which the explicit teaching of reading and writing takes place. In our book, *Reading Under Control*, we examined the teaching of reading, its history, its methods, its routines, resources and recurring issues. This companion volume does the same for writing which, as a process, develops alongside reading, provided that both are taught and supported as rewarding, meaningful and purposeful activities. Many physical, cognitive and affective demands are made on children as they develop as writers and we inspect all the various elements in this book. Teachers and student teachers should be strengthened in their understanding of how writing can be taught and valued, and they should be enabled to create a breadth and variety of writing experiences.

The contributors have been able to include accounts of teachers and children at work thanks to examples supplied by their students, their colleagues, and classroom teachers with whom they have worked. In particular they would like to thank Sarah Arscott, Jan Avery, Angela Buckle, Karin Doull, Gaye Grundy, Ruth Hunter, Gail Kelly, Fiona Kemp, Alexandra Law, Jeune Persaud, Heidi McCluskey, Susie Midgeley, Sue Robson, Sue Smedley, Alison Townsend, Geraldine Woods and the teachers at Horn Park and Cardwell Schools, Greenwich. We are also most grateful to Maggie Hancock.

We apologise for not attributing the dictation passage which occurs on page vii. We have been unable to locate its source.

And thanks also to Conrad Guettler and Mark Pawley for patient support and unflagging interest.

Judith Graham and Alison Kelly
University of Surrey Roehampton
February 2003

Introduction

A teacher dictates this passage to his class of 80 nine-year-olds:

> While hewing yews, Hugh lost his ewe
> And put it in the hue and cry.
> You brought the ewe back by and by
> And only begged the hewer's ewer,
> Your hands to wash in water pure.

The children write carefully in their copybooks using copperplate handwriting. Older children – monitors – walk up and down the rows to check that the children are working hard and sitting up straight.

This is what a writing lesson might have looked like one hundred years ago when learning to write consisted of imitating adult models – copying or tracing letters, memorising spellings, and transcribing passages from the Bible, Latin grammar or, for light relief, Aesop's fables. Younger children would write on slates so their efforts were no sooner accomplished than they had to be rubbed out in readiness for the next exercise. The nearest the children got to their own compositions is described by Sybil Marshall:

> The teacher showed the children an object of some sort, and from the entire class, ranged in their rows of desks before her, she elicited 'facts' about the object which could then be written down, e.g. 'We have a plum. The plum is red. It has a stone. The plum grew on a tree.' The sentences, composed by the teacher from the children's hesitant observations, were then written by her on the blackboard, from where the children copied them in whatever form of script they had been taught to write.
> (1974, p. 2)

Now, take a leap forward one hundred years. A Reception class has been visited by a storyteller. One of her stories is a Native American creation tale about how the sun came into existence. Later, Matthew (age 5) dictates a story of his own to his teacher which she writes down for him:

> Once upon a time there was no such thing as a dog. There were just dogfish alive, until one day a dogfish came out of the sea and it started to live on land. While he was living on land some very peculiar things happened. He started to change. Instead of scales, it was fur. Instead of no neck, it had one. Instead of flippers, it had a tail. Instead of fins, it had legs. Until one day he was a dog! This way life on earth has developed ever since.

Despite the role reversal, both the Victorian teacher dictating and the contemporary teacher taking dictation could be described as being 'in control' of the teaching of writing. Both based their practice on prevailing views of the writing process, of the nature of learning and of the relationship between child and adult. The Victorian teacher would have believed that 'We must not expect young people to invent matter, what they write should be infused into them' (John Walker 1801, in a book for teachers, cited in Michael 1987; p. 313), and his concern would have been to give children adult models to imitate with an emphasis on correct spelling, handwriting and grammar. The contemporary teacher is just as concerned that her children use these aspects correctly, but knows too that composing is important and is giving her young writer the opportunity to compose with greater fluency than he would achieve if left to transcribe by himself. Early behaviourist thinking lies behind the often punitive Victorian regimes, where wrong spellings or poor handwriting could lead to the ultimate negative reinforcer – the cane. The contemporary teacher's interaction with a younger child suggests a more collaborative enterprise, where her adult model of expertise is still privileged but where it is exercised in a way that empowers the younger writer. The point is that we know much more now about the writing process and about the learner, and we bring this to bear on our teaching. Chapters 1 and 2 of this book chart the developing understanding about writing which has moulded the ways we teach writing.

We write this at a time when multiple changes have occurred in the teaching of literacy in primary schools. The framework of the *National Literacy Strategy* introduced in 1998 takes the National Curriculum for English as its starting point and goes on to prescribe exactly what we should teach and when; never before has the teaching of writing (and reading) been so externally controlled. There are many rich and imaginative suggestions for work and you will find that we make close links with these and the framework throughout the book. However, there are points to be made here about such tight external control – one potential hazard is that it may actually be disempowering for teachers as it can take away the need to rationalise and stand back from practice. An imposed framework tells us what we 'should' be doing, which is always superficially attractive but, in the process, it takes away the need for analytic thinking about what we practise. The changes that Pat Pinsent and Rebecca Bunting describe in their chapters came about partly because of the critical inspections teachers gave their own work in the light of new research. We would not want to lose sight of the role teachers and researchers have always had in shaping and understanding good literacy practice.

In *Reading Under Control* (2000) we said that 'control in any area springs from a secure understanding of processes and enabling practices'; it is this belief that motivates the structure and content of *Writing Under Control* and we suggest that such a feeling of control is more important than ever today. After the historic update provided by Chapters 1 and 2, we move firmly into the early twenty-first century classroom with an account of the many different writing routines that are needed for the effective teaching of writing. In this chapter, Anne Washtell links these routines with the *NLS* framework and materials and includes discussion of the resources teachers need as well. She also makes important points about the role of parents in children's writing lives. The next two chapters tackle the two distinct aspects of the writing process: composition and transcription. In Chapter 4, Fiona Collins looks at the demands of narrative, nonnarrative and poetry writing and describes ways of supporting and scaffolding children's understanding of the complexities of composition. In Chapter 5, Alison Kelly looks in detail at the three separate aspects of transcription: spelling, punctuation and handwriting. Liz Laycock's chapter shows how crucial close observation, analysis and assessment are in shaping teaching, monitoring progress and setting targets. She adds an informative section on National Curriculum assessments. In Chapter 7, Judith Graham draws the threads of the book together through its analysis of differences in the writing from children with literacy difficulties, gifted writers, boys and girls, and children with English as an additional language.

In a chapter new to this edition, Cathy Svensson offers two case studies of children with the specific learning difficulty, dyslexia. The detail she offers illuminates areas including what is meant by an inclusive classroom and an Individual Education Plan.

This book offers another framework then, one which is clearly linked with the *National Curriculum* and the *NLS* framework, but which is intended to offer you, the teacher or prospective teacher, a sense of control in all aspects of the teaching of writing. This sense of control is one which is achieved through clear understanding of all of the above; it is about knowing where we have come from in the teaching of writing and of how current views have shaped and changed practice. It should also arm you in readiness for any new initiatives that may be on their way!

There is another kind of knowledge that is important too; personal control also comes about when we feel confident about the subject we are teaching. An important strand of this book deals with the subject knowledge teachers need, at their own level, to inform their planning and assessment.

A confident grasp of the following will empower your teaching:

- the nature and role of standard English   Chapters 2, 6, 7
- word level knowledge   Chapters 5, 6, 7, 8
- sentence level knowledge   Chapters 2, 4, 5, 6, 7
- text level knowledge   Chapters 2, 4, 6

Chapter 5 also contains glossaries which will help you with technical terms.

Recent developments focus teachers' attention on individual components of the teaching of writing and there is a risk that more global considerations about writing become obscured. In our work with student teachers, we often gather writing histories in which our students attribute their writing confidence and competence as writers to such experiences as: a teacher becoming excited or informed by a piece of their writing; a teacher setting up a dialogue in writing with them enabling the work to be extended over a long period ('interactive writing'); the incentive of a diary or attractive notebook for private writing; the realisation that writing can, on some occasions, meet a creative need such as might equally be met by making a painting or a piece of music; the excitement of seeing ideas come forth as you write; the understanding that writing can, at difficult times, serve as a solace and an outlet for strong feelings; the satisfaction of seeing a piece through to a perfect end product and the reward of having others respond to and appreciate our work. These personal revelations about the role and power of writing are very relevant to your appreciation of the writing process and should frame and inform the reading of this book.

For children to be in control of writing a confident grasp of all aspects of the writing process is needed and this is why we are so insistent that an important strand of teaching writing is developing a healthy curiosity about language. Such curiosity should be fostered both with regard to the shapes and features of texts (narrative, non-narrative etc., Chapter 4), and with regard to the transcriptional aspect of writing (spelling, punctuation and handwriting, Chapter 5). We want children to delight in the curiosities and challenges of our spelling and punctuation systems rather than be fearful or inhibited by them. A prevailing theme of the book is ensuring that our teaching leaves children clearly free to attend to particular aspects of the writing, whether this is attention needed for developing the structure of a story, character delineation, sentence construction or appropriate punctuation.

As in *Reading Under Control*, our preoccupation is with good teaching and with doing the very best possible work with children. Learning to write is an extraordinary feat and, as children become writers, we get glimpses of them at their most active, creative and imaginative. Children can surprise and delight us, as they learn that writing enables them to 'create worlds' (Smith 1984; p. 152). The Dogfish story (p. vii) contains many different influences, ranging from the traditional story Matthew had heard in school to the final line which he told his teacher he had heard on a video soundtrack. Yet its freshness both startles and engages the reader. When children discover that they can create such 'secondary worlds' then it is their turn to feel in control and empowered.

CHAPTER 1

From Copying to Creation: the teaching of Writing before the 1980s

Pat Pinsent

TEACHING WRITING BEFORE 1960

Let us look at the experience of an imaginary English teacher – Mary Angell – who was born in the 1930s. Her early schooling, broken up by the Second World War, included such things as making many copies of 'headlines' in a copperplate hand. The intention of this (which seldom succeeded) was to inculcate handwriting skills, but the process also provided unwanted and decontextualised information, such as 'Linseed oil is derived from flax'. The whole process certainly conveyed the lesson that copying from adult models was the way to learn. This was supported by copying passages from books chosen by the teacher, and reproducing from memory stories read to the class. Twenty years earlier there had been isolated, more imaginative initiatives such as that quoted by Shayer (1972) of a teacher who said, 'The best way, indeed the only way, to learn to write is to try to write'. He went on to provide interesting assignments like describing a sea-monster (p. 81) but if Mary's teachers had heard about these they gave no indication of this in their lessons.

At grammar school, Mary's English education was extended by grammatical exercises and the requirement to write compositions about abstract topics such as 'Patriotism' or letters to non-existent recipients about holidays which did not take place. Comprehension, précis, and accurate renditions of literary texts selected for examination rounded off the English curriculum. Mary therefore internalised the message that correct set pieces were what mattered.

When she went to college in September 1953, to be trained as a teacher on a two year course, Mary received conflicting messages. It was difficult to reconcile the narrow approach of 'Methods' (practical teaching approaches) courses with the kind of 'child-centred' approach which was beginning to appear in Educational Studies (educational theory). One of her assessed essays had been based on a quotation from Robert Browning:

> ... To know
> rather consists in opening out a way
> whence the imprisoned splendour may escape,
> than in effecting entry for a light
> supposed to be without ...
> (Paracelsus 1835: I)

You may recognise this as a poetic 'empty vessels' type of argument!

Mary started work in a secondary modern school with many naive hopes about her career but little firm grasp of how to teach her subject, as what she had learnt at college tended to replicate the way she had been taught herself. The kind of English teaching expected from her gave little credence to her pupils' bringing with them to school any kind of inner light, or even any kind of knowledge about life or the writing process. The sole audience for writing in school was the teacher, and so little were the results valued that exercise books, once full, landed in the wastepaper basket. Mary felt that if she had been teaching younger children, there might have been more opportunity to liberate her pupils' 'imprisoned splendour'. In fact, there were very similar pressures in primary school (with the eleven-plus examination) and no greater understanding of children's development as writers.

CREATIVE WRITING

In 1963, Mary, now Mrs Bright, returned to teaching after six years of bringing up her own children. She found herself readily welcomed, despite her secondary background, in the local primary school. Confessing herself out of touch, even in her own subject, she was heartened to read Sybil Marshall's *Experiment in Education* (1963) which had just been published. Marshall describes teaching in a village school during and after the Second World War. She discovered, while teaching in a cross-curricular way which combined music, art and writing, that the quality of the children's work in all these areas was greatly improved. Mary recognised how the ideals of educational theory which she had found exciting in her Educational Studies initial training, and which had been fortified by her experience with her own young children, could be brought to life in the classroom.

At this period, 'creative writing', under various names, was in full swing in primary schools. Over the next few years Mary read and implemented with enthusiasm the recommendations of Margaret Langdon (1961), Boris Ford (1963), Sheila Lane and Marion Kemp (1967) and many others. The title of Alec Clegg's book, *The Excitement of Writing* (1964), conveyed the enthusiasm these writers brought to their subject, and, as in the other books, it also included a collection of children's own work, showing the immense potential of child writers. David Holbrook's *English for the Rejected* (1964) gave an account of amazing results achieved with young people who had been written off by society. All the books abounded in ideas of how to foster similar qualities in other young writers. Basil Maybury's *Creative Writing for Juniors* (1967) advocated working through sense stimuli of touch, sight and taste to encourage writing. He suggested using, for instance, music as a stimulus, blowing bubbles or, more daringly, setting fire to paper.

Behind much of this creative writing was more general theory. Sybil Marshall, who later became Reader in Education at Sussex University, acknowledges in *Creative Writing* (1974) being influenced by Suzanne Langer, on whose work Marshall's definition of creative writing is based. She says creativity is 'the ability to create one's own symbols of experience: creative writing is the use of written language to conceptualise, explore and record experience in such a way as to create a unique symbolisation of it.' (p. 10).

Mary sometimes found it difficult to avoid the creative writing lesson falling into a limited pattern like, 'Listen to this music … what does it make you feel … now write a story … ' Nor did she feel comfortable criticising writing which clearly came out of the children's feelings. Sometimes the results were not very interesting and she wondered if she really was using the best way of drawing out the children's own experience, let alone building on it. It was difficult for someone not trained in psychoanalysis to be alert to the 'symbolic meaning', to how 'children's creative work symbolises … the quest for integration of the identity … ' (Holbrook 1967). She knew too that she should not neglect the tools of the trade like spelling and handwriting and had to admit that her pupils' strengths in writing stories and poems might not always help them much in the more subject based curriculum of the secondary school, nor, indeed, with the practical written demands of life.

LANGUAGE AND LEARNING

It was partly because of feelings of inadequacy in this area, and partly to increase her professional standing, that Mary took advantage of the Open University's scheme to award credit rating for previous study, thus facilitating non-graduate teachers obtaining a degree. Teachers were particularly encouraged to select courses relevant to their professional interests, so Mary chose 'Language and Learning'. The course reader was entitled *Language in Education* (Cashdan and Grugeon 1972) and among the papers included in it were several particularly relevant to the teaching of English. Mary read with interest James Britton's 'What's the use? A schematic account of language functions'. This article had a practical aim in mind, the classifying of 2000 pieces of writing from pupils aged 11 to 18, and it also was convincingly grounded in the earlier theoretical studies of Harding (1937), Langer (1951) and Moffett (1968). Although Britton's classroom based research was initially concerned with secondary school pupils, it was not long before its results filtered into primary schools by way of the Bullock Report, *A Language for Life* (1975).

The Bullock Report, which appeared in the concluding year of Mary's degree studies, became sacred scripture to Mary and her colleagues. The language functions identified by Britton and his team in 1972 were described thus in Bullock:

> The three main categories... are Transactional, Expressive and Poetic. The Expressive is the central one. It is language 'close to the speaker', often the language used by intimates in a shared context... it provides the tentative stage through which a pupil's new thinking must pass on its way to the comparative certainty of knowledge.
> (p. 165)

The Transactional mode is defined as using language with the intention of getting things done, as in advertisements or regulations, while the Poetic mode, not confined to poetry only, stands back from the subject described. Elsewhere in the Bullock Report, attention is given to the kind of audience for which children are writing (themselves, the teacher or the wider world). The recommendation is also made that pupils should have the opportunity to draft their work before submitting the finished article (pp. 166–7).

Mary began to incorporate a variety of different forms of writing that were not simply based on the expressive and sometimes poetic functions which she had up to now generally been demanding from her pupils. Rules about how to behave in school, advertisements for imaginary or even real products, accounts of events the children had experienced, all began to vie with story as outcomes of the English lesson. Her other lessons changed too. Instead of insisting that her top primary pupils write up scientific work in dictated formulae, she let them use an expressive mode to note for themselves what they had actually observed. She created opportunities for her children to write for real audiences. Like other teachers throughout the country, she encouraged her pupils to write to children in other schools, to local newspapers, to suppliers of educational material, as well as recognising the fact that they might well write for themselves alone, in personal journals which she promised she would not even attempt to look at unless invited.

Mary soon discovered that Britton's work was probably the best known out of a body of writing emanating from a number of educationalists influential in both initial and in-service teacher education. An account of the genesis of this movement was to be found in John Dixon's *Growth Through English*, first published in 1967 and reprinted many times. Based on a conference held for teachers of English in America and UK at Dartmouth, New England, in 1966, it presents the various paradigms of English teaching, the 'skills' model and the 'cultural heritage' model, before expressing its own endorsement of the 'personal growth' model, in which writing should express something that the writer feels is worth saying:

> Language is learnt in operation, not by dummy runs. In English, pupils meet to share their encounters with life . . . in ordering and composing situations that in some way symbolise life as we know it, we bring order and composure to our inner selves.
> (p. 13)

Mary and her colleagues were aware that some theorists such as Frank Whitehead (1978) did not welcome the approach of Britton and others to writing, but had she been asked her opinion she would have argued that the different functions had been very useful in extending the kinds of writing of her pupils, and their consciousness that they were writing for someone.

BEGINNING WRITING

Soon after completing her Open University degree in 1975, Mary found herself for the first time teaching a Reception class. At the same time, her taste for study had led her to start work on a Master's degree, so it seemed a natural development to look into the writing of these very young children. As someone initially trained for secondary teaching, she had always dreaded having, as she saw it, to impart so much basic knowledge to children who had not even made a start on literacy, so it came as something of a surprise to learn from the researchers, and from her own observations, that children in fact brought much more knowledge about writing into school than she had ever given them credit for. Margaret Clark's influential study of 32 children who were literate before going to school, *Young Fluent Readers* (1976), while focused predominantly on reading abilities, showed that many of these children were interested in writing even before they were four.

Mary was particularly fascinated by Marie Clay's *What Did I Write: Beginning Writing Behaviour* (1975), which charts the way in which children's earliest marks can be seen as representing discoveries of 'real' writing. These discoveries are only possible when the child sees people writing. Clay says:

> The linear scribble that fills the lines of a writing pad has, for the child, all the mystery of an unfamiliar code. It stands for a myriad of possible things but does not convey a particular message. The child seems to say 'I hope I've said something important. You must be able to understand what I've said. What did I write?'
> (p. 48)

Interpreting the 'linear scribble' of the five year olds in her class was both challenging and satisfying, but she wished she had known more about children's abilities when her own children had been young.

Mary also began to value the children's inventive attempts at spelling, and she learnt that as early as 1971, the research of Charles Read had explained how children use their awareness of the sounds of letters to enable them to write words without being explicitly taught by a teacher or parent. Carol Chomsky's 'Write now, read later' (1971), with its message that children could learn to read by creating their own spellings, was also congenial, particularly because it chimed in with her own discovery that young children could be helped towards reading by means of their own writing. An approach which recognised this was the 'Language Experience' approach which was published as

Breakthrough to Literacy (McKay *et al.* 1970). This material comprised plastic 'Sentence Makers' and little word cards which children could use to make their own line of writing, based on their own experience and what they said about it. Then they could transcribe it onto paper and draw a picture to go with it. She had seen it in use in other primary classrooms, but had some reservations about the repetitive sentence structures that emerged and the need to put all the little pieces back in the right places in their individual folders.

Mary's research and work with Reception class children had shown her that teaching writing and reading did not mean introducing them to something totally unfamiliar, but was a matter of helping them to build on what they already knew. She wanted her own small-scale research project to examine the nature of children's prior knowledge, so the kind of longitudinal study that Glenda Bissex had made of her own son in *GNYS AT WRK: a child learns to write and read* (1980) attracted her as a dissertation topic. The most important thing she had learned was never to underestimate young children.

Another revelation was the work of the Russian cognitive psychologist, Vygotsky, whose writings had been translated and published from 1962 onwards. On the subject of writing, Vygotsky was both provoking and illuminating. His account of the difficulties which young children face in learning to write made the process of teaching them seem almost impossible. The high level of abstraction required in order to 'replace words by images of words', to address 'an absent or imaginary person' without any real motivation, and to be aware of the necessary alphabetical symbols to put all this down on paper (1962: 98–9), sounded as if it was well beyond her pupils, and certainly gave her an understanding of why some of them found learning to write problematic. Yet elsewhere Vygotsky's explanation of the 'zone of proximal development' gave her more encouragement as it showed how children might in fact learn this difficult process. He says, 'What a child can do with assistance today she will be able to do by herself tomorrow' (1978: 87). Mary realised that she had often found herself assisting pupils with the beginnings of writing and noticed that they were on the verge of achieving independence but needed just that little extra guidance towards it. The 'zone of proximal development defines those functions that have not yet matured but are in the process of maturation' (1978: 86).

CHILDREN'S WRITING DEVELOPMENT

Having worked with the youngest and the oldest pupils in the primary school, Mary Bright was naturally interested in the ways in which children's writing developed, and what might be expected from them at different ages. She found the Crediton research project (1980), directed by Andrew Wilkinson, gave her some information. The team had investigated the writing abilities of children aged seven, ten and thirteen, using a framework for analysis based on stages of cognitive, affective, moral, and stylistic development abstracted from the theoretical work of Moffett (1968) and Britton (1982). While the categories Wilkinson provides were far too complex for daily use in the classroom, Mary found that looking at a few pieces of children's writing in detail was quite illuminating. She felt that any research which makes the teacher more aware of some of the factors entering into child writers' perceptions about what they are doing, what they want to do, and who they are writing for, provides a useful tool for the teacher. Wilkinson and his colleagues remark that the work of Britton has the limitation of perhaps over-stressing the cognitive aspect, and ignoring the many others which enter into the child's writing development. Wilkinson also reminds us that 'We need to make assessments of children's development in order to help them develop further. In other words, assessment is to be regarded rather as a teaching than as a measuring device' (pp. 223–4).

As Mary handed in her dissertation in 1980, she pondered many things. How she taught English now was a world away from the copying and conformity to adult models that had been part of her childhood. She knew much more of approaches which put the child at the heart of the process; she knew the pros and cons of creative writing; she found understanding of functions, forms, and audiences enriched the range and quality of writing in her classroom; she looked at her very youngest children's writing with new eyes and understood her supportive role more clearly; she knew how valuable it was to analyse closely individual pupils' writing.

She reflected too that she had learnt most about the teaching of writing by engaging in her own writing. Many theorists she had read seemed to pay relatively little attention to the writing process as experienced by adults. Perhaps that was something for the future.

Further reading

Allen, D. (1980) *English Teaching since 1965. How Much Growth?* London: Heinemann.
Marshall, S. (1963) *An Experiment in Education.* Cambridge: Cambridge University Press.

CHAPTER 2

From Process to Genre to Strategy: recent developments in the teaching of writing

Rebecca Bunting

This chapter discusses approaches to the teaching of writing in primary schools from the early 1980s to the early twenty-first century. It provides an overview of significant development which is necessarily selective and general, since a detailed historical survey of the period, with an account of why certain approaches and trends prevailed, would be the subject of an entire book.

The last twenty or so years have seen radical changes in the pedagogy of writing and resources for writing. In addition, rapid advances in ICT have challenged our views of how and why we write and have generated expectations on the part of children about how they will learn. There is frequently a gap between teachers' and children's ICT expertise which teachers can find disconcerting.

There has been a growing understanding about writing on the part of teachers and researchers, particularly in relation to the nature of the process of writing and the nature of writing itself. This period has also been the subject of controversy both about methodologies for teaching writing and about the very purposes of writing in school. Formerly it was teachers who exercised their professional judgement in the teaching of writing; now, writing is a focus of public debate, driven by economic and social concerns and regulated by public policy.

UNDERSTANDING THE PROCESS OF WRITING

Process writing

Copying and behaviourist approaches to writing have been replaced in recent times by an emphasis on the process of the writing rather than the end product. In a process approach, or process writing as it is has also been described, teachers recognise that much more attention should be paid to the development of a piece of writing, as writing is more than the simple eliciting of a product by the teacher; it is a process that involves thinking and shaping meaning. There are various stages to be gone through in the production of the final piece of writing and young writers need support with these stages. A process approach views children as authors and treats their written work as creative and, most importantly, meaningful. Children's difficulties are treated as normal writers' difficulties, rather than failures of ability: so, for example, errors and misunderstandings need to be worked on, as a professional writer would, rather than punished by the teacher's correcting pen. A process approach encourages children to take more responsibility for their own writing, including decisions about revisions, corrections and presentation. Graves (1981) uses a property image in arguing for this approach: he says that 'owners' of their work are far more likely to take care of their 'property' than those who 'rent' their work from the teacher, to whom it really belongs. This image conveys the importance of children's interest and engagement with the writing process.

Very important in a process approach is the distinction between the composition involved in writing and the transcriptional aspects of writing such as spelling, punctuation and handwriting. Smith (1982) relates the composition aspect to the role of the author, and the transcription aspect to that of the secretary, a useful distinction for the developing writer. Fluent writers can attend to both these aspects concurrently, though with different degrees of attention, whereas young writers, Smith argues, need to attend to composition first and transcription later. Both are necessary and important but teachers should not try to develop the transcriptional skills at the expense of encouraging thinking and composing skills. This philosophy is in complete contrast to an approach which requires children to labour at spelling and punctuation exercises before being allowed to do some independent writing.

A process approach often involves children reflecting on their own writing. This reflection could be on the content of the written product, such as commenting on why certain decisions were made about what to include in the writing, or on the actual process of writing, such as how an effort was consciously made to vary sentence length. Such reflection develops children's metacognitive awareness, that is, their conscious understanding of their learning, and their metalinguistic awareness, in that their understanding of language is foregrounded. The reflection is often achieved through the use of writing journals or writing partners, where children conduct dialogues with the teacher or their partner about their writing (see Chapter 3).

A process approach also involves strategic and supportive intervention by the teacher during the process of the writing, rather than the teacher sitting in judgement when it is all finished. Smith (1982), rather ghoulishly but appositely, describes the traditional marking of an end product as 'manicuring the corpse', trying to do something to improve the situation, make it look better, when it is too late. In this traditional model, children see writing as largely for assessment by the teacher, and they have only one attempt at the writing before handing it in, in what Richmond (1990) described as 'a fairground shooting game where you only have one shot'. These lessons about writing remain with us even much later in our lives, as Smith comments: 'Sitting on the shoulder of many writers is the wraith of a school teacher, waiting to jump on every fault of punctuation or spelling, on every infelicity of expression' (Smith 1982: 13).

One book in particular caught teachers' imaginations about the possibility of opening up the classroom as an environment to support writing development through a process approach. In *Writing: Teachers and Children at Work* (1983), Donald Graves advocates a workshop approach which focuses on the needs of the writer and uses the 'real' writer as a model. Graves carried out a longitudinal study of children learning to write in New Hampshire, USA and his findings led him to advocate a model of writing which incorporates pre-writing activities (such as brainstorming ideas), drafting, editing, proofreading and publishing. In this model, children are permitted to choose their own topics for writing, helped to revise their work for publication and, most importantly, encouraged to reflect on their own development as writers, sharing and collaborating on their work with their peers and their teacher (Graves calls this 'conferencing').

Graves also argues that teachers should themselves write with and for their children because teachers cannot teach writing without understanding the processes the young writer is going through and without being able to demonstrate aspects of writing to the learner: 'We don't find many teachers of oil painting, piano, ceramics or drama who are not practitioners in their field' (1983: 6).

Graves' influential model for teaching writing clearly complements Smith's promotion of the distinctions between composition and transcription in teaching writing. Together, they set an agenda which began to shape the teaching of writing in the 1980s and 1990s in the USA and beyond, with its emphasis on the writer's needs and the facilitating role of the teacher.

As the process approach gained momentum, so the centrality of the key concepts of audience and purpose for children's writing emerged. These concepts were not new; even in 1975, the Bullock Report (see Chapter 1) was arguing that children should be writing for audiences other than the teacher, because 'if a child knows that what he [sic] is writing is going to interest and entertain others, he will be more careful with its presentation' (p. 166). However, it was really greater accuracy that was the spur behind the Bullock advocacy of audience; more recently, a sense of audience is seen as central to writing development because it gives children experience of writing different kinds of texts for a variety of readers and of handling the complex relationship in their writing between writer and reader. This means that a writer has to make decisions about, for example, levels of formality and has to consider how explicit to be in the writing in relation to what the audience already knows. These are key skills in becoming a writer but it is only relatively recently that they have been seriously considered in the classroom.

Writers need a sense of audience because the intended audience influences the tone, nature and form of the writing. Writers also need to understand the purpose of their writing and that writing differs according to both audience and purpose. Without this understanding, children are writing in an abyss, with no sense of why they are writing, what their intentions are in writing, and for whom they are writing. This point is persuasively argued by Vygotsky who is critical of a Montessori nursery where the children's writing diet consisted of perfectly copied messages and greetings. Writing was taught as 'a motor skill and not as a complex cultural activity' (1978: 117). It follows, then, that children need experience of writing for a range of audiences and a range of purposes and that opportunities for these must be made in the classroom. When the purpose for writing extends beyond practising skills, the writing curriculum becomes reinvigorated and refocused.

Writers have to compose and order their thoughts, and many teachers have become more aware of the cognitive processes involved in writing: writing engages thinking and deepens reflective thought. For example, Scardamalia and Bereiter's research into composing processes (1985) addresses the question of how writing enhances knowledge and brings about different kinds of thinking. They argue that writing involves the creation of a synthesis between what the writer wants to say on the one hand, and textual constraints on the other. They explore the inevitable but valuable tension involved in simultaneously handling the content, the audience and the type of writing.

Understanding young children's writing

A process approach is not restricted to relatively competent young writers. Children in the very early stages of learning to write can benefit from an approach which recognises that they have intentions as writers, that they are active in the process they are learning, and that through writing they are learning about the world and how to represent it in written language. The practice of tracing, then copying the teacher's writing, and then constructing simple sentences from key words, has become less acceptable. Teachers have become more aware of what Teale and Sulzby (after Marie Clay, see Chapter 1) call 'emergent literacy'. Teale and Sulzby (1986) argue that emergent is a significant term because 'it connotes development rather than stasis' and that as researchers have looked increasingly closely at literacy learning in very young children, they have come to the conclusion that 'it is not reasonable to point to a time in a child's life when literacy begins. Rather, at whatever point we look, we see children in the process of becoming literate, as the term implies' (Teale and Sulzby 1986: xxv).

Emergent writing (also known as 'developmental' writing, see Chapter 5) is an aspect of emergent literacy. An emergent writing approach recognises that children know a good deal about writing from a very early age. As we saw in Chapter 1, the marks children make represent meaning, and what parents often describe as scribbles are more often patiently and painstakingly constructed communications, as children learn both that language is a symbolic system for expressing meaning and that it has rules of usage. Perhaps the key point about emergent writing is that the writing is 'for real', not a rehearsal for proper writing later, or a series of actions to be practised for when the real writing starts. Children are active 'meaning makers' (Wells 1987), a view of the learner which is very different from that of the passive child copying letters.

An emergent writing approach encourages creativity and invention: it frees children from the fear and constraint of making mistakes and encourages them to experiment and to feel successful in what they have produced. The teacher can then respond to and monitor development as the children begin to learn about the writing system. For example, teachers can see that children's invented spellings are logical and can recognise the strategies the children use as they move through the developmental stages of spelling, from a stage where there is an imperfect match between sound and written symbol, to more or less fully accurate spelling (see Chapter 5 of this volume). In an emergent writing approach, children are encouraged to hypothesise about spelling rather than relying on spellings supplied by the teacher. In working out how to represent sounds for themselves, phonemic awareness is developed, a key skill in learning to read (see Adams 1990 and Chapter 5 in this book). Teachers can also see how children handle the grammatical aspects of writing and can monitor children's development and support them in moving onto the next stage, so that the children are learning transcription through composition, the skills through the process as a whole, rather than focusing on the skills first.

An emergent writing approach accepts that writing does not start and end at the classroom door. Teachers today are more aware than ever of the importance of children's cultural backgrounds and experiences and of the need to build on these educationally. In terms of writing, it means that teachers recognise that children already exhibit literate behaviours, that they are aware of some of the functions of writing and that they come from families and communities where writing is thought of and used in particular ways.

Understanding about cultural and linguistic differences

In school, particular kinds of writing are taught. Outside school, different social and cultural groups will have different attitudes to, and different ways of using writing, some of which will accord with schooled practices and some of which may even be in conflict with them. For example, Street (1995) describes Philadelphian adolescents with empty exercise books in school but notebooks and scrapbooks full of things like raps and messages out of school. These young people have resisted the kinds of writing the school values and have forged their own uses for writing and forms of writing outside school, a good example of Graves' idea of 'ownership' of writing with a more political edge.

Literacy is often viewed as a neutral technology, a set of skills you just learn to use, but many researchers and teachers argue that it is far from neutral, that literacy involves specific ways of representing knowledge and developing understanding. Some suggest that schooled literacy is too narrow in its conceptualisation of writing and that it inducts children into too limited a range of writing competences. Street (1995), for example, draws a distinction between an autonomous model of literacy, defined as a single, dominant kind of literacy, and an ideological model, one which recognises a multiplicity of literacy practices, specific to particular cultural contexts. A number of longitudinal ethnographic studies have examined the interface of these different literacy practices: for example, Heath (1983), in her study of three communities in the United States, examines the nature of these differing literacy events across the communities, demonstrating that the children in each community are inducted into very different literacy practices and learn differently about what writing is for and how it is used. More recently, and in an English context, Barton and Hamilton (1998) have studied the literacy practices of people in Lancaster, and there have been a number of studies of the literacy practices of children and families in minority ethnic communities which draw similar inferences.

So for teachers to 'build' on children's backgrounds means more than asking them about their lives outside school: it means recognising that their literacy knowledge comes both from the school context and the home culture and that their experiences of writing will not be uniform. The teacher therefore needs to value and nurture the types of writing done at home, at the same time as introducing children to the kinds of writing done in school (see Chapter 3 for a discussion of links between home and school).

A recognition of home literacy practices is particularly important for children for whom English is an additional language (EAL). For these children, in the past, special provision separated them from contexts in which they could read, write and speak English naturally. They were taught discrete skills before engaging with real writing. They were treated as though they were starting from scratch in their literacy development, yet many of the children were literate in a language other than English and such practices served only to hold back their development.

Teachers have become more aware that the needs of bilingual writers are very similar to those of first language writers. In addition, recent developments in understanding of EAL indicate the vital importance socially and cognitively of supporting the first language at the same time as enhancing the additional language, in reading, writing and speaking and listening. For example, Baker (1996: 136 and 142) analyses research into bilingualism and thinking and concludes that 'the judgement of the clear majority of researchers tends to be that there are positive links between bilingualism and cognitive functioning' and that bilingual children may have an increased communicative sensitivity and increased metalinguistic awareness, an understanding of, and sensitivity to, language.

UNDERSTANDING THE NATURE OF WRITTEN LANGUAGE

Alongside developments in understanding the process of writing, there have been significant developments in teachers' and researchers' understanding of writing as a system, of the linguistic characteristics of written language. There are two main ways in which teachers' greater linguistic understanding of language is influencing practice in the teaching of writing.

Spoken and written language

The first area of increasing knowledge about the nature of writing is its relation to other modes of language, particularly to spoken language. Teachers need to understand something of the relation of spoken and written modes of language because, in learning to write, children have to learn to operate in a secondary discourse (speech is the first discourse they learn) and to put their language into written form.

Further, children have to move through a significant psychological stage of development in which they realise that written language represents speech which in its turn represents what they see, experience, feel, etc. Young children learn about representation or symbolism – making something stand for something else – initially through their play: 'a piece of wood begins to be a doll and a stick becomes a horse' (Vygotsky 1978: 97).

Their early drawing efforts reveal their developing understanding of the ways that they can represent on paper the things they see in the world. This is what Vygotsky calls 'first order symbolism'. Writing involves a move to 'second order symbolism' because it is about understanding that the written word 'horse' stands for the spoken word, which stands for the horse itself; it is 'the creation of written signs for the spoken symbols of words' (1978: 115). The teacher's role is to help children through this transition. If teachers can understand how children are learning to operate in the secondary discourse of writing they may be better able to understand what the children are trying to convey and to discuss and explain differences in spoken and written language with them.

Speech and writing clearly differ in their processes: speech is more context dependent; usually takes place face to face, so is more interactive; can use all the resources of body language, intonation and volume; and is characterised by false starts, repetitions and hesitations. Written language must convey its meanings without face to face contact; must be more explicit; is usually non-interactive, more planned and less spontaneous; and relies on punctuation and other written features such as capitalisation or fonts to make its effects. Writers have to predict responses or misunderstandings and must be much more aware of the needs of the reader.

There is, however, a danger in thinking that speech and writing are totally different systems. Sometimes speech can be like writing, as in a formal lecture or public speech, which would be more like written language than speech. Similarly, some writing is very like speech, such as personal correspondence or messages on notepads or emails. The important point here is that children need to understand that the purpose of the writing, and its intended audience, will determine the level of formality of the writing and that this in turn will determine the form of the writing.

There is a good deal of evidence to indicate that speech and writing also have different grammatical and syntactical organisation. Information units are bundled, or 'chunked', differently in speech and writing. In speech, the main linguistic unit is the clause. In writing, clauses are connected and related to each other into sentences, then sentences are linked into paragraphs and so on. Basically, sentences are made from clauses and the task facing the writer is how to connect the ideas in the clauses. Writing, therefore, requires decisions about what the main ideas are, what is subsidiary, in which order to place things, and which information is secondary to the main information units of the sentence. It also requires the handling of grammatical features common in writing but not in speech, such as certain subordinate clauses.

In relation to continuous prose, a reader can revisit what has been read to check any misunderstanding or to follow a line of thought, so the structure can be relatively complex. In speech, the communication is more linear and transient and a listener cannot keep checking what has been said, unless through repeated interruptions. So learning to write involves both developing control over the sentence and learning to be more explicit, and linguistic research can provide useful insights into these aspects of writing development. For example, Kress (1982) charts the development of control of the sentence in children's writing and argues that apparent irregularities or mistakes can be viewed differently by teachers once they understand how the child is moving from a spoken to a written mode of thought. Perera's research (1989) into whether children write as they speak, as is often suggested, found that this was not actually the case. Children increasingly edit out typical speech forms from their writing as they become more familiar with written language, demonstrating the importance of reading to writing development.

For many children, learning to write means adding standard written English to their repertoire. Writing is almost always conducted in standard English, though the style, register, and genre will differ, whereas spoken language could be in the standard or another dialect. Teachers need to understand that as well as moving from spoken to written mode, children may be having to adapt to and use standard written English forms and that such forms may be quite different from those with which children are familiar.

The books children read provide models for writing, not just at the level of the content, or the genre, but also at the syntactic level, where children absorb linguistic structures. This is one of the reasons why it is important for children to hear written language read aloud which is more challenging than they could read alone. The written language which children hear then provides a resource for their own grammatical and syntactical composing.

Texts and genres

The second area of linguistic knowledge which is having an impact on practice is that of a genre-based approach to teaching writing. This involves identifying the language features and structures characteristic of certain common written genres and teaching children explicitly about them.

Essentially, different types of writing have recognisable patterns of structural organisation and linguistic features. Genres are socially recognised text types (though precise definitions vary somewhat) and the argument is that in teaching writing, generic forms should be explicitly taught. Research in the 1970s carried out by Halliday on behalf of the Schools' Council, and continued in the 1980s and 1990s in Australia by Martin *et al.* (1987), among others, looked at the teaching of English in the context of developments in linguistics. In its later stages, and in relation to writing development, their research involved the extensive collection and analysis of writing done in school. They identified a small range of genres as predominant, yet found that little attention was given to the structure and linguistic content of these genres in the teaching context. In other words, the range of writing experiences the children were having was limited and little attempt was made to explain to children how certain kinds of texts are structured and what their characteristics are. In a British context, similar concerns have been raised about the kinds of writing done in school. In the more distant past, the Plowden Report (DES 1967) was very critical of the amount of story writing done in primary schools and similar concerns were raised in two further

HMI reports (DES 1978 and 1982), which found in primary schools inspected a good deal of copying, much use of exercises in text books and, in terms of the range of types of writing carried out in school, a predominance of personal expressive writing and story writing. Later, in 1993, Ofsted found little had changed: inspection evidence indicated 'excessive copying and a lack of demand for sustained, independent and extended writing' (Ofsted 1993: 8).

Linguistic research into the teaching of writing identified a number of principal genres, but in practice, many children were experiencing only a small number of these text types. The main genres are described as: recount (chronologically ordered retelling of events: 'last week I went to my nan's'); report (classificatory descriptions of processes and things: 'whales are mammals'); procedure (explanations about how something is done: 'the first player throws the dice'); explanations (of how something works or why something occurs: 'the sea causes the pebbles to move up the beach'); discussion (argument from a range of perspectives with conclusion: 'should fox-hunting be banned?'); persuasion (persuasive writing promoting one point of view: 'I think fox-hunting should be banned'); and narrative ('there was once a village where nobody grew old'). In early writing, other common genres are identified, such as labelling ('this is my teddy') and labelling/observation ('this is my teddy and I love him').

Whether this is a sufficiently inclusive list is an interesting question, but it does reflect the *National Curriculum* requirement for range in writing. The main question and contentious issue in genre-based approaches is to what extent the teaching should be explicit about specific linguistic features of texts and what the pedagogical implications are of direct teaching about linguistic forms. Most teachers feel reasonably comfortable talking about the audience for a piece of writing and how this will shape the language used, such as formal or informal, or the general form of the writing. However, beyond this, at the more detailed linguistic level, such as the type of verb used in a particular genre, or the implied question and answer structure of newspaper journalism, many teachers feel less secure and sometimes quite out of their depth. Lewis and Wray (1995) report from their research into teachers' practices in teaching writing that, when asked about writing:

> most teachers tended to concentrate their replies on the writing of narrative texts and that there was a general lack of knowledge of the range of texts, and at the least, a lack of a shared vocabulary with which to discuss text types. (The research) supports the hypothesis of Ofsted, that teachers need to improve their own knowledge about the 'structures, functions and variations' of language.
> (p. 11)

We might expect teachers to be more confident in the area of narrative, a common enough feature of primary writing, but even the writing of narrative receives little support in terms of the explicit teaching of generic features. In fact, the term 'story' is often used to refer to both narratives and recounts and for some children writing a story means writing a recount, rather than an actual narrative, with stages such as orientation and complication (see Chapter 4). Recounts are by far the most common genre in primary schools, which raises questions about whether children are experiencing the necessary range, particularly in relation to the requirements of the *National Curriculum*. Research into genre theory suggests that the narrow range of writing done in school should be extended to prepare children to write more socially relevant genres, so that writing is more meaningful in the 'real' world, though they also recognise that certain kinds of writing are expected in the curriculum and the formal examination system and must be taught. Teachers should be trying to achieve a better balance of genres but this is also problematic: for example, Barrs (1994) argues that the main problem with what the theory advocates is that it does not relate well to what we know of children's development as writers. Most writing by children, she says, mixes genres and does not reflect the kinds of genres identified by linguists. Such genres should not be deemed 'failed adult genres', but developmental genres in their own right. To expect children to write specific structures, and to expect teachers to adopt codified rules for writing, stifles writing development and is inappropriate in the primary classroom.

Genre theory purports to be a social theory of writing development because it identifies and teaches kinds of writing which are more significant in the world than the narrow diet of writing many children experience in school. What children learn to write, as well as how they learn, becomes an issue of entitlement and empowerment. How teachers move forward on this will depend on their view of the purposes of writing, and their understanding of the linguistic issues involved.

A NEW APPROACH? THE NATIONAL LITERACY STRATEGY

The *National Literacy Strategy (NLS)* arose from a concern about the variability of standards of achievement in literacy across schools nationally. The Government felt that literacy was too significant an aspect of children's development and entitlement to be left to chance and that intervention was necessary to establish a model to control and shape how literacy should be taught in primary, and subsequently secondary, schools.

The strategy marks a very significant change in the relationship between teachers and the government, in that for the first time, both the content of the curriculum and the methodology are prescribed. Its Framework for Teaching prescribes a syllabus for reading and writing for short- and long-term planning and specifies the orientation of a daily hour of explicit literacy teaching (the Literacy Hour) which requires 'systematic, regular and frequent teaching of discrete aspects of language such as phonological awareness, phonics, spelling, grammar and punctuation'. Its linguistic premise is that language can be studied at three levels, the word level, the sentence level and the text level. Activities are organised in a managed framework which reflects this distinction.

Initial national targets for pupil achievement particularly, but not exclusively, in the area of writing have not been met. Writing has been identified as a continuing problem: there are significant discrepancies between boys' and girls' levels of achievement, particularly in Key Stage Two and in the achievements of children from some of the minority ethnic groups. The Strategy can enable purposeful attention to written language and structured opportunities for its development but there is a view that the Framework provides too few opportunities for sustained writing in schools across the curriculum, and that the Strategy has led to a reduction in the time available for English teaching.

CONTROVERSY IN THE TEACHING OF WRITING

The *National Literacy Strategy* is only the latest manifestation of controversy in the teaching of literacy. Literacy has, for a long time, been a controversial aspect of education, because people have differing views about what counts as being literate. Lay and professional views often come into conflict and writing is in the firing line because it is more tangible than reading: employers, for example, actually see writing, whereas weaknesses in reading are less visible. Standards of literacy, in terms of writing, focus almost exclusively on transcriptional aspects and on the grammatical aspects of composition (and on narrow aspects of each) and public judgements on these are widely reported in the media. Whether standards are declining is a very complex matter, partly because of the problem of the validity of comparative studies of standards in writing: the measures to be used, the changing demands on writing, the scale of the sample and its replicability all serve to make comparisons across time difficult. The assessment required in the *National Curriculum* may enable better comparisons to be drawn in the future, but even this national data will not necessarily give a full picture of writing standards, other than in relation to transcription. As Brian Cox (1991), chair of the group which proposed the curriculum and assessment for English in the *National Curriculum*, remarks, 'the best writing is vigorous, committed, honest and interesting. We did not include these qualities in our statements of attainment because they cannot be mapped onto levels' (p. 147).

In terms of pedagogy, writing is controversial because of debates about what children need to know about language: the question is whether children need to know about the forms of the English language in order to be able to write, or whether knowledge about forms emerges through writing. Knowledge about language has been seen as important for children in several government reports (DES 1984, 1988 and 1989) and the *National Curriculum* includes this area under 'Language Study and Variation'. There was always a concern that separate, decontextualised language teaching would be insisted upon and that a more holistic and process approach to language development would be ignored. However, an insistence on drills and exercises has not emerged: for example, there is a definite intention in the *National Literacy Strategy* to ensure that children's knowledge about language is contextualised in their own reading and writing and that learning about the forms of the English language arises from meaningful contexts. Nevertheless, a national strategy will necessarily be open to varying interpretations by those implementing it and there is varied practice in schools in this respect.

INTO THE NEW CENTURY

This chapter has considered change in the teaching of writing. Some of this has arisen from research and publications which have influenced practice. Some has been regulated by government. In the new century, the *National Literacy Strategy* is setting a revised and refocused agenda for the teaching of reading and writing.

Information and communications technology (ICT) brings even greater challenges for the teaching and learning of writing, with new technologies for writing and new genres to be learned, offering immense possibilities for writing development: Graves' model for writing becomes more manageable through the applications of ICT, particularly in relation to editing, proofreading and publishing. Manual transcription may soon be seen as less important than the development of keyboard skills, even in very young children, though the resource and training implications are considerable. The national networking of schools opens up significant opportunities for new audiences for writing, new kinds of information texts to be read, and new ways of sending and receiving writing. Text messages are an emergent genre, texting now a ubiquitous verb and experience among the pupils we teach.

Writing remains under scrutiny. Literacy is again being drawn into the political and moral agenda for social inclusion. More than ever, teachers need to feel that they have writing 'under control', and are secure in what they do to develop children as writers, so that the best of the past can combine with the new initiatives of today.

Further reading

Fullan, M. *et al.* Institute for Studies in Education, University of Toronto (2001) *Watching & Learning 2. OISE/UT Evaluation of the Implementation of the National Literacy and Numeracy Strategies. Second Annual Report.* London: DfES.

Gamble, N. and Easingwood, N. (2000) *ICT and Literacy.* London: Cassell.

Hodson, P. and D. Jones (eds.) (2001) *Teaching Children to Write: the Process Approach to Writing for Literacy.* London: David Fulton Publishers.

Riley, J. and Reed, D. (2000) *Developing Writing for Different Purposes. Teaching about Genre in the Early Years.* London: Paul Chapman Publishing.

Williams, M. (2002) *Unlocking Literacy.* London: David Fulton Publishers.

CHAPTER 3

Routines and Resources

Anne Washtell

> Miss, you hold my hand and show me how to write.
> (Katrina, 5.0)

INTRODUCTION

These words, spoken in frustration by an inexperienced young writer, indicate the crucial and central role of the teacher in enabling children to succeed as they begin to take control of writing. In order to provide effective intervention and support, teachers must establish a set of regular, well understood, purposeful classroom writing routines which will permit the understanding of all elements of the writing process to develop.

In this chapter, we look at a selection of commonly used writing routines, some or all of which you are likely to find in use in your classroom. As each writing routine is discussed, it will be linked, where appropriate, to the *National Curriculum (NC)* (DfEE 1999) the *National Literacy Strategy* (NLS) (DfEE 1998b) and the *Curriculum Guidance for the Foundation Stage (CGFS)* (QCA 2000). A clear indication of suitability to particular age ranges will also be given. Two other NLS documents that you might want to have by you for reference purposes as you read this chapter are *Developing Early Writing (DEW)* (DfEE 2001) for the Foundation Stage and Key Stage One and *Grammar for Writing (GFW)* (DfEE 2000) for Key Stage Two. In addition, the Ofsted report, *The National Literacy Strategy: the first four years 1998–2002* (QCA 2002), provides a useful perspective.

What are writing routines and why do we need them? Writing routines offer regular opportunities for children to develop the strategies and skills that underpin the writing process. We need to provide these opportunities and we need to provide them regularly so that no important element of writing is neglected and so that each child's needs are met. Key routines that we discuss in this chapter include such routines as shared and guided writing, drafting and writing partnerships.

Some writing routines may function at the level of regular practice with an emphasis placed on the learner, while others, for example, shared and guided writing, are used by the teacher to make aspects of the process explicit to the children prior to independent activity. We need, therefore, to provide children with a well-balanced range of writing routines in order that they do not become over-reliant on a narrow field of strategies and skills at the expense of others. Limited provision of routines by the teacher could lead to serious weaknesses and ultimately difficulties in the children's development and growing independence as writers. Therefore, building a selection of writing routines into medium- and short-term planning is essential. If we do not think carefully about writing routines at the point of planning, we cannot guarantee balance and variety in terms of the strategies and skills that we want to encourage children to use.

PLANNING FOR WRITING ROUTINES

The Foundation Stage

Young children learn actively: they manipulate, they experiment, they hypothesise and they practise. Sound planning for this age range recognises this and the *CGFS* offers a planning framework underpinned by clear principles about early years education. The 'Communication, language, and literacy' area of learning in the *CGFS* comprises strongly interdependent strands. Thus, the teaching of writing will be bound up with children's play, with their speaking and listening, their reading, their manual dexterity, and their growing awareness of sounds and letters.

Those teaching children of Reception age are responsible for inducting them into the key routines of the Literacy Hour – it is expected by the end of the Reception year that the children will have experienced a full Literacy Hour – and therefore the objectives for Reception in the *NLS* (for which the *NLS* has produced additional guidance (DfEE 2000)) should be consulted. This guidance acknowledges that we must take into account children's personal, social and emotional development as well as their literacy needs. Literacy routines such as shared reading and writing, guided reading and writing are recommended as well as regular opportunities to engage in a range of planned independent learning activities where skills that have been taught in shared and guided work can be experimented with and applied in a variety of contexts including play and outdoor activities (2000: 6).

Key Stage One and Key Stage Two

As the *NLS Framework* is now well established in most schools, the key literacy hour routines are likely to be evident in planning throughout the school. Nevertheless, before planning your writing routines, it is important to read the school's agreed policy on writing as you may find that particular routines, approaches and resources are prescribed for each year group.

The school will also have a long-term plan that will provide further detailed information about the progression of skills, genres and forms of writing to be taught as the children move up through the school. This information is frequently documented on a term by term basis, year group by year group, and is intended to form the framework from which teachers write their medium-term plans (also known as Schemes of Work). It is important to note at this point that the *NLS* offers many different examples of planning in its publications. For the Foundation Stage and Key Stage One, *DEW* and *Progression in Phonics* (2000) are helpful and for Key Stage Two, *GFW*, and *Spelling Bank* (DfEE 2001) can be consulted as well as the *Year 6 Planning Exemplification* (2003). There are CD-ROMs for some of these documents which contain resources to support your teaching. The *NLS* section of the Standards website http://www.standards.dfee.gov.uk/literacy offers online planning material, ideas and other useful links.

It is helpful when writing medium-term plans to think about the three types of planning identified by SCAA (1995b) and central to the *NLS*: these are 'blocked', 'linked' and 'continuous'. Blocked planning essentially describes a discrete unit of English work, for example, in Key Stage Two, a series of lessons over a period of four weeks to develop children's knowledge of the linguistic features of writing argument and persuasion. A helpful example of 'worked' blocked planning is given in Part 3, Section 5 of *GFW*. The planning is for a Year 5 class, Term 3 and is based on the compelling novel *The Midnight Fox* by Betsy Byars. It is engagingly written in a personal way by the class teacher.

Linked planning, as its name suggests, involves linking writing to another area of the curriculum to provide purposeful writing in a range of genres. An HMI report (2002) provides a persuasive example of a PSHE lesson taught by a Year 5 teacher in which she demonstrates how to write a scientific argument. It shows how the teacher helps the class to apply their knowledge of the structural and linguistic features of the persuasive genre in order to meet the PSHE objectives for the session. For a history topic such as World War Two the class might undertake writing in various genres, for example, diary entries of a soldier returning home or report writing after the first evacuation of children to the country. Children should apply their knowledge about reading and writing learnt within the Literacy Hour to enhance the quality of their work in all areas of the curriculum.

Continuous planning (sometimes known as 'drip-feed') includes those routines which require regular practice, week in, week out, such as handwriting and spelling patterns (see Chapter 5).

Finally, short-term planning (usually on a weekly basis) expands the material contained in the medium-term plans to provide weekly and daily outlines for teaching. The *NLS* teaching units provide much of the detail needed at the short-term planning level. For suggestions on teaching strategies, *DEW* offers a teaching sequence for Year 2 (124–30) and *GFW* has ideas for interactive teaching strategies at sentence level. By referring to the documentation at all stages of planning, you can check on your learning intentions and outcomes as well as the appropriateness of the work for the differing needs of your class.

Planning for progression and target setting

Knowledge of what is achievable and desirable at certain ages will help us to ensure progression in our planning as well as providing suitable levels of challenge in our teaching. Targets for individuals, groups or indeed the whole class can then be more easily identified. Pages 30–1 of *DEW* map the end of Reception *NLS* target statements for writing onto the Foundation Stage early learning goals and pages 53 and 85 summarise what most children should have learned to do in their writing by the end of Years 1 and 2. In this particular document the components of writing are 'stranded out' in terms of phonics and spelling; handwriting; style: language effects; style: sentence construction; purpose and organisation and process. By keeping these strands in mind decisions about differentiation and meeting individual needs can be much more precise. Such decisions are, of course, based on previous observations and assessments.

The Literacy Hour

The *NLS Framework* takes you through the daily Literacy Hour and explains each of the key teaching strategies and routines (see Chapter 2). By paying careful attention to the actual teaching strategies at whole class, guided group and independent levels, the Literacy Hour aims for a balance between writing which is 'modelled' (where the teacher takes responsibility through, for example, demonstration) and independent writing (where the child takes responsibility for his/her writing). *DEW* reminds us of the importance of talk in the development of writing and offers a teaching sequence (pp. 14–6) which starts with class discussion and making a plan for the writing with the children. Shared writing follows in which the teacher writes for and with her class, prior to their independent but still supported efforts (see sections below).

Writing outside the Literacy Hour

Because writing sessions in the Literacy Hour are quite short, it is important to sustain children's enthusiasm for writing outside the Hour. This can be done in Reception by making provision for writing and other forms of representation through children's play activities, and routines such as the child dictating to the teacher, or another adult. In Key Stages One and Two, opportunities for writing outside the Literacy Hour can be identified through linked planning (discussed above) and also by making provision for sustained periods of time where children can write, uninterrupted, and at length (extended writing). It is important also, that we make connections for children between writing skills and strategies targeted in the Literacy Hour and their purpose and application in other curriculum areas. Children may also take writing home to complete (which may or may not be set as homework) and many schools encourage children to bring in writing done at home.

SHARED WRITING

I first heard the term 'shared writing' in the mid-1980s. It was used by teachers and staff attending courses in London at the Centre for Language in Primary Education (CLPE). Shared writing was the natural development from another literacy routine known as 'shared reading'. Shared reading's roots can be traced to New Zealand and the work of Don Holdaway (1979) whose ideas were based on what he described as 'the bed-time story cycle' where certain characteristic routines (including returning to familiar texts and engaging in highly interactive dialogue) regularly took place between parents and children as they shared books. He felt that this experience was so enriching for children that it could be replicated in the classroom by means of enlarged texts. Through the use of big books, A1 size posters, the use of projected ICT material or carefully enlarged pieces of individual children's writing, the whole class or groups of children can learn collaboratively about any aspect of the reading or writing process that the teacher chooses to focus on. The teacher takes the lead and 'scaffolds' (to borrow Jerome Bruner's term) the children's learning by modelling skills and strategies that she wishes the children to experience and learn for later independent use. Through explicit and highly interactive teaching the children are introduced to new areas of learning but they also revisit and consolidate previous experiences. Most importantly, through the collaborative nature of shared reading and writing, the teacher can set high expectations by placing the children in what Vygotsky calls 'the zone of proximal development' (see Chapter 1). In so doing, the children are led towards new areas of knowledge and skills which they would not have found independently.

Shared writing can be undertaken with any age range and, importantly, with the whole class; it can be used for short tasks or more extended pieces of work. The teacher acts as scribe (taking the transcriptional strain) thus freeing the children to participate fully in the creation of the text and to learn about the writing process, *at the point of writing*, from an experienced writer. This practice was a key feature of Graves' process approach (see Chapter 2) and it is something that the *NLS* endorses as it shows how writers make choices and decisions 'at the point of writing rather than by correction' (DfEE 2001: 13). In order for this to be effective, the teacher needs to be clear about her teaching objective(s) for each session and she needs to make sure that she provides a spoken, explanatory commentary as she writes. She uses 'writerly' language, constructs a 'writing plan' with the class, rehearses sentences orally, rereads, encourages automatic use of punctuation, checks misconceptions and works with the class on common errors (2001: 13).

When we engage in shared writing we need to balance our own explicit, direct teaching about the writing process with asking the children searching questions which relate to our teaching objective(s) and which encourage good quality, focused teacher/child interactions. By listening to children's responses, we can attune ourselves to their current conceptual understanding or misconceptions about the writing process and differentiate further questions accordingly. For example, in response to the question, 'Where should I start writing this text?' a child might point to the bottom of the piece of paper. Noting the child's misconception, the teacher might then ask the same child a more closed question such as, 'Can you point to the top of the page and show me where to start writing?' We can also encourage the children to take on specific, previously introduced technical terminology, such as 'verb', 'paragraph' or 'speech marks'. We can develop children's use of metalanguage (a language with which to talk about language) by framing questions in such a way that they are required to try to use the terminology in their answers and explanations.

This talking about writing or 'talk for writing' as the *NLS* phrases it, helps young writers make the move from dependence to independence as they begin to learn how to make explicit their implicit knowledge about how written language works. These collaborative opportunities to reflect on the writing process will be especially supportive to those children who have learning difficulties, those for whom English is an additional language and indeed, for very able pupils as well. Children will be listening to and absorbing knowledge and, understandably, it may take time before all children feel confident enough to share their ideas with the whole class.

Currently, three different types of shared writing have been identified by the *NLS* for teachers to work with. These are: teacher demonstration; teacher scribing and supported composition. Not all of these would be used on every occasion.

Teacher demonstration is, as its name suggests, teacher led. As she scribes in front of the whole class, the teacher models how to write a text and will speak her thought processes aloud so that the children can hear how she goes about composing a stretch of written text. While thinking aloud the teacher will maintain a clear focus on the stated objectives for the session. For example, in a session focusing on conventions of direct speech in story writing the teacher says, 'I must start a new line here because I've got a new person speaking.' Contributions from the children are not sought at this stage but they should be engaged in active listening, perhaps by being asked to save their questions, comments and opinions until later.

Teacher scribing enables children to make contributions that build on the teacher's initial demonstration. Using the above example, when the teacher reaches the point in her script when speech on a new line has been sufficiently demonstrated, she will ask the children what it is that she needs to remember as a new character starts to talk. Paired talk could be used here ('Tell the person next to you what you think it is I have to remember to do.')

Supported composition shifts the focus onto the children's composition. The teacher may ask the children to record a conversation, for instance, between parent and child at the supermarket where the child is demanding sweets. Typically, the pace will be swift and the children will work individually or in pairs writing in their note books or on dry-wipe boards. As soon as the writing is completed the children's examples are held up so that the teacher can make an on-the-spot assessment. Successful examples are reviewed with the class and misconceptions addressed. The teacher can then decide whether further practice is needed before the children work independently. The intention here is that supported composition should form a bridge between shared writing and guided or independent writing.

GFW indicates that in Key Stage Two the time spent on shared writing can be extended from the usual 15 minutes to 50 minutes especially when the class is engaged in extended supported composition. Such longer slots may need to be punctuated by two or three 'mini plenaries'.

The following examples show how these different types of writing can be orchestrated in work with younger children. A Reception class took a favourite book with a repetitive, predictable text, *The Monsters' Party* (Story Chest 1980), and rewrote it as *The Nice Monsters' Party*. The pattern of the story was simple: 'What can this nice monster do? He can dance, that's what he can do.' This patterning of the story was first modelled for the children through teacher demonstration. By composing the first sentence of the new version for the class it was possible to move easily into teacher scribing. At this stage they substituted new action words, such as 'leap' for 'dance', and invented a surprise ending for the story which went as follows: 'What can I do? I can jump in the cake like a kangaroo.' The draft was reproduced as a big book, illustrated by the children and reread many times. The children also re-enacted the book in role play. At Text level the activity provided a model of a simple narrative structure and at Sentence level it drew attention to the idea of questions and how we punctuate them. At Word level the class discussed how some of the alternative verbs might be spelt. Some children used graphic knowledge to draw attention to 'long' words and 'short' words.

An alert teacher can always provide a real purpose for shared writing with young children as contexts arise from everyday events. In a Reception class, a child suddenly left the school midway through the term. The children wanted to send her a message in the form of a big poster. Through shared writing the teacher scribed the short and simple message, 'We love you so much Katrina.' Having reread the message together through shared reading, the children spontaneously began to play at spotting the letters of their names in the text. This proved an exciting and intense activity which lasted for approximately ten minutes with everyone participating at increasing levels of complexity. I include this example as a reminder that children are as capable as teachers at initiating purposeful opportunities for learning. In this very young age group, the skill of playing with and manipulating language must be nurtured and encouraged.

Shared writing is a flexible teaching tool to use with children. It can support any aspect of composition and transcription. In Key Stage Two, it can be used to model the linguistic features of more challenging writing genres, such as arguments or reports (see Chapter 4 on writing frames). Shared writing can also be very effective in teaching children skills which we as adults may take for granted. One such skill is that of note taking. Through the shared reading of an enlarged extract from an information text, the teacher can demonstrate how to use the skills of skimming and scanning to extract information, listing key words and points. Useful strategies and techniques can be demonstrated, such as using simple abbreviations which can speed up the note-taking process. For example, when writing notes about the Gunpowder Plot, a teacher used teacher demonstration to show the class how to use the initials of the conspirators rather than writing their names out in full. So, Guy Fawkes became 'G.F.' and Robert Catesby 'R.C.' (A similar example is given in Chapter 5 but this time in the first draft of a child's independent writing.) To read more about teaching note taking see Chapter 4.

When resourcing shared writing, teachers may prefer to work with a flip chart and felt pens; alternatively, you could use the board, an acetate on the overhead projector or a data projector. The size and appearance of the teacher's handwriting is a further consideration, especially if children are seated at some distance from the writing. For supported composition the children need access to either easy-to-handle note books or dry-wipe boards and pens. The *NLS* publication *ICT in the Literacy Hour: Whole Class Teaching* (2001) and its accompanying CD-ROM provides examples of classrooms where, for example, the computer, interactive whiteboard and data projector are being used for whole class teaching (see also section below on Writing on the Screen and list of useful websites).

It is important that a proportion of the shared writing drafts are reproduced as finished products. The type of product will be determined by the type of text being produced. For example, a story text could be reproduced into a home-made big book which the children go on to illustrate and reread. Other texts will become posters, captions, sentences, letters to be posted or word lists to go on the wall. Some material will be word-processed.

The following is offered as a checklist for what can be modelled through shared writing:

- A sense of purpose and audience: voice (formal or informal); planning; drafting; revising; proofreading; presentation (publication).
- Content and features of different types of texts: linguistic features; structural features (such as paragraphing); vocabulary choices for specific genres; words, phrases; grammatical features; use of connectives to sequence and structure text.
- Transcription skills: punctuation; spelling; handwriting; editing; proofreading; layout; organisation; presentation.
- Self-help strategies: correcting mistakes; rereading; discussing; peer conferencing; collaborating; using resources.

GUIDED WRITING

Guided writing takes place during the twenty minute group work session within the Literacy Hour. The children are usually taught in ability groups, in follow-up work to shared writing. In its pure form the *NLS Framework* envisages two guided groups to be taught within the twenty minute time slot each day with each group receiving ten minutes of direct teaching time. In other words they are the focus group(s) within the group work part of the Hour. If we stay with the example above of children writing dialogue, this is the context in which the teacher recaps and refines depending on the level of understanding the children in the focus group have reached.

The intention is that the other groups will be engaged in independent activities. However, as teachers have gained ownership over this routine, there has been some variation from the original pattern. For example, some teachers have felt that a full twenty minute session once a week per guided group, is a more effective use of time. Other teachers have found that, despite promoting strategies for independence during this time, it is very difficult, or indeed inappropriate, for all children working in the independent groups to be left largely unsupervised and with the expectation that they will not interrupt the teacher. A common solution in the Foundation Stage and Key Stage One is to designate classroom assistants to help support the independent groups or indeed to teach another guided group. Also, it is not uncommon to see specially trained classroom assistants working alongside the teacher with targeted groups using the *NLS*'s support materials (*Early Literacy Support, Additional Literacy Support* and *Further Literacy Support*).

In addition, both *DEW* and *GFW* provide significant shifts in terms of the perceived effectiveness of guided writing in leading to independence. *DEW* deals very briefly with guided writing and does not see it as a necessity in leading into independent writing. Instead, the document would seem to imply that supported composition, the third phase of shared writing, is a much stronger conduit to independence. A similar message is to be found in *GFW* with shared writing being acknowledged as 'the most significant and influential teaching strategy in the Literacy Hour' (2000: 17). The key issue here is the effective further teaching and practice of the objectives that have been demonstrated in the shared writing session. The document does go on to accept the obvious advantages of working with a group – these are often psychological/social advantages – but states that much of the guidance provided for shared writing is equally applicable to guided writing. Significantly, guided writing is seen as 'an additional supported step towards independent writing, where the onus is on the children to make decisions, compose and revise their own texts.' (p.17). Three major purposes for guided writing in Key Stage Two are stated:

- to support children in planning and drafting their own work;
- to revise and edit work in progress;
- to provide differentiated support for particular groups.

(2000: 17–8)

One of the main advantages of guided writing is that the teacher can teach 'at the point of writing' just as she worked earlier in shared writing. The small group allows her to give targeted help where it is needed. Despite Ofsted (2002) reservations that guided sessions are not as efficient as supported composition, many teachers still find that the small guided group is an important context for scaffolding children's learning. There will be schools where guided writing is very much part of practice and policy and you will find you can explore its potential for yourself. In those schools that move straight from supported composition to independent writing, you will make judgements about whether the routine of guided writing still has a place.

INDEPENDENT WRITING IN THE LITERACY HOUR

Independent writing features prominently in the Literacy Hour during group work and can be challenging, albeit for different reasons, for both pupils and teachers. Since the *NLS* was introduced, this writing routine has undergone considerable refinement, and, as we shall see, a certain degree of redefinition.

We will first discuss children in the Foundation Stage and Key Stage One by reminding ourselves that in *DEW*, the third element of the teaching and planning sequence is entitled 'independent but supported writing'. The idea is that the children will undertake 'independent writing at an appropriate level to complete, insert into, extend, modify, etc. work that has been started in the shared task' (2001: 14). This underlines the important point that independent writing should be seen as a carefully scaffolded move from a task that has been worked with through shared writing and may not necessarily always use guided writing as a 'stepping stone'. The strong message here is that, for the inexperienced writer, independent writing cannot be viewed as a disconnected, separate entity because the odds against success are too heavily stacked against younger and less experienced writers. The teaching and planning sequence suggested in *DEW* (2001: 18) is:

- talking for writing;
- writing plans;

- teacher demonstration;
- teacher scribing;
- supported composition;

and this sequence is intended as 'preparation' for independent writing. The idea is that in independent writing the children will apply their new understandings. As their confidence and competence grows in one area then the scaffolding can be carefully reduced. It needs to be remembered though that in a new area of learning or when working with fresh objectives, the need for scaffolding (working with the above sequence) is more than likely to be necessary again. In this way of working children need not feel frustrated or defeated by the challenges of moving into independence. There is further guidance in *DEW* (p. 14) on ways in which shared writing can be used to scaffold independent writing.

The model is similar at Key Stage Two. *GFW* (2000: 16–7) also makes the point that guided writing may not 'always be used as a stepping stone into independent writing' (2000: 16). The recommended planning and teaching sequence to scaffold the move into independent writing is anchored in shared writing at the levels of teacher demonstration, teacher scribing and supported composition. Moving through this sequence will serve as a preparation for independent writing. *GFW* offers a range of ways in which shared writing sessions can be used in order to scaffold independent writing. The tasks that are listed, such as 'infilling', writing endings or changing texts, provide focus, structure and support so that the child is not presented with a blank page and the simultaneous challenge of marshalling the full gamut of writing skills. These types of tasks fit in with the time constraints of the Literacy Hour and are likely to be manageable. As with the Key Stage One teaching and planning sequence, the aim here is to reduce the scaffolding around independent tasks – the pace at which this occurs is left to the teacher's judgment. All this comes with a health warning about being 'careful not to allow structure of this kind to lower expectations' (2000: 17). The aim is for children in this age group to attain an adequate level of independence in their writing so that they can hold their own in secondary school. But, if well handled, this planning and teaching sequence should see many more children attaining autonomy in their writing.

Ofsted (2002) reports that independent and group work has shown 'modest' improvement. Over the last three years Ofsted has identified several factors which have contributed to this improvement. It appears that it is helpful if teachers:

- give pupils numerous opportunities to work on group and independent writing tasks which build on earlier shared text work;
- increase the level of challenge of these writing tasks;
- organise the independent and group tasks more skilfully. (QCA 2002, para. 39)

The major cause of difficulties occurs when teachers ask pupils to work independently on tasks which have not been demonstrated or explained clearly to the whole class resulting in children being unclear about what they should be doing and failing to develop their independent writing skills.

UNAIDED WRITING

Unaided writing is the routine in which children work completely on their own. It involves the child marshalling all of his or her existing knowledge of the writing process in order to produce pieces of writing. In its purest form, as the word implies, the child is expected to write without turning to the teacher for support or referring to resources such as dictionaries. It is this kind of writing that is assessed in the National Curriculum Assessments for English.

With the youngest and least experienced writers, unaided writing is sometimes referred to as 'emergent' or 'early' writing. You may also hear this kind of writing described as 'early mark making' or 'pre-alphabetic'. This can be a puzzling and yet intriguing experience for adults as they watch the boundaries between writing and other representational systems, such as drawing and numbers, apparently overlapping at the point of writing (see Chapter 2). Confusingly, children's own perceptions of the meaning of what they have written may shift: they may attribute no meaning at all to their writing or, on subsequent 'rereadings', they may provide different meanings every time. (For a more extended discussion of this see also the section on 'Responding to unaided writing' later in this chapter.)

Research evidence does suggest that from a very early age children are more than able to write (or communicate meaningfully on paper) for real purposes and audiences. Shirley Payton (1984), in a case study of her daughter Cecelia, provides evidence of the child's early attempts at compiling shopping lists and writing letters to friends. Both Payton and James Britton (1982) show us that very young children want to communicate meaningfully in their writing and will do so initially using non-alphabetic systems of representation. James Britton describes the 'pretend writing' of a young writer explaining how she gradually makes the crucial move from what Vygotsky calls 'drawing objects' to 'drawing speech'. Figure 3.1 provides an example of a very young Reception child's sandwich list compiled in just the same way as her teacher daily compiles a class dinner list.

The list reads, 'Egg sandwich, cheese sandwich, cheese sandwich, cheese sandwich, salad'. A close look at the three central lines reveals that she has represented the words 'cheese sandwich' in a consistent way. Despite its non-alphabetic appearance, the writing is not random but systematic. Such opportunities for self-generated practice are most important in the Foundation Stage, where children will spontaneously play with the writing system in the way that Marie Clay (1975) describes. These kinds of early attempts at representation and ascribing meaning are acknowledged in the *CGFS* when they draw attention to the fact that children 'draw and paint, sometimes giving meanings to marks' (2000: 64).

Whatever their age, when children engage in unaided writing, the text that they produce may well appear unconventional in some respect. Whether it be in its appearance, layout or spelling the unaided writing will provide valuable information about the child's current stage of development and understanding of the writing process. In practice, the teacher will make judgements about interventions and the level of support the child needs in order to succeed but the writing produced will largely be the result of the child's own efforts. The success of unaided writing as a routine rests on the degree of confidence and independence that the young writer has. All children, whatever their age, should have the opportunity and materials to engage in unaided writing and need to be provided with the strategies to support them in their endeavours.

From the assessment point of view, unaided writing is essential as it is only through the child's own written products that we can gain an accurate understanding of his or her current development and thus measure the effectiveness of our teaching. This point is demonstrated by the two pieces of writing by five year old Tommy.

The two pieces were written on the same day. Tommy's previous experience had largely come from working with *Breakthrough to Literacy* materials (see Chapter 1) and he had only recently begun to make the move into the unaided writing routine.

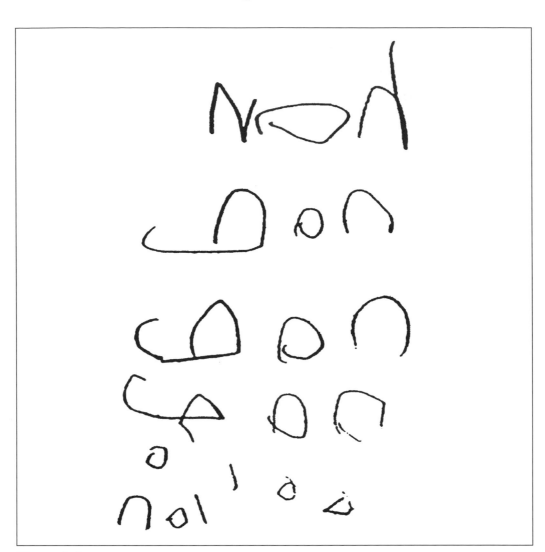

Figure 3.1

The first example (copied from *Breakthrough to Literacy* materials) reveals information about his handwriting and copying skills while the second is written completely unaided and reveals a wider range of information about his understanding of the writing process. The second one reads: 'Danny Farley and I play out'. Figure 3.2 shows that Tommy is able to copy successfully with good control from the printed model provided by the Breakthrough materials. In his unaided writing, Figure 3.3, it is immediately noticeable that Tommy's handwriting seems much less controlled. It is bigger and the letter formation is a mix of upper and lower case. However, he does show an awareness of directionality, an understanding that words must have spaces between them, an appreciation that sentences must end with full stops and a confidence in trying to spell all the words for himself. These two pieces provide evidence about Tommy's transcription skills but it would be necessary to offer other writing routines, such as dictated writing, to form a better impression of his compositional abilities.

Figure 3.3

Resourcing unaided writing

Children are not going to be drawn into unaided writing unless they have access to resources. Available space varies in classrooms but some kind of central and accessible collection of resources is always possible. A writing area provides an incentive and might include some or all of the following resources (depending on the age of the children).

- rough paper
- card and paper (various qualities, colours, sizes, shapes)
- loose-leaf folders
- envelopes and headed notepaper
- blank greetings cards, postcards
- blank official forms to fill in (e.g. travel agent, paying in slips)
- ready-made address books, diaries, birthday books
- material for book covers
- ready-made blank books (variety of qualities)
- book-making material (needles, thread, bookbinding tape)
- boards for book covers, ready-cut blank pages
- clipboards, bulldog clips, paper clips, staplers
- pens, pencils, felt pens, crayons, highlighter pens
- handwriting books, cards, sheets, line guides
- erasers, sharpeners, sellotape, glues, scissors and trimmer
- calligraphy materials, stencils, Letraset.

Additional items might include:

- post box
- notice board and messages board
- easel, large sheets of paper, thick felt pens
- board and chalks
- computer with simple instructions on word-processing packages
- ABC books, alphabet frieze, dictionaries, thesaurus
- display space for children's writing and books
- books such as *The Jolly Postman* (Allan and Janet Ahlberg) and *The Diary of Neil Aitkin* (Cartwright and Campbell).

Displays might include:

- examples of different kinds of writing
- suggestions for starting points for writing
- ideas for drafting
- ideas for finding spellings and lists of current high usage spellings
- class rules about maintaining the writing area.

(See Chapter 5 for more on transcriptional aspects of the above.)

A selective trawl of the above list of ideas should provide materials that are suited to the needs of different age groups. Calligraphy materials, for example, would be aimed at Key Stage Two. Health and safety considerations should be addressed before resourcing a writing area. Ground rules for use of the resources can avoid stock being improperly used (see the section below on resources and self-help strategies).

Contexts for unaided writing

It is, without doubt, a definite plus if we can provide contexts for purposeful writing activities. It is not uncommon in the Foundation Stage or Key Stage One to see a writing area or an office set up for the children, or for the home corner to be resourced as a context for role-play and writing. A typical example might be a cafe, where the waiters and waitresses write in role as they take their customers' orders. Older children will also find role-play, or writing in role, provides a valuable context for writing and you will find examples of this in Chapter 4.

It is very important that we actively encourage boys to see unaided writing as a worthwhile activity for them. Evidence from QCA (1998) found that some boys tended to use dedicated writing areas less than girls but responded to role-play areas where the writing was purposeful, for example, using a note pad in the large construction area. We should try to provide writing materials and create purposes for writing in the areas that boys might prefer to play in. Setting up a 'B & Q' store, 'Wickes' or 'Homebase' might hold more appeal for boys. Play in these contexts may give rise to large posters for writing out prices, safety rules and order pads to be used with customers. This is not to say, of course, that boys should not be encouraged to write in the usual writing areas as well.

Responding to unaided writing

You may hear some very young or less experienced writers providing a running commentary as they represent their ideas on paper. When children bring us their writing, it helps to raise their awareness about writing as a mode of communication if we can encourage them to try to tell us what they think their writing says. In the early stages, their versions may vary from one reading to another, which reflects the lack of stability of children's early concepts about print. You may feel that it is appropriate to make a conventional transcription of what children say so that you can refer back to it in future rereadings or for assessment purposes. A tricky challenge for the inexperienced teacher occurs when the child brings a piece of 'pre-communicative' (see Chapter 5) writing and says, 'You tell me what my writing says.' Such a request is characteristic of some early writers and the teacher can: comment on and name all the different letters that have been used; talk about the use of letters from the child's name in the writing; discuss spaces between words; discuss the length of words; point out repetitions and consistencies. If the child has accompanied the piece of writing with a drawing or diagram, this may well provide helpful clues and cues for discussing the intended content. Later, working with a different writing routine such as shared writing or dictated writing the teacher can continue to help the child to make the important connection that print holds meaning.

The empowerment of unaided writing

Unaided writing is also supportive to children who wish to write on topics that are of particular interest or importance to them, for example a lengthy story in chapters, or an ongoing diary or journal. *The National Curriculum* Programmes of Study in Key Stage One acknowledge this need. Figure 3.4 is a piece of extended writing undertaken independently by a Year 2 writer which clearly indicates the positive benefits of spending a concentrated, uninterrupted period of time drafting a piece of writing.

on the 22nd May Dominique came to my house to stay over night. First Dominique Played a game. Then my mum told us to clear up the mess that we had made. Me and Dommique Made 4 Model of a dolls house with all the old stuff. Then My Mum called and we We had to go upstairs and wash. When we had washed and put on our night dresses We went downstairs to eat an apple each. We Played a game. What you had to do is guess something that begins with a and the second Person has to guess something diffrent and the so on and on. Then My Mum said it was time to go to bed. So we had to go upstairs to bed. (My guest had My old bed) Just before We got to sleep My Mummy Kissed us goodnight. We were asleep in no until we woken up at ten o'clock. We got back to sleep by reading books. In the Morning Me and Dominique went downstairs and had our breakfast. After breakfast we went upstairs to get dressed. When Me and Dominque got in my room We Went in the Secret Passage. When we got in we Stayed in there For a long time. After half an hour we took our Clothes and Went back in the Secret Passage to dress in: to our clothes. After that we Played some games until Louise Came to pick her up.

The end

Figure 3.4

The child's piece exudes her determination to recount her adventures and she does this in an entertaining style, for example, with the use of parenthesis. She had not been directly taught about brackets but she seizes her opportunity in this piece of writing, using them appropriately, to make a direct address to her reader. For a first draft this example reveals few surface errors but unaided writing can also be a very effective way of helping children to learn how to go on to redraft, revise, edit and proofread their writing (skills which they are required to master in Key Stage Two).

Most important of all, unaided writing is empowering for all children who love to write and feel the need to write, no matter what their level of skill. For these children, working and playing with words or shaping and polishing an idea, is as satisfying and absorbing as the mixing of colours is to an artist. It is these children who may go on to write, whether it be for a personal or public audience, throughout the entirety of their lives.

Confidence and self-help strategies

Children will require a wide range of self-help and self-monitoring strategies in order to sustain their independence and avoid frustration and loss of confidence. Donald Graves (1983) characterises children of seven or eight as moving into a phase where they become very self-conscious as to whether their writing looks right or wrong. Some children by this age are only too aware of their shortcomings, especially in relation to their spelling power. Some children are very fearful of unaided writing because it requires them to take risks, thereby making mistakes, and some simply dislike the thought of their writing looking 'messy'. (See discussion on learning styles and strategies for independence in spelling in Chapter 5.) Other children will be struggling with several aspects of learning to write, for example, the getting of ideas, and will need very achievable short-term goals set to help them (see Chapter 7). Setting an achievable target to be secured by an agreed date is one way of helping such writers move forward. Involving children themselves in the target setting process will also help raise their self-esteem and self-awareness. For example, a Year 3 child, Tom, who needed to remember to use full stops in his unaided writing agreed a three step plan with his teacher: 'When I finish a piece of writing I will remember to read it aloud, to put in the full stops and then show my teacher.' You will find further self-help ideas in the next section.

It will already have become clear in this chapter that writing routines are underpinned by a careful balance of direct teaching and collaborative and independent activity. Our observations of children while engaged in teacher led and independent writing activities will inform us of areas of strength and elements that require further teaching from us (see Chapter 6). In the Literacy Hour, the ability to utilise self-help strategies is crucially important during the period when the teacher is targeting groups for guided reading or guided writing. The groups engaged in independent work need a wide range of strategies to enable them to maintain their independence and avoid disturbing the groups working with the teacher.

These strategies for independence are not learnt overnight. They will require repeated demonstrations from the teacher, especially in the early stages. McCormick Calkins (1983) describes these as 'mini-lessons'. In the early days with a new class, monitor carefully what makes the different routines operate smoothly. Identify strategies that promote independence within each routine and explain these to the children. Check how successfully the children cope with the self-help strategies that you give to them and make amendments as necessary. One of the best ways to work on self-help strategies is to involve the children themselves by discussing the problem with them and asking them to offer solutions. One class solved their spelling queue problem by devising their own self-help poster which children had to follow before asking help from an adult. In this way, we are helping children to reflect on the problem for themselves and encouraging them to take control of possible ways of managing it. (See also Chapter 5 under Independence and risk taking.)

There follows a self-audit that can be used when preparing to promote self-help strategies and independence in the classroom or to review existing strategies and resources. The intended target audience for the audit is student teachers evaluating issues in their own practice or newly qualified teachers who are in the process of organising and resourcing their first classrooms.

Resources

Have I:

- made essential writing resources permanently available?
- got fixed places for permanently available resources?
- made available everything that the children need for specific activities? (may vary according to writing task)
- got enough resources to go around the groups?
- ensured that the resources are within reach?
- told the children where to find the resources they need?

Ground rules for using resources

Have I made clear to the children:

- what they can/cannot help themselves to?
- the use and care of shared resources, e.g. rubbers and sharpeners?
- that some items can only be used by a limited number of people at any one time, e.g. computer?
- that they should only take what they need?
- that some scarce resources can only be used for limited periods of time when they are *actually needed* within an activity?
- that they should handle expensive resources carefully?
- that anything that is borrowed must be returned to its place at the earliest possible time?
- what to do with left-over resources that need tidying up?

Writing resources which require careful organisation

Dictionaries, word banks and word books

Have I:

- checked that a suitable range is available?
- taught the children in shared sessions how to access dictionaries?
- created word banks of words in current high usage, e.g. key words for class topic (illustrated if necessary)?
- made alphabet strips available to help locate the position of letters in dictionaries?
- set ground rules for the use of personal word books?
- drawn up a reminder poster on how to succeed in finding a word?
- promoted independent spelling strategies?
- taught the use of the thesaurus and encouraged children to use it?

- made use of word bank facilities on ICT packages and drawn these to the children's attention?

Self-help strategies and the individual child

Getting started

Have I:

- carefully explained the process and purpose of the writing routine to be practised?
- drawn attention to self-help strategies that may come in useful?
- taught or re-taught specific self-help strategies?
- made a set of attractive and briefly worded 'reminder' cards of key points (colour coded depending on aspect of writing process, e.g. pink for spelling, yellow for punctuation etc.)?

Getting stuck

Have I:

- demonstrated to the class what I do when I'm stuck with my writing?
- agreed with the child that self-help strategies must be tried first?
- encouraged the child to have a go at solving his/her problem using his/her own ideas and initiative?
- encouraged peer group support at solving problems?
- encouraged the child to move on to next part of task which s/he can do independently and then go back to the problem area?

If all else fails

Have I:

- told the child which relevant, alternative 'holding' activities can be carried out?
- agreed a last resort system of making contact with me if help is absolutely essential?

DEW (2001: 19) provides some writing focused suggestions to help children when they get stuck.

COLLABORATIVE WRITING

Unlike supported composition, in this routine, children work together, *independently* of the teacher, to produce a shared written text. The text could be written on a dry-wipe board, large piece of paper or composed on screen. As it requires a high level of cooperation, collaborative writing is probably best suited to the top end of Key Stage One and to Key Stage Two. For children to succeed in this writing routine, the groups should be small (preferably even numbers) and carefully constructed to ensure compatibility. The ground rules for participation should also be clearly explained and, ideally, everyone in the group should take a turn to write with the mutual support of the other group members. This activity can work very effectively as part of the Literacy Hour. A Year 2 class had listened to a rereading of a story in the first part of the Literacy Hour and had been asked to retell the story orally in their groups and then rewrite the main sequence of events to accompany a set of pictures. The pictures had already been sequenced and stuck on to a large piece of paper in the previous session and the children's main task was to compose and then write their sentence to accompany each illustration. This independent writing group supported one another, taking turns to suggest possible sentences, agreeing on the best one and then working in pairs to write the sentences down. Children who were waiting for their turn to write, either helped with suggestions for spellings or wrote a rough draft of their sentence on smaller pieces of paper. In the plenary session, the group read their story aloud to the rest of the class.

DRAFTING

For many years in schools, it was usual for redrafting to be in the form of a 'fair copy'. Bullock *et al*. (1975) make brief reference to the place of drafting in the classroom but it is through the work of Frank Smith (1982) and Donald Graves (1983) on the writing process that we have come to a better understanding of what drafting is and its role in the writing process for primary age children. As has already been indicated in Chapter 2, Smith and Graves were concerned that all too often children were being asked to write 'one-off' pieces of writing which tended to lead to an overemphasis on the presentational aspects of writing at the expense of the content. Through his classroom based writing workshops, Graves began to help teachers to see the value of asking children to redraft their work. Central to Graves' approach was to make the whole writing process explicit to children (from pre-composition to publication) and to promote independence in their approach to writing. By the mid-1980s, teachers in this country were encouraging drafting as a routine. For many children this proved to be a liberating experience, although others found it challenging to be asked to redraft their work. In confident hands, the approach worked successfully but it soon became clear that a sense of balance was needed. Questions were raised such as: did every piece of writing need to be redrafted? If so, how many times? Wasn't there still a place also for 'one-offs'? Was redrafting necessarily appropriate for all children? Did redrafting entail copying out the complete text again or using editing techniques such as 'cut' and 'paste'? Did children see the purpose (i.e. of improvement) of redrafting? How much support was given to children in redrafting techniques? The *National Curriculum* helped to some extent to clarify the way forward as far as drafting was concerned, placing drafting carefully within a clear progression for producing pieces of writing by requiring children to 'plan', 'draft', 'revise', 'proofread', 'present' and 'discuss' their work.

It is now commonplace for teachers to introduce the idea of drafting with younger children through oral redrafting. This can be demonstrated by reading aloud from a short passage during shared writing and, through teacher scribing, by involving the children in decisions about improving the text. Alternatively, an individual child's own writing can be discussed and suggestions made about how it could be improved. This requires sensitive handling and the teacher will need to have modelled examples of 'good questions to ask'. One of the early *NLS* videos provides an illuminating example of a young child sitting in the 'Author's Chair', reading her draft aloud and then taking questions and suggestions for improving her text. The teacher then offered the child several alternative ways of undertaking a small piece of redrafting. The suggestions all avoided the need to write the whole piece out again.

Shared writing can also be used to model, through teacher demonstration, drafting techniques, including planning, moving paragraphs, marking omissions, changing vocabulary and refining sentence structure. If the children are paired up as 'writing

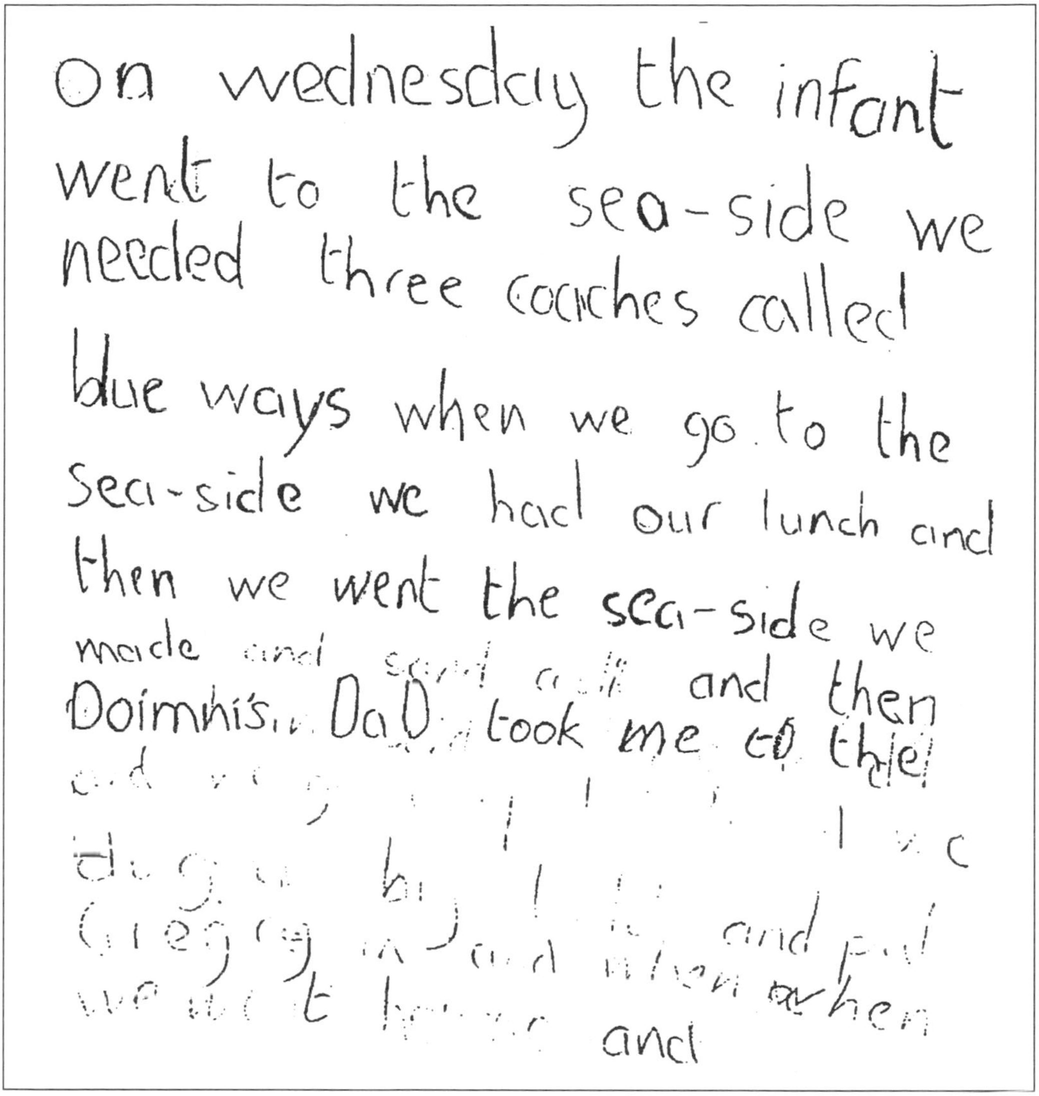
On wednesday the infant
went to the sea-side we
needed three coaches called
blue ways when we go to the
Sea-side we had our lunch and
then we went the sea-side we
made [illegible]
Doimhis Dad took me to the
[illegible]
[illegible]
[illegible] and [illegible]
[illegible] when
and

Figure 3.5

partners' they can support each other with all aspects of drafting, including proofreading. It is also worth teaching the children some basic editor's marks and encouraging them to use them as they draft. Suggested marks include:

- ^ the omission mark;
- circling spelling or alternatively using a wavy or straight line (under a word);
- 'sp.' in the margin to mark spelling errors;
- // to indicate a new paragraph is needed.

The word processor is another tool which children can use in the drafting process. Editing functions such as clicking on 'cut' and 'paste' or dragging across sections of text can assist in the easy movement of paragraphs and sentences while the range of fonts and print sizes provides plenty of scope for the final presentation of pieces of work. However, as the word processor can conceal the different drafts that are produced, it is useful, occasionally, for assessment purposes, to keep a sample of the 'complete life history' of children's pieces of writing which shows the progress from initial plan through to the final copy.

Finally, some children want to redraft their work because they can see the value of improving it. Figures 3.5 and 3.6 are from a Year 2 child who speaks English as an additional language and show marked developments from first to second draft.

Figure 3.6

Figure 3.5 is a recount of a school trip to the seaside. The child became dissatisfied with his work, tried to rub sections out (which accounts for the apparently poor quality of the Figure) and finally asked if he could start again on a fresh piece of paper. Before doing so, we had a brief discussion on the areas that were causing him difficulty and he was given some ideas on improving the content and the sentence structure. This resulted in a second draft, Figure 3.6, which proved a much more satisfying piece of writing. Not only does he add more detail about his trip but he has also tried to regularise his sentence structure and punctuate the piece. There are, of course, still some errors, including confusions over the use of the apostrophe, but the child was much happier with the second draft. For assessment purposes, both drafts provide a wealth of information about the child's growing ability to take control of the writing process and to monitor his own work.

WRITING WORKSHOPS

The idea of the writing workshop comes from Donald Graves (1983) and his research associate Lucy McCormick Calkins (1983). As the name suggests, writing workshops involve the whole class writing together (although not necessarily at the same stage in the writing process). The aim of writing workshops is to make the different stages of the writing process explicit to children and to enable them to work independently by taking their pieces of writing through from 'pre-composition' to 'publication'. It was intended that children would learn how real writers work by drafting, redrafting, revising, editing and proofreading their pieces, prior to publication. As you will remember from Chapter 2, the emphasis of Graves' work was on ownership and children taking an active rather than passive role in their writing.

Teachers who have implemented Graves' model have been impressed by the degree of independence and confidence his approach gives children. They have managed to reduce some of the pressures caused by the mechanics of writing and they have helped children focus more closely on content. While it is unusual to see writing workshops operating in quite these ways today there have been many spin-off practices which we almost take for granted. These include: 'everyone writing together'; demonstrations or modelling by the teacher (recognisable now in shared writing as teacher demonstration); writing response partnerships; talking about the different stages of the process with children; mini-lessons and bookmaking. Publications produced by the National Writing Project (1989–91) describe aspects of good practice which clearly show the influence of Graves' work.

WRITING PARTNERSHIPS

In school, the child's first and most significant writing partner is his or her teacher. It is the teacher who usually provides the first audience and initial response to a piece of writing. The teacher's feedback may also include constructive criticism and guidance on improving the piece of writing. However, as a context for responding, writing partnerships between children can also be very effective and this writing routine is well suited to the Key Stage Two age range. The Programmes of Study (1999), 'Planning and Drafting', 2f states that children should be given the opportunity 'to discuss and evaluate their own and others' writing'. Donald Graves sowed the seeds of writing partnerships through what he termed 'conferencing'. He recommends that conferencing should be a routine part of the drafting process and that initially the teacher should demonstrate to the class how to respond in a positive and constructive way to a piece of writing. He suggests that the teacher starts by using one of her own first drafts in order to help the children learn how to respond.

For this routine to work, children need to learn how to ask purposeful and worthwhile questions and how to offer comments in such a way that they do not undermine their partner's confidence. Graves offers two powerful prompts to help children to begin to do this effectively. The first is, 'Tell me something you like about your writing', to be used when the piece is first read aloud. This gives the writer confidence and helps him

or her to begin to evaluate the quality of the work. The second prompt, 'Tell me something you want to know more about', is asked by the writer to his or her partner, after
the piece has been read aloud. The intention here is to help the children develop their
sense of audience by identifying gaps in the writing where more detail or information is
required. Ways of operating writing partnerships do vary. Some children are asked to
swap their writing, while others read their drafts aloud to one another before their partner responds (see also the example of the Author's Chair in the section on Drafting). The
idea is to get the first responses directed towards the content. This could include suggestions for clarifying points, grammatical expression or choice of vocabulary. Suggestions
might also be made in relation to the cohesion of the piece and sequencing of ideas. At
the proofreading stage the response partner might focus on the presentational aspects
including spelling and punctuation. Lucy McCormick Calkins (1983) provides some
detailed examples of how children were inducted into responding to each other's writing. She lists a series of questions which the children found helpful, including:

- What is the most important thing you are saying?
- Which is the most important part of your story? Why?
- Are there places where you could describe more?
- Is there any other way you could order this?
  (pp. 129–30)

With careful induction into being sensitive support partners, children can be helped to
reflect on their writing and evaluate it. Partners need to be paired thoughtfully.
Friendship and compatibility might be one basis for struggling writers while for the
most able children in the class, pairing by ability might provide more challenge and
lead to improvements in the revised drafts of children's writing. For all children it can
be the site where they help each other in the setting of achievable targets. Some of
McCormick Calkins' ideas outlined above could be adapted for use in supported
composition sessions within the Literacy Hour.

DICTATED WRITING

A five year old told me a wonderful 'chapter' story which was full of vivid description and interesting twists of plot. When she had finished, I asked her to write her
story down. Slowly and laboriously she managed to write one sentence, 'I love my
dog.' She stopped in dismay, saying, 'I've done my best' and I, as her teacher, was
also left feeling disappointed. Between the two of us, we had lost that wonderful
story. This example will probably sound familiar to many teachers of young children and I include it here to illustrate the gap between the child's potential
competence as an author and her performance as a writer. As a result of years of
being told and read stories at home, this child was a skilled 'author' but she was
also a very inexperienced writer in terms of the 'secretarial' skills (i.e. knowledge
about the spelling and handwriting system, see Chapter 2). For this child and many
others like her, dictated writing is an important routine as it maintains, sustains and
develops the child's skills as an author while the child begins to come to grips with
the physical aspects of the writing process. Dictated writing, as its name suggests,
involves the teacher (or other adult) working on a one-to-one basis with a child in
order to scribe for the child. It is distinctively different from shared writing, not only
because it is on an individual basis, but also because the teacher transcribes exactly
what the child dictates. It is a labour-intensive routine, but teachers are surprised
and delighted not only by the extended pieces of writing that can result, but also

by the complexity of the language structures used and the richness of vocabulary. You may at this stage want to look back at the 'Dogfish' example we gave in the Introduction.

Liz Laycock (1996) provides an important account of several young children and their dictated stories. She reminds us that to create and tell stories is a very human activity: 'In telling our stories, putting our fears, doubts, excitements, joys or sorrows into words, we are shaping them in order to make sense of them, both for ourselves and for the listeners' (Laycock 1996: 54). This may in part explain why this writing routine is so popular with many young children. She analyses the narrative structure of stories dictated by children in a Reception class showing that such young children already know a great deal about how narratives are constructed.

Although dictated writing is usually thought of as a Foundation Stage routine, it is acknowledged in the Key Stage One Programme of Study for writing that pupils should 'write extended texts, with support (for example, using the teacher as writer)' (p.48). This routine also has considerable potential for children who are in difficulties with writing or who are disaffected by writing. For this reason, children may be asked to tape stories in Key Stage Two for the teacher to transcribe later on (see Chapter 7). Alternatively, a suitable voice-activated word processing computer package could be used. Whatever the age range, dictated writing can be turned into valuable reading material for the children.

TEACHER DICTATING TO THE CLASS

'Dictation' has a rather old-fashioned tone, but one Year 5 teacher has a successful continuous routine called 'You are my secretaries'. On one occasion the class had been writing letters of complaint and the teacher decided to read them a letter she had composed to provide a further model of the linguistic features of the genre. She then asked them to 'take a letter' and dictated a short passage to the children. This was followed by pair or group work where the children compared the versions that they had written down and then they extended these to produce a final version. The plenary session was then used to read out and defend their versions. Ruth Wajnryb (1990) has developed a method of dictation to young children which is also suitable for children for whom English is an additional language where she reads a passage to her listeners several times with the children noting down as many words each time as possible. In pairs the children then attempt to reconstruct the whole text.

Although dictation is not mentioned in the Programme of Study, many teachers find it a useful routine to use occasionally, especially when they are trying to gain direct feedback on a particular aspect of the child's knowledge of the writing process. Dictation, in its traditional form, places heavy, simultaneous demands on the child's working knowledge of the writing system. These days, teachers may choose to use the technique rather more flexibly than the nineteenth-century teacher you read about in the introduction to this book. For instance, the teacher might use it to consolidate a specific teaching point on spelling which would take the form of dictating a short, specially tailored piece of writing rather than a lengthy stretch of text which tested everything. In this way, teachers could reinforce teaching objectives about genre, sentence structure, punctuation, paragraphing, layout, spelling and handwriting. The dictation of short stretches of text could be used sparingly for diagnostic purposes within guided writing sessions to help confirm children's consolidation of a particular target or objective.

COPYING AND TRACING

As with the previous routine, copying and tracing have had a long and at times controversial history (see Introduction and Chapter 1), especially in terms of their overuse at the expense of those other routines which place more emphasis on the active participation and hypothesising of the child. However, copying and tracing routines are still commonly practised in Foundation Stage classrooms, and with some children in Key Stage One who might still benefit from them. They are important routines for several reasons: they help in the child's physical development by improving hand/eye coordination and by providing opportunities to refine the child's fine motor skills; they play their part in developing the child's growing awareness of print by drawing his or her attention to key concepts about print; children seem to benefit from the time that these routines give them to reflect on their writing – and they love the neat end product!

Go into any children's bookshop and you will see plenty of attractively produced, graded, exercise books that focus on copying and tracing. The tracing activities teach children about directionality and familiarise them with the key movements that underpin handwriting and letter formation. The task is made achievable for the child by virtue of tracing on top of a 'good model' of the particular pattern to be practised. It could then be argued that through tracing the child gets a 'feel' for handwriting (see Handwriting in Chapter 5).

In Foundation Stage classrooms, teachers will plan, at a continuous level, a variety of tracing-related activities to help children practise the necessary skills involved in learning how to hold and control a writing implement. The child may trace over a wide range of pre-drawn outlines of everyday objects and shapes. Literacy-related tracing activities will include tracing over handwriting patterns, tracing over individual letters of the alphabet to develop knowledge of shape and orientation and, most significantly, tracing over the child's name. Kinaesthetic provision will also be made for independent experiences arising from tracing, such as, writing in wet sand, tracing the finger over raised letters, or finger painting. Some of the routines described here are also used with older children with serious literacy and fine motor difficulties (see also Chapter 7).

For many children, copying marks the first stage towards independent handwriting. The first word that most children copy, with some degree of accuracy, is their name. Through name writing they will begin to develop an awareness that letters can be written in both upper and lower case. The *CGFS* expects children to recognise the letters of the alphabet by shape and sound. They are also expected to learn how to write their names. One of the Early Learning Goals for handwriting states 'use opportunities to help children form letters correctly, for example when they label their paintings' (QCA 2000: 67). By participating in a range of the routines discussed above, young children can begin to develop this knowledge. It is important to talk with children when they undertake these tasks in order to find out what they find easy and difficult about the activities. Copying and tracing without teacher intervention tend to be very passive activities and, therefore, less useful.

Another common practice in Foundation Stage classrooms is to ask the child to compose a sentence which the teacher writes down. Then the child copies underneath. It is important to offer a good model of handwriting and to remind children who are new to copying where to start writing. This could be done by marking the appropriate starting point on their page with a dot. You may find that some children try to write over your writing or copy words, or indeed letters, out of sequence. A Reception class teacher who observed this decided to introduce a midway step which she called 'overwriting'. In this procedure, instead of copying underneath, the child overwrites the teacher's handwriting. This forms a bridge between tracing and copying. The quotation from Katrina at the beginning of this chapter underlines the value of this kind of support.

Children meet a wide range of other forms of copying in the course of a day. Although a less common sight in today's classrooms, some children are still working with *Breakthrough to Literacy* materials. They may be asked to copy the sentences which they have made from word cards taken from their sentence makers. The sentences that are written are then intended to become part of the child's reading material.

In Key Stage One, the demands on copying rapidly widen as children will be beginning to copy words from books, including dictionaries or class word banks. They may also be copying work from the board which, in Key Stage Two, becomes an increasingly important routine. To make this workable for children, check that all the children are seated so that they can see the board properly and are comfortable. As with shared writing, your handwriting must be large and clear and, where necessary, cursive ('joined-up'). If the children are copying a list such as spellings, where accuracy is vital, make sure that no errors have occurred during the copying. Remember, it is a long distance from the board to the child's book and consider the act of memory involved in maintaining and holding on to the correct letter order. Try to discourage children from copying spellings one letter at a time (see Chapter 5 on developing visual spelling strategies). As accuracy is so important, it may well mean that you need to check the children's books after they have copied the list down. For some children, who have limited short-term memory spans, this kind of copying may prove too demanding. You may need to make other provision, for example, photocopying the list for them. The time may not be far off when you write on an 'interactive whiteboard' and the children are instantly able to download your writing directly onto the personal laptops. The report on this in the *Guardian* (20 May 1998) suggests that pupils will thus be able to avoid 'laborious amounts of copying'. As ICT plays an increasing role in classrooms we need to remember that there may also be losses. As explained earlier, manual copying has its own part to play in learning about writing.

In both Key Stage One and Key Stage Two, making fair copies of drafted writing marks the final stage in the writing process. The Key Stage Two Programmes of Study for writing state that children should 'prepare a neat, correct and clear final copy' (DfEE 1999: 56). Children may well be working from drafts that have been revised and edited and may need motivating to put in the final bit of effort. An awareness of the ultimate destination of the final copy will provide an incentive for the children, as will the provision of good quality paper and writing implements with which to execute the task. However, we need to balance the skill of being able to write neatly for publishing purposes against the obvious advantages of using a good quality desk top publishing package (see next section).

WRITING ON THE SCREEN

Over the last few years, the use of ICT to support the writing process has become a much more familiar sight in classrooms. Many schools now have networked ICT suites and most classes have their own computer with access to the internet including email. The range of 'easy-use' word processing packages is steadily increasing and improving: they can combine word processing with multimedia options and 'access' options such as speech.

In the Foundation Stage the children will need time to explore and play with the computer. 'Talking' programmes are especially useful as they give the child immediate feedback and guidance. (See the end of this section and Chapter 5 for further details of some of these packages.) If you have other adults in the class, you could plan for them to work with pairs of children composing collaborative pieces of writing directly onto the computer. Multiple copies can be printed so that the children have something immediate, that looks good and can be taken home. Further copies can be produced for display and record-keeping purposes in the classroom. Programmes such as *Easy Book* (Sunburst for WINPC or Mac, REM) enable children to put their work into the format of a real book. (See also Bookmaking below.)

The *NLS* publication *ICT in the Literacy Hour: Whole Class Teaching* (2001), via its CD-ROM, provides exemplification through video sequences with sound commentary of ways in which ICT can be used integrally, as a teaching and learning tool, within the children's literacy activities rather than an add-on after other work has been completed. A worked example for Year 2 shows a shared writing session where the teacher uses a laptop computer with a data projector. Working with the text *Jamil's Clever Cat*, we see the teacher moving from teacher demonstration into teacher scribing. This is a good example of 'teaching at the point of writing'. The teacher is able to model clearly for the children how writing choices are made, revised, altered and even deleted. An example for Year 6 takes place in an ICT suite. We see the teacher using the suite for whole-class teaching moving from shared reading and writing into independent paired work. A key focus is note-making and in order to do this for themselves each pair works with a text about the locality of the school taken from an internet website. The commentary which accompanies the video clip explains that the children are able to make notes by high-lighting text and dragging sections of the original text into the word processor. This use of ICT relieves a lot of the effort of re-writing and enables the children to retain their literacy focus of identifying the most important parts of the text to note down.

As they get more experienced, children will use the word processor to enhance the drafting stage of their writing. By being introduced to tools such as 'cut' and 'paste', grammar and spellcheckers and the thesaurus, they can undertake revising and editing tasks systematically and with less physical effort. Many packages now offer a wide array of fonts, tools and layouts, which will particularly support Key Stage Two children, who are expected to make decisions about layout and presentation and are also required to produce different finished products such as guidebooks and pamphlets. There is now a much better range of packages for creating newsletters, cards and posters.

ICT can also raise the self-esteem of struggling writers, especially those with handwriting and spelling difficulties. One example is *Clicker 4* (Crick Software www.semerc.com) which is equipped with special functions to support inexperienced or struggling writers. For example, through the use of 'Clicker grids' teachers can customise material which will support children's individual needs. This includes the facility to create bilingual talking grids. Some ready-made grids are provided with the package, for example, stories and descriptive writing. Examples from the story material are *The Three Bears* and *The Gingerbread Man*. Pictures of the main characters, key words and phrases are ready to use. The sequence of the story is set up on consecutive grids. When being used the actual Clicker grids sit across the bottom half or third of the screen. The grids contain demarcated boxes known as 'cells'. It is in these cells that the teacher can assemble a selection of pictures (for instance, about the seaside) and associated words or phrases that the child will need in order to fulfil a specific writing task. As the child composes he or she simply clicks the mouse on a particular cell and the picture, word, or phrase which is in the cell will appear on the blank part of the screen above the grid. In effect, clicking on a cell is equivalent to using the keyboard. The speech function options can be adjusted so that by simply clicking on a cell it will immediately say the word or alternatively, for a more confident writer, the speech function will only speak the text after a sentence has been assembled on the screen. By adjusting the different options the teacher can increase or reduce the level of support that the child requires. An additional package, *Clicker Sounds*, is recorded in UK English providing an alternative to Clicker's inbuilt speech function. (Further information about a selection of other packages is given at the end of the section.)

It is becoming more common to see children with specific learning difficulties using their own laptops for a wide range of class work and many programmes have been specifically designed with the struggling writer in mind (see examples in Chapter 5 for spelling and Chapter 7).

Children working in pairs seem best suited to the computer and in older classes these could be the pairings that have been set up as 'writing partners'. If access to computers is limited, then it will be necessary to maintain a rota system to ensure that all the children have a fair chance to use the packages. It is important to ensure that both boys and girls receive an equal opportunity to work with computers and it may help to monitor this on the class rota as well. Finally, remember that many children will already be highly computer literate because they have considerable experience of using computers at home (see Ben's story below). Encourage the children to share their expertise and acquaint yourself with the packages they are using outside school.

Computers require some regular health and safety checks. It goes without saying that we need to be mindful that responsibilities come with operating electrical equipment in the classroom. The *NLS* ICT CD-ROM discussed earlier in this section provides, in its 'ICT Considerations', a useful list of things that must be regularly checked. A website for further advice is also provided: http://www.becta.org.uk/technology/inforsheets/html/Hands.html. Ensure that the children become involved in some aspects of caring for these expensive resources. For example, ask them to take responsibility for letting you know when the printer is running out of paper or when they notice that the inkjet is low. Children will quickly understand the basic operating instructions but there is also a place for teaching them some simple troubleshooting dos and don'ts. Independence might be further promoted by displaying small posters or trouble-shooting cards which diagrammatically indicate how to resolve common, but minor difficulties.

The *NLS* CD-ROM mentioned above can be used to gain access to the following sites:

- http://www.standards.dfes.gov.uk
- http://besd.becta.org.uk
- http://www.naace.org

These sites provide a wealth of material including schemes of work, plans, resources, up to date ideas and information, links to other related sites and much more.

Some examples of ICT packages for writing

We conclude this section with a brief summary of a selection from the many packages now available. It goes without saying that, prior to laying out money, schools should trial inspection copies, look out for BETT award winners and consult authoritative services such as the ICT post-holder in school and BECTA. Most packages have further resources and linked additional packages.

Writing Focus www.semerc.com

Summary of package: claims to stimulate, encourage and improve pupils' creative and factual writing skills. Provides activities and contexts all linked to the *NLS*. Exemplar material is intended to model linguistic and literary features based on extracts from significant authors.

Features: pictures and words; shape poems; biography; comic strip; persuasive writing; diary; playscript; free writing; roving reporter.

Primary Writing Frames Fiction (5–7) email: sales@r-e-m.co.uk

Summary of package: a booklet gives starting points for writing by providing generic, re-useable writing frames. Links are made with *NLS*.

Features: Accompanying disc provides pictures, diagrams, subject specific vocabulary with built in dictionary.

I Can Write Version 2 (5–11) email: sales@r-e-m.co.uk

Summary of package: the main part of the package consists of writing frames which are organized into the key genres targeted in the *NLS* i.e. the six non-narrative genres and narrative.

Features: Each genre is accompanied by topic material. The package can be used for shared writing and the frames can be printed out.

Draft: Builder (5–16) email: sales@r-e-m.co.uk

Summary of package: claims that a three-step framework enables children to produce a 'high quality' first draft. The three steps are: outlining and mapping, note taking and drafting. This framework is supportive at a planning and an organisational level.

Features: Children are able to generate, manipulate and make connections which enables them to create a logically sequenced first draft of their writing.

Story Maker (FS upwards) www.spasoft.co.uk

Summary of package: claims that children aged five or even younger can use the simplest tools in the programme. Story Maker enables children to produce animated speaking and 'sounding' stories as an alternative to printing out the book.

Features: Figures can move, appear and disappear and even speak to us. There are plentiful back up resources e.g. 1,500 picture stamps, a library of sound effects e.g. dogs barking, and 20 different voices can speak the text. It also offers multiple text boxes, speech bubbles, background scenes, etc.

TalkingWrite Away (5–11) www.blackcatsoftware.com

Summary of package: *Write Away* itself is a well-established word processing package. *Talking Write Away* has additional supportive features for less experienced writers.

Features: In addition to the speech functions there are four levels of difficulty with each level having an increasing range of functions. Features such as word banks, pictures and learning functions are included.

BOOKMAKING

Bookmaking is about the final stage of the writing process: publication. Although it does not receive a direct mention in the current Programmes of Study for writing, its place is acknowledged in the *NLS* (pp. 20 and 29). Bookmaking sends out powerful signals to children that their writing will have an active future life and a real purpose. If we make books, we assume that we have a readership who will respond to and be interested in our efforts. Books made by children can form part of the class or school library collection and be read aloud at story time. Despite the obvious presentational and time saving advantages of ICT bookmaking packages (see the end of this section), I believe that children should still, at points in their primary schooling, be encouraged to make their own books, an activity which can easily be linked with Design and Technology. There is an intrinsic pleasure and appeal in the craftsmanship that hands-on bookmaking gives. As adults we often treasure and enjoy handling these early efforts at authorship because we can still see and, perhaps, even marvel at, the unique 'stamp' that our own handwriting brings. However, increasingly, time is of the essence, and for this reason hand-made books can be constructed with varying levels of sophistication from quickly made simple folded ones, such as concertina books, to the hardback, fully-bound variety. For practical suggestions consult Paul Johnson's *Children Making Books* (1995).

Some teachers include bookmaking resources within or alongside their writing area. Such resources include:

- variety of staplers (including long arm)
- small size trimmer
- comb binder
- needles, thread, scissors
- paper
- boards for covers
- bookbinding tape
- glue
- offcuts of wrapping paper or wallpaper (for covers)
- instructions and ready-made examples.

There is a financial implication here and bookmaking materials can be expensive to provide. However, the 'Blue Peter' spirit can prevail and alternative materials can be improvised quite easily. If space is limited, then a tray with compartments can be used to store the materials.

There are of course ICT packages that can take the strain out of bookmaking. One such is *EasyBook* and *EasyBook Deluxe* (KS 1–3 email: sales@r-e-m.co.uk). The idea with *EasyBook* is that children can write, illustrate and then print their work in book form. Its use can be organized in a variety of ways from individuals, to pairs, to small groups. This programme also has a clip art facility and speech support. Another programme that is well suited to younger writers is *Kidworks 2* (Davidson for WINPC or Mac) which helps children to create talking books. *Kidsworks Deluxe* (ABLAC on CD for WINPC and Mac) is a programme for all ages which enables children to write, record and animate stories, books and poems. It includes twenty-five story starts. *Pawprints* www.blackcatsoftware.com is a desktop publishing package that contains a range of design activities including illustrating poems and producing newspapers and can print to a wide range of paper, for example, from A4 to posters. Finally, *Textease* and *Textease Talking* can be used by a wide age range and provide flexibility in terms of manipulation of the words and images on the screen.

PARENTAL INVOLVEMENT

Although contact with parents is a routine of a different order from others discussed in this chapter, it is nevertheless of such importance that working with parents needs to be part of your daily practice if children are to make progress in writing, as in all other areas.

It was research into literacy before schooling such as that of Gordon Wells (1987), Glenda Bissex (1980) and Shirley Brice Heath (1983) which drew attention to the key role of parents in introducing their children to reading and writing. Parents have always helped their children with reading and writing but for many years teachers were either unaware of this or did not actively encourage such involvement. As recently as the 1980s, it was understandable and not uncommon to hear parents saying such things as, 'We don't want to go against school' and showing some wariness about becoming actively involved in their children's reading and writing. However, home-school reading partnerships (or PACT schemes, as some were known) began to flourish at about that time and marked the clearest sign of a shift in attitudes. Schools quickly realised that a two-way dialogue with parents was positively advantageous and supportive to children's development. Some schools took parental involvement a step further by using the 'parent conference' from *The Primary Language Record* (Barrs *et al*. 1988) as a method of providing two-way information about the child's development in reading and writing. Another appreciable advance has been the increased role of parents inside school, supporting reading and writing in the classroom. One of the most positive benefits has been that parents and teachers are able to communicate on a much more regular basis and share their expertise and understanding.

Many schools who have children who speak English as an Additional Language have been able to tap into the languages spoken and written at home. Parents have been approached to help with the translation of reading and writing material and to put stories and rhymes onto tape. Where writing is concerned, teachers have sometimes been surprised to discover that children whom they may have perceived to be struggling as writers of English are in fact, writing confidently in their home and community languages. *The Primary Language Record* and Hilary Minns (1990) provide further details on the importance of maintaining the child's first language in the service of learning a second. They also point out the value of teachers having an awareness of the home-based literacy experiences of EAL learners.

Parents can be involved at many levels in their child's writing development, both formally and informally. With the youngest children, at an informal level, a 'Home Writing' board or 'Our Messages' board in the classroom can encourage children to bring in pieces of writing they have done at home. Such pieces will come in all shapes or forms. They might be handwriting practice on the back of an envelope, a list of family names on a scrap of paper or a computer written story. In one class, a child brought in a copy of the alphabet written in Arabic script. Another brought in a story that he had written, which his parents had translated into Spanish. The resulting excitement and pleasure that the sharing of this writing has for both pupils and teachers indicates that it is a very positive and worthwhile activity to encourage.

Schools will have a whole-school policy on the involvement of parents and the level of commitment expected on each side. Some schools have established formal contracts with their parents in order to guarantee support for children's reading and writing development at home. It is not uncommon now to see short booklets or brochures which are given to parents, explaining the school's approach to reading and writing. These booklets may give detailed information about the ways in which handwriting and spelling are to be taught. In addition, information might also be provided about the school's marking policy for writing so that parents are not dismayed or puzzled by the teachers' response to the children's use of invented spellings. In Key Stage Two, parents may also be asked to participate in the school's homework policy which is likely to include the regular learning of spellings and writing assignments to be completed at home and brought into school. Relationships with parents are particularly important when you are dealing with children with learning difficulties.

Occasionally, both school and parents are unaware of the writing that children choose to undertake at home. There have been examples of children who have written 'novels' (stories with chapters) or have written their own collections of poetry or maintained diaries over lengthy periods of time. An example, involves a Year 6 pupil called Ben. Ben has worked hard with his writing at school and does what is required but writing is not one of his preferred activities. Outside school, Ben is a big fan of James Bond. Every other week, when his James Bond 'Fanzine' arrives, Ben eagerly seeks out the pack of collector's cards (which he trades with other young collectors). For the uninitiated, there are five types of cards: allies, villains, vehicles, gadgets and locations. Ben also enjoys spending time using the family's computer. With close supervision and monitoring from his mother and older brother, Ben has been allowed to download and copy suitable images from one of the James Bond websites. Not surprisingly, he is especially interested in downloading pictures of gadgets and vehicles. Unknown to Ben's mother, he taught himself how to use PowerPoint. He wanted to learn how to use PowerPoint because he wanted to devise a presentation about James Bond to entertain his family and friends. Completely unaided, Ben created a series of slides that were illustrated with a selection from the downloaded images which he had by now taught himself to animate. Each slide was accompanied by text. As a PowerPoint slide has a limited amount of space for text it worked like a sort of 'frame' which kept the text-based side of the enterprise containable for Ben. In order to view the show, Ben first makes his reader decode a secret message. Once into the main presentation the reader is immediately engaged as images appear on the screen from different directions and in different forms. To support the images and text, Ben has used sound effects. He is particularly fond of ricocheting bullets and the sound of breaking glass. When Ben's father eventually caught up with him he helped Ben to 'burn' a disc of his presentation and assisted in the creation of a distinctive label for his disc. To do all this work took Ben a considerable amount of time but what was noticeable to his parents was his high level of commitment and staying power as well as the huge enjoyment that he was gaining from his enterprise. Ben's father was so impressed with his son's creativity that he took the disc to work and presented the slide show to his colleagues with the wry comment 'If my ten-year-old son can do this, we as a company should as well!' The recognition of his efforts by his friends and family has done much to boost Ben's self-esteem and enthusiasm for writing. Having published his disc he also now sees himself as a successful and established author. When last heard of Ben was busy planning his next publishing venture!

Further reading

Baker, R., Franklin, G. and Meadows, J. (2000) 'Reading and writing with ICT', in Leask, M. and Meadows, J. (eds) *Teaching and Learning with ICT in the Primary School*. London: Routledge Falmer.

CLPE (1990) *Shared Reading Shared Writing*. London: CLPE.

Fisher, R. (2002) *Inside the Literacy Hour*, Chapter 5. London: Routledge Falmer.

Hall, N. and Robinson, A. (1995) *Exploring Writing and Play in the Early Years.* London: David Fulton Publishers.

Merttens, R., Newland, A. and Webb, S. (1996) 'Parental Involvement in Writing', in *Learning in Tandem Involving Parents in their Children's Education*, Chapter 4. Leamington Spa: Scholastic.

Topping, K. (2001) *Thinking Reading Writing: a practical guide to paired work with peers, parents and volunteers.* London: Continuum.

Williams, M. and O'Connor, L. (2002) 'Teaching 'write': Writing in the Literacy Hour', in Williams, M. (ed.) *Unlocking Writing: A Guide for Teachers.* London: David Fulton Publishers.

Composition

Fiona M. Collins

COMPOSITION AND RANGE

> Composition is what powers the writing. It is vital that the focus, in relation to children's writing, is first and foremost on composition, and that children perceive that this is so.
> (Barrs 1987: 2)

What is composition?

Composition is about creating ideas, developing individual voice and being able to write in different forms for a range of purposes and audiences. This chapter looks at what we understand by composition, its place in the writing process and how children can be encouraged to extend and develop their range of narrative, non-narrative and poetry writing.

As we saw in Chapter 2, there is a useful distinction to be made between 'composition' and 'transcription' in the writing process. Smith shows it in this way:

Composition	*Transcription*
(author)	(secretary)
getting ideas	physical effort of writing
selecting words	spelling
grammar	capitalisation
	punctuation
	paragraphs
	legibility

(1982: 20)

Composition, like any imaginative or creative process, involves a willingness to take risks and impose order on one's thoughts. It is important that children do not feel constrained when writing by difficulties in controlling the secretarial aspects; as Barrs says 'the focus...is first and foremost on composition.'

The *National Curriculum* Programmes of Study for writing recognise this distinction with separate headings for Composition and then for transcriptional skills (Punctuation, Spelling, Handwriting and Presentation). For Composition the emphasis in Key Stage One is on vocabulary, sequencing, full sentences, awareness of purpose and audience and the role and influence of the literature children read. In Key Stage Two the emphasis is on purposes and forms; widening vocabulary; linguistic and stylistic choices; organising text and, again, drawing on books read. For both Key Stages a range of forms to be covered are identified.

The *NLS* endorses this range, and adds that:

Literate primary pupils should:

- know, understand and be able to write in a range of genres in fiction and poetry, and understand and be familiar with some of the ways in which narratives are structured through basic literary ideas of setting, character and plot;
- understand, use and be able to write a range of non-fiction texts;
- through reading and writing, develop their powers of imagination, inventiveness and critical awareness.
(1998: 3)

Writing is explicitly taught within the framework of English, whether it is in Literacy Hour or in other English sessions. However, children are also asked to write in other curriculum areas, such as history, geography or science. Thus progress and development can be fostered and monitored in writing across the curriculum.

Audience, purpose and context

Audience, purpose and context help the young writer to develop a voice and gradually control the written word to make meaning. Children often write with a particular audience in mind such as other members of the class, younger children, their parents, the local community or a specific organisation. These audiences may be known or unknown. For young children, it is important that audience is identified from the outset because it helps with decisions about tone, choice of language and structure. The *National Curriculum* requires that Key Stage One children write for 'teachers, other adults, children and (the writers) themselves' and at Key Stage Two this range widens to include 'the wider community and imagined readers'. The *NLS* gives detailed and specific suggestions for children to vary 'appropriateness of style, vocabulary and presentation' according to audience. Sometimes such real and varied audiences are difficult to contrive, and writing in role, discussed later, can be used as a context to provide imaginary audiences.

The purpose of the writing also affects composition, whether it be to entertain, persuade or explain. Purpose influences the linguistic structure of the piece and helps the child consider the language choices to be made. The purpose of the writing also links with the form that the writing will take, maybe a letter, diary or pamphlet. It should not be forgotten that one form of writing can be used for different purposes and different audiences; just think of all the different types of pamphlets you see in a week, some informing, some persuading and some warning.

The context for the writing provides purpose and gives the writer direction and involvement in the piece; a purposeful context can also be motivating and encouraging. Writing arising from a class story or poem can stimulate children to write imaginatively, in the role of authors creating imaginary worlds and characters. The provision of role-play contexts for writing is most important for children.

As well as teacher provided contexts, children are often motivated to write from their own interests, reading and life experiences. Television and video stories, characters and events are important influences and frequently appear in children's writing, sometimes in the same story as favourite book characters. Such influences can affect the plot of the story, pace, style and the use of dialogue. The influence of popular culture is often short-lived as one fashion replaces another. However, although the particular programme may disappear, the impact of popular culture on children's writing will always be apparent.

The links between reading and writing are strong and widely recognised. The more children read, the more their work reflects wider horizons, the more they employ book language to create feelings, thoughts and questions, the more they experiment with plots, themes and ideas. The *NLS* acknowledges this: 'Writing is closely linked to reading – the two activities reinforce each other... The context of pupils' reading, i.e. the texts, gives structures, themes and purposes for much of their writing' (DfEE 1998: 5). CLPE investigated this link further in their year long research project *The Reader in the Writer* (Barrs and Cork 2001). The project explored the influences that quality literature, along with specific activities such as drama, reading texts aloud and discussion, had on the writing of Year 5 children. As stated by Barrs and Cork:

> ... we (also) wanted to track the influence on children's writing of the literature that they read and studied. In doing this, we wanted to look not only at how challenging literary texts influenced their writing *stylistically*, but also at how they affected their deeper understanding of the way in which meanings can be explored, developed and communicated through writing. (p. 26)

The evidence was clear that children's writing had been marked by the exposure to quality texts in terms of the quality of the language used, the complexity of their sentence structures and their ability to sustain narrative voice and perspective. Some children gained more from the project than others but the work reflected clearly that by bringing the text alive through expressive reading aloud, regular discussion of the narrative and exploring the themes and issues within the stories through drama all the children made progress in their writing.

As well as experiencing quality literature, first-hand experiences and interests also colour much of children's writing and indeed are at the heart of all talented composition. Many small boys will turn all their stories into football accounts as you can see in this five-year-old's story:

> A Match at Wembley
> Once there were eleven tigers and eleven lions. All the lions and tigers fans came to Wembley stadium. They were going to play a football match. Everyone in the whole nation came to watch...

It is however sometimes difficult to persuade older children that their experiences merit written exploration and attention but writing about what you know intimately nearly always results in better writing.

In this discussion on audience, purpose and context, we should remember that writing is not always in the public domain. It is also for thinking and learning. It is important that children are encouraged to write down their feelings or to use writing to reflect on what they have actually learnt, for instance, in a science lesson. Myra Barrs argues that activities that link writing and learning are just as important as those driven by audience and purpose and she quotes Katherine Perera: 'Writing is not merely a way of recording speech, but a different form of language in its own right which can lead to different forms of thinking' (1991: 1).

Types of writing

Writing can be divided into two broad categories: narrative and non-narrative (or fiction and non-fiction). Although these are loose categories and there is some overlap, they are helpful as the separate characteristics of each can be identified and deliberately used by new writers. Note that poetry can fall into either category: many poems tell stories (narrative) but many are the expression of strong feeling and opinions and have no narrative element.

The characteristics of narrative writing are: characters, settings, problems, solutions and resolutions. Narratives may be set in the present, in another time, in this country or another place. They may be realistic or fantastic. The main purpose of narrative writing is to entertain the reader. In children's literature, there are many different types of narrative writing such as traditional tales, adventure stories, historical stories and personal narratives. The *NLS* requires children to write from personal experience, to compose myths, fables, traditional tales (typically predictable and patterned), playscripts and poems (which will not always be narratives). By Year 6, the children are expected to be reading and writing, at least in modest ways, such narratives as mystery, humour, sci-fi, historical and fantasy. The requirement to parody a literary text (Year 6.2) clearly depends on secure understanding of narrative features.

Non-narrative writing, unlike narrative writing, is not just to entertain (although it often does) but is written for different purposes and for different audiences. It is not about specific characters and their problems but is about general matters, processes and arguments. It comes in different forms and aims, amongst other things, to inform, persuade and instruct. These different purposes and aims give rise to the many different text types, or 'genres', that are characteristic of non-narrative writing. You will remember from Chapter 2 that genres are socially recognised text types, or 'different kinds of writing that have different functions in written discourse and in society' (Barrs 1991: 9). The genre influences the overall structure of the text and language choices made. The work of Maureen Lewis and David Wray (1995) for the EXEL project was established to look at ways of improving children's writing in different genres. They identified six non-fiction genres used regularly within our society (recount, report, procedural, explanation, persuasion and discussion) and they argue that children need to understand the structural and linguistic characteristics of the genres.

Katherine Perera (1984), among others, classifies writing in a rather different way. Rather than using narrative and non-narrative she employs the terms 'chronological' or 'non-chronological'. In other words, writing can either be structured and organised with reference to time, or not. The *NLS* bases its definitions of chronological and non-chronological writing on Perera, defining them as 'writing organised in terms of sequences of events' (*NLS*: 75) or 'writing organised without reference to time sequence' (*NLS*: 83). Examples of chronological writing are: directions to a particular place; a recount of a day visit; a recipe or a mystery story. You will see that this list includes both narrative and non-narrative writing. All of this is not intended to confuse; the fact is that chronological writing, narrative or non-narrative, is easier for young writers to manage than non-chronological writing and thus there are implications for your teaching. For those of you working with older children, you will need to pay careful attention to the planning of non-chronological writing which becomes more of a challenge once you lose time and sequence as an organiser. You will see this if you consider the organisation of these examples of non-chronological writing: reports written in science or geography, a discussion about hunting, or an argument for the banning of whale killing in the world.

The *CGFS*, *NC* and *NLS* provide suggestions as to which types of writing should be taught. For instance, children in the Foundation Stage will typically be writing captions and lists. Key Stage One children will be experimenting with messages, instructions and notes and by the end of Key Stage Two they will have added explanations, playscripts and reviews to their repertoire. There is also guidance, particularly in the *NLS*, about poetry writing and the different forms from riddles in Year 2 to linked haiku poems in Year 6.

Children as writers

From a young age most children feel the need to communicate. As they see adults responding to print in and out of the home they will start to understand the different purposes for written communication. Wanting to communicate in writing themselves arises when they see writing actually happening so children who play at taking an order in a café have been fortunate to see this use of writing in their own lives. The adult purposes and forms of writing become ever clearer and children start to copy these. They write letters to Father Christmas, prescriptions whilst role playing doctors and nurses, lists of friends to invite to their party and notices banning siblings from their bedrooms. These non-narrative forms of writing, which have their counterpart in the adult world, often occur within the realm of narrative play so, long before children arrive at school, they know a great deal about imaginary worlds and the roles that writing can play in such worlds. As we saw in Chapter 3, they will also be able to compose narratives even if they do not have the transcriptional skills with which to record these.

So when children arrive at school, they know a great deal about writing – about stories and non-fiction forms of writing. As children grow older, research suggests that some boys lose interest in narrative and do not want to write stories so it is most important that their natural inclination to write about facts is recognised through balanced teaching of a range of genres. (This does not mean that story becomes marginalised; it may mean we have to think carefully about the stories we are sharing in our classrooms.) The Key Stage Two tests, from 2003 onwards will not always require the children to write a piece of narrative.

Some children are able to compose in different languages and, as you will remember from Chapter 2, this biliteracy is cognitively healthy and needs to be actively encouraged. Composing involves thinking and if you are thinking in one language and being asked to write in another it may not be very easy to be fluent. If this is recognised by the teacher, opportunities can be provided to discuss, plan and compose in first languages, in the early stages of writing. At a later stage the move can be made into English. You may find that children are more comfortable writing straightaway in English when the writing is in school curriculum areas (science, geography etc.) whereas stories, which may spring from early experience in the mother tongue, may be more readily composed in that first language. At an early age some children will experiment with both languages together and there may be evidence of such code-switching in their writing. (See Figure 5.6 and Figure 7.3 later in the book for examples of this.)

Where linguistic diversity is valued and the children's use of different languages and dialects is actively promoted, there are exciting possibilities for joint composition. Two nine-year-old girls worked intently together to produce a dual-language text in English and Turkish. What you will notice in Figure 4.1 is their delight in offering this 'new' translated version which lures the reader in with the promise of 'jokes all the way along'.

Teaching new text types

Whether teaching narrative, non-narrative or poetry the same sequence of teaching can be followed.

Reading aloud

The teacher needs to read aloud the new text type in order that children can compose in the same genre. Hearing a piece of prose or poetry read aloud helps the child listener to hear the language and 'voice' of the poet or author.

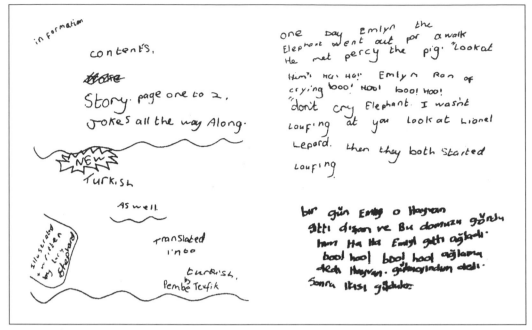

Figure 4.1

Non-narrative writing also needs to be read and discussed so that children can tune in to the rather different structures and rhythms that belong to non-narrative genres.

Analysis

After such immersion the class need to be supported in analysing some of the different linguistic and structural features of the text. For instance, if you are wanting to teach the children about the procedural genre you might offer them a recipe with all the verbs deleted in order to draw their attention to the use of the imperative.

Teacher modelling

Now the teacher builds on her children's emerging understanding and models the writing through sharing her thought processes as she writes in teacher demonstration. She may make use of a writing frame if she intends the children to use one in follow-up work.

Supported writing

Then children need to be supported in their independent writing efforts. This can be achieved through teacher scribing and supported composition within shared writing or by using an appropriate writing frame in guided group work.

Writing independently

Writing independently is always the goal of any teaching about writing and thus children should ideally be given the opportunity to compose their own text, whether for a known or unknown audience, and then be encouraged to reflect on the effectiveness of this writing.

NARRATIVE WRITING

Stories have a basic structure: a beginning, a middle and an end. Children quickly realise this from hearing stories read and reading themselves. They also learn about this basic narrative structure from watching cartoons and dramas on children's television. Narratologists have analysed the structures of stories in order to show common patterns or story grammars and such descriptions can help our work with children. For instance Hoey (1983) gives us the following labels which could be easily understood and used by children: 'Situation', 'Problem', 'Solution' and 'Evaluation' (by which Hoey means how everything turns out and what has been learned).

At Key Stage One children may write stories that include familiar characters, settings similar to where they live, and personal experiences. They may also write about characters taken from fiction, exotic settings and fantasy experiences. Such stories may be simply structured with a beginning, perhaps taken from a traditional story ('Once upon a time . . . '), an event, and an ending with a resolution ('. . . and we all went home for tea'). Some young children may also write stories that are a series of linked events rather than including a problem or an inciting moment which is significant in narrative structure. The *NLS*, in acknowledgement of this, has placed emphasis on teaching different aspects of story writing, which build on children's natural interest in narrative and books. The Framework states that pupils should be taught 'to write about events in personal experience linked to a variety of familiar incidents from stories' (Year 1.1) and 'to use story settings from reading, e.g. redescribe, use in own writing, write a different story in the same setting' (Year 2.2). The question of how children develop their narrative writing is complex. Some young children's narratives will display surprising complexities of plot with narrative twists, chained episodes and the introduction of minor characters. (This is especially true when they are given the opportunity to dictate their stories, see Chapter 3.) This ability to handle complexity may have been acquired through wide reading rather than through being explicitly taught within the primary classroom. However, we cannot depend on this. As some children get older, they may experience problems with narrative writing such as: poor structure, lack of focus, too many linked incidents, poor endings or unwarranted shifts in narrative voice. The *NLS* suggests explicit teaching at Key Stage Two of the component parts of narrative writing including character descriptions, narrative view point and story structure in order to aid young writers in the craft of writing narrative.

Teaching narrative writing at Key Stage One

This section provides a case study on fable writing carried out with a Year 1 class.

In planning this scheme of work the teacher had to think about the particular features of a fable, how to help children understand the structure of a fable and how to give them support in writing a fable for themselves. She started by reading a selection of Aesop's fables (including *The Fox and the Grapes*, *The Frog and the Stork*, and *The Boy who Cried Wolf*) and she discussed the differences and similarities between them.

The following sequence of activities was intended to encourage the children to think about narrative structure, choice of language and how the plot is linked to the moral. She wanted the children to see that each of the fables has a moral, a structure in common, and uses animal characters.

After the initial readings children retold a fable to one another, showing how important oral storytelling can be for such work as it brings about real personal engagement with the story. (It is particularly appropriate for stories like these that have been told for generations by word of mouth.) After this, the children carried out two written activities: a cloze procedure where they had to replace certain words in the story thus focusing their attention on the meanings of words in context, and a storyboard activity to help them reflect on the sequence of main events in a fable.

The children were then asked to write their own fable using animal characters and including a moral. Before the actual writing started the children brainstormed relevant opening lines such as: 'In a far away land...', 'There was once...' and 'Long, long ago...' After this the children discussed how such stories could end and two possibilities were decided on: either the characters learn a lesson or they meet a sticky end.

Finally, the teacher wanted to extend the children's use of vocabulary so she discussed descriptive words that the children might use in their writing. Together they compiled a list of useful adjectives which might suit the different characters ('curious', 'greedy', 'vain', 'massive', etc.). These were written on the board as a reference point for the children.

To help their thinking about structure the children were given a storyboard planner on which to plot the basic events of their fable. Michael's completed planner is shown in Figure 4.2.

Figure 4.2

After the planners were completed, the children discussed them with the teacher allowing her to respond to their attempts. This discussion is all-important, as it provides a context for the children to develop their thinking and creativity and also to be shown any problems in their story structure. Then, with their planners beside them, the children started their own independent story writing. The teacher continued to discuss their writing with them and enabled the kind of development below by Rebecca. This is the first draft of her writing:

The Cow and the Mirror
Once upon a time in a far away land lived a cow. The cow was very vain. The cow kept looking at herself in the mirror. One day the mirror smashed.

At this point Rebecca thought she had finished, but after discussion with the teacher she continued:

... into tiny pieces. She found a river and she went closer and saw her reflection. She got so close that she fell in the water. She was very sorry for herself and learned her lesson not to be so vain.

The completed story is more sophisticated in structure, with the moral linking quite clearly with the events of the story.

Finally, here is Michael's completed fable:

The Tiger and the Zebra
In a hot country called Africa there lived a bright orange tiger who was so proud of his stripes. The tiger really couldn't think of another animal that had them. Every day he went to show off to the other animals. Then he went to sleep feeling very very proud of himself. When he woke up and went to show off to the other animals he saw a zebra and that zebra had stripes just like him. He was very upset with himself. He was so upset he couldn't sleep or speak to other animals because he was so upset. The moral of the story is don't show off.

In this we see Michael's grasp of story 'grammar'. He provides an opening 'situation', a tiger living in Africa. The 'problem' is that the tiger believes he is the only animal with stripes and thus becomes very vain; the 'solution' is that he sees the zebra and realises other animals have stripes; and the 'evaluation' is that he learns a lesson which is not to show off. Such well organised, lively and coherent writing is a direct result of the teacher's well thought through approach to the teaching of narrative structure in fables.

Traditional stories are not, of course, the only narratives to be worked on at Key Stage One. Children will want to write in many other ways and it is important to support and respond to their interests and efforts.

Teaching narrative writing at Key Stage Two

In this section, the teaching of more complex narrative aspects such as characterisation, more varied beginnings and endings, settings and descriptions, and narrator's point of view are considered.

Tantalising beginnings and satisfying endings

A good beginning will engage readers and encourage them to want to read on. They will want to go on to discover the story, answer questions that have been posed and to fill gaps that have been left by the author. Many an author hints at secrets that will be revealed later in the book (as in the opening of *Gulf* in the example below). Reading a range of literature allows children to experience different beginnings and consider the ways that authors engage the reader's attention. Some use arresting dialogue: '"Where's Papa going with that axe?" said Fern' from *Charlotte's Web* (E. B. White); some involve us immediately with the character's dilemmas: 'I loved my brother. Right from the start. But did I love him enough? You shouldn't use people you love. Maybe what happened to him was all my fault...' *Gulf* (Robert Westall); and some shock us with the drama of the opening statement: 'When Bill Simpson woke up on Monday morning, he found he was a girl' *Bill's New Frock* (Anne Fine).

As children develop their reading and writing so their personal beginnings start to diversify. Below is a selection of Key Stage Two beginnings that mirror the different categories discussed above:

> And what do you think you are doing in my garden? snapped Mary.
> (Year 6)

> Suddenly everything went dark, I panicked.
> (Year 5)

> It was on a Sunday evening when I went to church to say my prayers, when all of a sudden a beam of light shone down on me.
> (Year 6)

However, it is not only the first few lines that make an impact on the reader; it is also the first page. Comparing interesting and dull first pages will help children think about their own writing. Try looking at the first page of a book like *Cold Shoulder Road* (Joan Aiken). What is it that makes us want to read on?

> Every night, around nine o'clock in Cold Shoulder Road, the screaming began. It came from the end house in the row. It was not very loud. The sound was like the cries of the gulls who flew and whirled along the shingle-bank on the seaward side of the road.
> People who lived in the road (there were not many of them) took no notice of the screaming. It's the gull, they thought, or the wind: or, whatever it is, it's no business of ours.
> Only one person felt differently, and she lived next door to the house from which the screaming came.
> Night after night she clenched her hands and stood trembling by the window.
> Something has got to be done, she thought. Something must be done.
> At last she did it.

The impact of repeated words ('gull', 'screaming'), short paragraphs and the closing focus on the girl with her clenched hands who is going to take action all contribute to the power and tension of this opening.

Completing a story may be difficult for the young writer, especially if the organisation of the story does not support a conclusion. Often children's stories conclude weakly with 'I woke up and it was all a dream' or 'I went home to have my tea'. To move children on from this stage it is important to discuss endings of favourite novels with the class, to find out if they were satisfying and left a feeling of 'Yes, I agree with this'. As with beginnings, different endings do different things: some answer questions, some leave questions unanswered and some raise new questions. Endings can entail physical movement, for instance a person walking out of sight along a road, a character travelling to a new country or getting into a car and looking back. All these leave the reader with the impression that the story is moving on, and that the narrative continues even though the book has finished. These and other techniques discussed here leave the reader with a sense of fulfilment in the narrative and it is worth spending time with children looking at interesting endings such as this one in Michael Rosen's *The Bakerloo Flea*:

She told me I was the first person she'd ever told the story to, and told me never to tell anyone. The scandal would be terrible. I don't know whether to believe her or not.

Such work will help children reflect on their own writing, just as Ricky (Year 5) did: 'It was a really exciting story. Only I knew who the burglar was till the end when I revealed ALL – like on the telly!'

The key to a good ending lies in the planning and structure of the story, although this will not always come when you start the planning. Once the writer has established the basic structure of the plot and started writing then the ending or resolution will fit more easily into place. To end with a satisfying ending, here is Rachel's (Year 6) 'epilogue' to her World War Two family saga, *Father at War* (see p. 63):

I never saw Mrs Whitby again, but I will never forget her. Some memories cannot be forgotten. Like the war, not that a war is an easy thing to forget, with all its deaths, bombs, battles. I want to forget the war, like waking up from a bad dream, but as much as I try I know I will never forget it.

Planning and structuring plots

As well as engaging the reader's attention at the beginning of the story, the writer needs to build up the plot and 'focus on language to create effects, e.g. building tension, suspense, creating moods, setting scenes' (*NLS*). As we saw with the fable example, thoughtful planning helps children to be creative and imaginative within a scaffolded approach.

Young writers often find the structure of a story difficult to manage and as a result their stories may become a lengthy string of events which then loses the reader. As Jamil, a Year 6 writer commented 'You have to work your way down and when you get to the middle and end you have to decide. You've been writing the first paragraph and then you have to jump into something else. Description is okay but what happens is difficult.' QCA make the same observation as Jamil: 'A lack of structure is evident in the frequency of ineffective endings of narrative. Stories often begin well, but endings do not link back to openings or offer satisfying solutions.' (2001)

The *NLS* framework attempts to help young writers structure their narrative writing and understand the significance of order within the plot. However, unless a child is allowed the time to write a complete story she will not be able to put into practice what has been learnt during the Literacy Hour. Many schools arrange for at least one slot of extended writing each week so that longer pieces of writing can be shaped and completed.

A young writer needs time to think and create as story writing seldom happens instantaneously. Ideally, time should be taken to think about and internalise the task. Some children will draw during this time, others will discuss their ideas with their writing partners (see Chapter 3), and others will search for inspiration in earlier pieces of writing and in books. Preliminary work on characters and setting could be carried out during the Literacy Hour while the extended writing itself could be done outside this period when the children have the time needed to work on longer pieces.

Story planners or prompts help structure narrative, as well as prompting ideas. Some children will need more structure than others and it is advisable to differentiate according to need. Below is an example of some planning prompts that can be adjusted to meet the different needs. These could be organised in clearly delineated sections.

Story planner
Who are you writing the story for (audience)?
What is the story about (plot)?
What type of story is it (adventure, horror, fantasy, historical or other)?
Who are the main characters?
Where and when is the story set?
Who is telling the story and how much do they know (narrator's voice)?
What is the first sentence? Have you interested the reader?
Ideas for the ending? (These can be added to as you are writing the story.)

Giving children a clear structure to follow supports creativity in their writing as the following example, from a Year 3 child, shows. The story imitates Jill Murphy's book *On the Way Home* but the young writer has added her own reasons for the accident:

Rosie was going home to tell her Mum she had a bad knee. On the way home she met her friend Harry.
'Look at my bad knee!' exclaimed Rosie.
'How did you do it?' gasped Harry.
'Well,' said Rosie. 'There was wild horny bull over in the calm countryside but luckily I managed to close the gate and he banged his head and the gate banged my knee and that's how I got my bad knee.'
'Oh my!' gasped Harry.
Then she met her friend Lucy.
'Look at my bad knee!' gasped Rosie.
'How did you do it?' asked Lucy.
'Well' said Rosie. 'There was an angry aqua dolphin and it tried to drown me! But luckily I got out of the water so I couldn't drown but when I got out I tripped over and that's how I got my bad knee.'
'Oh my!' screamed Lucy.

And so the story continues with Rosie making up a different reason for her bad knee every time she meets a friend. This tight framework gave support to the young writer and in doing so allowed for the child's imagination to create different situations in a most successful manner.

Characterisation

At Key Stage Two the *NLS* requires work on characters stating that pupils should be taught to, 'write character sketches, focusing on small details to evoke sympathy or dislike' (Year 4.1). From early in Key Stage One the *NLS* encourages teaching linked to characterisation such as writing simple profiles of characters in stories that the children know (Year 1.2) For children to develop characters in stories, they need to consider the techniques writers use to depict character. An obvious technique is to give character details through the narrator's description of what the character looks like, their past, their thoughts and their actions. A second device is to allow characters to reveal themselves through direct speech. An author can also show us the character through the thoughts of other people in the story. To draw on all these techniques it is useful to give children a checklist of questions:

- What does the character look like?
- What do other people think of them?
- What are the typical things this character would say?
- What are they seen doing?

The most common of these techniques, narrative description, is explored below and concludes with a piece of writing by a Year 6 girl, Rachel, which demonstrates all the above techniques in her competent characterisation.

Young writers need to be reassured that they can draw from the people they know, their friends and family, as well as people they read about. Many teachers ask children to compose descriptions for their classmates to identify. They can be reminded of memorable characters they have met in their own reading (Harry Potter or maybe Dahl's Big Friendly Giant) and help them to see how the author uses the above techniques. Consider a passage such as this initial paragraph from a short story by Bill Naughton where he introduces us, through a narrator's description, to the main character:

> Spit Nolan was a pal of mine. He was a thin lad with a bony face that was always pale, except for rosy spots on his cheekbones. He had quick brown eyes, rather stooped shoulders, and we all knew that he had only one lung. He had had a disease which in those days couldn't be cured, unless you went away to Switzerland, which Spit certainly couldn't afford. He wasn't sorry for himself in any way, and in fact we envied him, because he never had to go to school. (1970: 20)

Using such a passage, you might ask the children to highlight the things they learn about Spit in one short paragraph: his appearance, his disability, his poverty and his positive outlook. From this activity, the children could then carry out a 'search' for similar objective descriptions in their reading.

To conclude this section, here is the beginning of the third chapter of Rachel's World War Two saga:

> Father At War
> A few days after the scene in the dining room there were hasty goodbyes at the railway station, my mother talked on about eating well and not getting to sleep too late until my father gave her a brief hug, a quick peck on the cheek and disappeared into the crowds of uniformed men.
> 'Well that's your father off,' she said briskly to us and tickled me on the tummy, I stared back at her with big eyes.
> 'Well come on' she snapped as if cross at me for not laughing as my tummy was very ticklish. When we got home mother busied herself in the kitchen making tea. Mary, George and I scrambled up the stairs and into Mary's room where we all sat on the bed and talked. We talked about the war and all the changes that would come into our lives. We talked about father and what he would be doing now. Mary was scared and she and I cried, me clinging onto Mary like a rag doll.
> George was brave and stern now that he was the man of the house but I often saw a flicker of fear pass through his eyes.

In shared text work, the teacher could show the class how Rachel has portrayed the mother's character through narrator's description ('she snapped'); through an account of actions (she 'tickled me', she 'busied herself in the kitchen'); through direct speech ('Well, that's your father off!') and through other characters' thoughts (she 'talked on about eating well'). The class could then go on to look at how she has characterised Mary, George and the narrator.

Point of view

A story can be written in the first or third person although most narrative writing for children is in the third person. Narrators may, in 'omniscient' mode, tell us everything a character or characters are doing, thinking and feeling. Alternatively, narrators may only 'report' on their characters' actions and leave readers to infer how they must feel and think. Just as in first person narratives, a single character is usually the focus of the narrator's attention. We as readers usually have no problem in knowing who is the character to watch. Writing in the first person is something children will be doing readily in their recounts: 'We were in Lanzarote and we went to the lagoon. I said to my Mum "Can't I go scuba diving with Emma my new friend I met at the swings?"' (Year 4). However, making the kind of shift to first person narrative writing that Rachel, in the above examples, does so successfully usually requires teacher support. Children need to understand that the first person narrator does not have to be them, but may be a fictitious person telling the story from his or her point of view, as the wolf does in *The True Story of the Three Little Pigs* (Jon Scieszka):

> Everyone knows the story of the Three Little Pigs. Or at least they think they do. But I'll let you into a little secret. Nobody knows the real story, because nobody has ever heard *my* side of the story.

Considering another person's perspective can be difficult but placing children in imaginary situations allows them to write successfully as a particular character, as this Year 5 writer has done taking the role of the dormouse in her revisiting of the Mad Hatter's tea-party:

> The Mad Hatter and the March Hare were having their tea. I was asleep. Alice had just sat down after the Mad Hatter had said, 'No room!'. Alice started telling us her story when all of a sudden she brought Dina into it. Dina is her cat!
> 'Cat!' I yelled. I jumped up and ran into the Mad Hatter's arms. The Mad Hatter asked the March Hare to give him some treacle to put on my nose. I love treacle. After that I was put back in the teapot and I went back to sleep.

Alongside planning, an important aspect of any young writer's work is the continuing discussion and feedback that usefully takes place during the process of writing. Guided writing is the ideal place for this to occur. One of the most significant teaching points is when a teacher intervenes or supports a young writer while they are actually in the process of writing. Teacher intervention can occur at any point in the writing process, whether the group is just beginning a story or is in the middle of a draft. A supportive and sensitive comment or suggestion can help the young writer's understanding of structure, perspective and voice. Even when the work is complete, sharing with an audience will also give children opportunities to sharpen their writing.

Narrative writing engages children's imaginations. It allows them to explore the literary world for themselves and become real authors. In order to do this children need careful support and structure offered through interactions with both books and teachers.

Further reading

Corbett, P. (2001) *How to Teach Fiction Writing at Key Stage 2*, London: David Fulton Publishers.

Goodwin, P. (1999) *The Literate Classroom*, Chapter 11. London: David Fulton Publishers.

Hodson, P. and Jones, D. (2001) *Teaching Children to Write*, London: David Fulton Publishers.

Sedgwick, F. (2001) *Teaching Literacy*, Chapters 1–3. London: Continuum.

Thomas, H. (1998) 'Working with Story Structure', in *Reading and Responding to Fiction: Classroom Strategies for Developing Literature*, Chapter 1. Leamington Spa: Scholastic.
See also Scholastic *Writing Guides* for fiction.

POETRY WRITING

> Reading and writing poetry helps me understand myself, clarify my thoughts and see things in a new way. It keeps the mind alert and also satisfies that basic urge we have to create something unique.
> (Brownjohn 1994: 15)

Young children demonstrate an early interest in playing with rhyme and rhythm. Songs, advertisements, TV jingles, nursery rhymes, rhyming stories, finger and action rhymes foster and exploit this early delight in language. As they get older they find that poetry comes in different forms, not always rhyming, and is to be found on the page as well as in the ear. They learn that words in poetry have been memorably ordered to represent feeling. They learn that Walter de la Mare can evoke moonlight perfectly, just as Michael Rosen can sum up how they feel about a younger sibling.

Children will find out about these joys when enthusiastic adults surround them with the work of many poets. We need to read a great deal to them and let the poems and poets do the work for us. We can be sure that poets like John Agard, Charles Causley and Christina Rossetti will work their magic! Sandy Brownjohn reminds us that 'The teacher should be interested in and enthusiastic about poetry; otherwise the children themselves will be indifferent towards it' (1980: 85). Many schools have found that a visit from a poet who shares his or her working approaches results in increased confidence and interest in writing poetry. By sharing and enjoying poetry children will realise that they too can represent images and feelings through words which they choose and work on with care. Six year old Claire did just that with her first poem:

> Out in the playground
> Mark stands at the top of the slide
> Afraid to come down.

In the above example, Claire has not only worked from her own observations and understanding of feeling, but she has also benefited from her teacher's help in looking at form, in this case the three line haiku. Such inspection of form is an important part of teaching children to compose poetry. The *NLS* states that Reception children should build on their knowledge of poetry by 'retelling, substitution, extension, and ... shared composition with adults'. In Years 1 and 2, the *NLS* suggests that such work should be extended through language play, through inventing their 'own riddles, language puzzles, jokes, nonsense sentences etc., derived from reading; ... tongue twisters or alliterative sentences' (p. 30). Sandy Brownjohn states: 'I separate all the individual details which go to make the whole. Every part is understood as it is conquered' (1994: 7). Brownjohn advocates that teaching different techniques to children will develop their skills as composers of poetry, encourage them to play with language, give them the freedom to manipulate words and allow them to control what they say. She suggests that a great deal of this type of work can be carried out through games and puzzles. Her 'The Furniture Game' (1994: 19) helps children with description and develops their use of metaphor and simile. It is a guessing game with one child thinking of a person that the rest of the children know and describing this person as a piece of furniture, a plant, a type of food and a time of day. The following example comes from a Year 4 child. Look at the way in which the exercise has enabled her to follow her three similes with a metaphor:

> She is like a cushion
> She is like a sweet smelling rose
> She is like a cheesy pizza
> This person is an afternoon person.

This child and her classmates were being encouraged to appreciate the effects you can create through manipulating language. Just four lines of this sort of work can be put on the page and begin to look like a poem.

At this stage children need to know that there are formal ways of crafting poetry and they will enjoy experimenting with these. In the *NLS* there is comprehensive coverage of the forms that can be shared and taught across the primary age range. Some are specified for introducing to younger children (playground chants, tongue twisters) and others are for older children (e.g. limericks, riddles). The teacher can model these different forms in shared writing. However, it may be helpful to understand that many poetic forms can be regarded as frameworks that children will use at any age if they know about them, to help shape their writing. The success with which they do this will be determined by maturity, experience and ability, and obviously by the appropriateness of the form; if you want to lament your cat's death you are more likely to choose the form of an elegy rather than a limerick.

One such form that all poets enjoy is shape (or concrete) poetry, where the poem is written in the shape of the object that is being written about. A very young child might enjoy making a shape poem to represent a snail. George Herbert, the seventeenth century poet, made a sophisticated shape poem in the shape of angel's wings. Figure 4.3 is written by a Year 4 child in the shape of a rose.

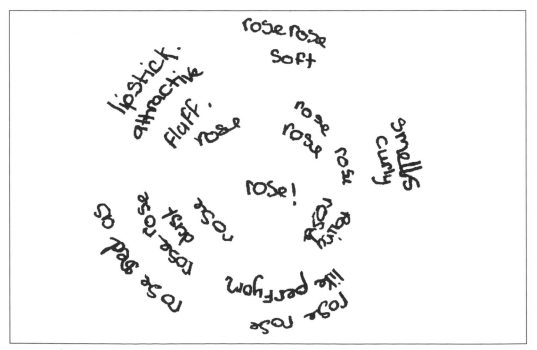

Figure 4.3

As well as being given support with technique and form, children need to be aware that poetry springs from many different starting points but particularly from 'personal or imagined experience' (*NLS*: 39). Michael Rosen, a poet who has inspired many children in recent decades, believes that better poetry is written if children value their own experiences ('I broke my mum's vase yesterday'), using the actual words that people speak ('That's my favourite vase you've broken') and their own responses and feelings ('Why does she keep going on at me? She shouldn't have left it in the sink anyway.') All of this can be the stuff of their poetry. 'My point in asking children to write down what people say and what they think, is that this is knowledge they already possess. It isn't something they have to concoct or translate' (1989: 43). Jill Pirrie (1987), a teacher who has worked with many children, believes that the close observation that she encourages in her children, whether it be of ants in the grass outside the school or of how they feel about a promise being broken, is what lies behind an effective poem.

Such work can be particularly empowering for children who are regarded as 'low achievers'. If these children work with familiar content, with a prescribed and supportive framework, and with no expectation that they have to write at length, then they have a real opportunity to compose successfully in ways that they may not be able to do in prose. As Sandy Brownjohn states:

> Teachers should be prepared to be surprised by the good quality of writing that may soon be in evidence from children who were hitherto low achievers. In fact, it is not always the most able children who write the best poetry in schools.
> (1994: 5)

In the writing of poetry the points that are made throughout this book about process (issues such as drafting) and product (issues such as presentation and publishing) are particularly significant. When children are working on what are often quite short stretches of text, then the motivation to shape and work on writing is enhanced. Children's poetry should not only be published, decorated and displayed but also performed to other children and parents. Many teachers make anthologies and tape collections of children's poetry which are highly motivating. All of this will contribute to the sense of audience and purpose with which they can approach the composing.

Teaching poetry writing involves experiencing poems, exploring words and language, looking at different forms and believing in the validity of one's own experience. 'The pursuit of form, coupled with the encouragement to revise and refine first impressions, leads writers back to their experiences and makes them respond more deeply to them.' (Tunnicliffe 1984: 151).

Finally, Figure 4.4 is a lullaby, a song written to lull babies to sleep, but in this case written for the sleepy dormouse in *Alice in Wonderland*. Influenced by Clare and Helen's reading and their knowledge of the form, this poem still contains their voices in its final cautionary advice. Notice also how they have enjoyed presenting their poem.

Further reading

Hiatt, K. and Rooke, J. (2002) *Creativity and Writing Skills, Finding a Balance in the Primary Classroom*. London: David Fulton Publishers.

Morgan, M. (2003) *How to Teach Poetry Writing at Key Stage 1*. London: David Fulton Publishers.

Morgan, M. (2003) *How to Teach Poetry Writing at Key Stage 2*. London: David Fulton Publishers.

Dormouse's Lullaby

ock-a-bye Dormouse,
In the teapot.
Sucking your treacle,
And sleeping a lot.
When nightfall comes,
You will climb up the spout.
But do watch out,
'Cause Queenie's about!
                                    by Clare and Helen

Figure 4.4

Rosen, M. (1989) *Did I Hear You Write?* London: Andre Deutsch.
Sedgwick, F. (1997) *Read my Mind: Young Children, Poetry and Learning.* London:
    Routledge.
See also Scholastic *Writing Guides* for Poetry and PCET posters (and teachers' notes)
    for Michael Rosen and Roger McGough.

NON-NARRATIVE WRITING

> At all key stages more children choose to write narrative rather than non-narrative and
> generally the standard of writing is higher in narrative. (QCA 1998: 14)

This statement shows how important it is to give children a broad experience of
writing non-narrative, as well as narrative. For many children narrative may be the
easier form to manipulate, but by giving them a range of different experiences and
support, non-narrative writing can become more attainable and more purposeful.

As has been said, non-narrative writing in primary schools covers a range of
purposes and forms and children need to be given opportunities to write in these, in
meaningful contexts, for clearly defined purposes and for specific audiences. In this
book there are examples of very young children writing lists, captions and labels. At

Key Stages One and Two non-narrative writing occurs across the curriculum as, for example, children label diagrams in science, and write diary accounts in history, captions in geography and instructions in design and technology.

Cross-curricular links

Most of the examples of writing discussed in this section come from different curriculum areas. However the language and structural features of these different types of writing will be taught explicitly within the Literacy Hour. For instance, in Year 2, instructional, explanation and non-chronological report writing are all taught. Non-chronological report writing is taught in Years 1.2, 2.3, 3.1, 4.1, 5.2 and 6.1 which indicates how much there is to learn about this genre and how this can be taught in a logical progressive way. An important point to remember about the link between the *NLS* and other curriculum areas is the need for children to apply their understanding of the text type they are learning about. Thus when a class is learning about non-chronological report writing in the Literacy Hour they need to use this type of writing in either science or geography in order to understand the genre completely. In the primary classroom report writing is often asked for in geography or science lessons. Here is an example of a Year 5 child's writing in science:

> Igneous Rocks
> Rocks are sometimes formed from a red-hot liquid that has cooled down and slowly hardened. This type of rock is called igneous. Here are some examples of igneous rock: granite, basalt, diorite, obsian and andesite. Another example of igneous is pumice. It is cooled lava that comes to the surface of the ground. People sometimes use it to clean dry skin off their feet. Granite is a quite a common rock. It is hard, tough cooled molten lava. The speckles are really compact crystals mixed into the lava, which can't be seen to the naked eye. It can be pink, white or grey and sparkly. The whole of Dartmoor is really one big block of granite. But one thing the stones look completely different and I think I know why. It is because the pumice is made on the surface and so it gets more air and that's why it looks bubbly and smooth but granite on the other hand is made under the surface and does not get so much air and that's why it is so solid.

This is a competent piece of writing that demonstrates the way in which a report is structured and all its characteristics. It includes an opening general statement, use of technical vocabulary, generalisations and the use throughout of the present tense. As a class teacher you could use such a well structured piece to show the class, perhaps on an OHP in shared text work, how to organise this genre. (As a teacher you would note that the personal tone of the hypothesis at the end is not strictly a feature of reports, but you would nevertheless be pleased to see how writing, thinking and learning unite at this point.)

Within many of the foundation and core subjects writing is used to help children think and learn, to remember what they have learnt and to give the teacher some evidence to assess their learning. One example of this is seen in Figure 4.5, an explanation of a vehicle designed and made in a Design and Technology lesson.

The diagram gives the reader a clear idea of what the vehicle looks like. It is labelled, with arrows to show the different parts of the vehicle. The text does not have an opening paragraph as most explanations do, but the diagram may act as such.

A subject such as history gives children opportunities to write in a range of genres for different audiences and in different contexts. A topic such as the Victorians will allow older children to write explanations of the growth of the Empire, newspaper

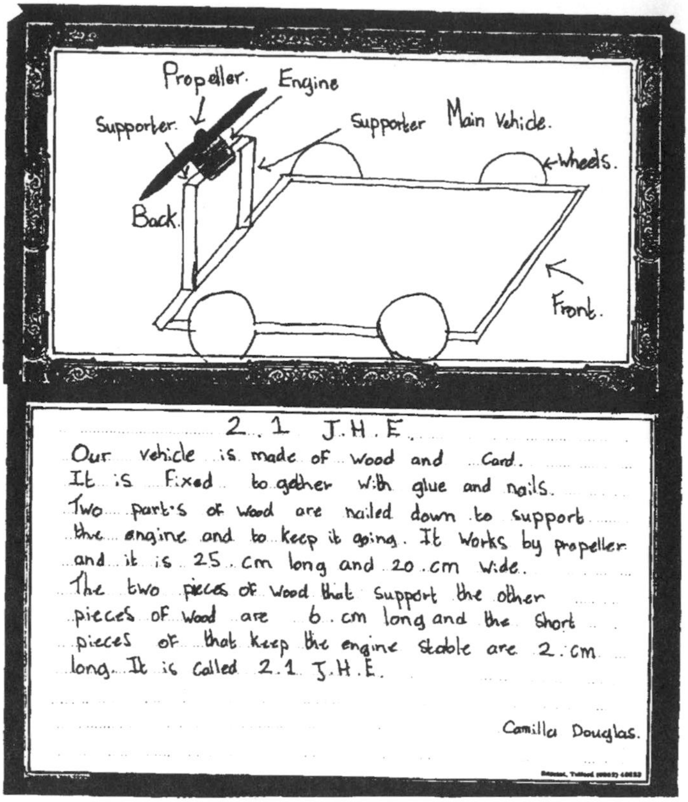

Figure 4.5

reports that argue for the abolition of child labour or discussion papers on whether to
have the Great Exhibition or not. The *NLS* states that 'Teachers will need to provide
opportunities for practising and applying new skills in independent work at other
times. Most of this practice should be productively linked to other curriculum areas'
(p. 14).

Teaching about genres

Generally, as children move through the key stages, non-narrative writing features
more strongly across the curriculum. To help children learn about different non-
narrative genres of writing: recount; explanation; report; procedural; argument and
discussion, it is important for the class teacher to model these for the children. This
can be achieved through shared writing, with the whole class or in a guided writing
group, which allows children to investigate the structure, language and purpose of the
genre. It is important to have examples of such writing displayed in the classroom for
the children to read and explore themselves. Reading and discussing information
books will also help children hear and understand the different language patterns and
features of texts, as will exposure to information books in group and guided reading
sessions. Lewis and Wray (1995) argue that the careful support that children need in
writing different genres can be provided by 'writing frames' – a series of prompts

specific to a genre. In the worked example below, a procedural genre (recipe writing) is being taught. The example demonstrates how a writing frame can be used. In the following section we are going to focus on the teaching of one specific genre – procedural – in order to illustrate both the teaching strategies and also progression.

Procedural writing

The procedural genre is one of the easier genres to understand because it records a sequence of events in time (chronologically), and aspects of it can be taught to children of all ages. Procedural writing can cover any set of instructions which uses a series of sequenced steps: instructions for playing a game, using a video recorder or building a model. The *NLS* recommends that in Year 2 children 'write simple instructions, e.g. getting to school, playing a game' and 'use models from reading to organise instructions sequentially . . .'. At Year 5 in the *NLS*, pupils are expected to write '. . . instructions for loading computers, design briefs for technology, rules for games'.

As discussed in the introduction of this chapter, when introducing a new text type to children it is important to read and analyse the text. A selection of recipes (*NLS*, Year 3.2), for instance, is shared with the children and used to explore features of this type of writing. The use of imperative verbs such as 'stir', 'shake,' 'fold' or 'beat', the layout and organization of the text and the use of adverbs in describing how to carry out the actions are all features of this genre which the teacher would focus on. The following is a selection of investigative activities that the children could attempt before beginning their own instructional writing:

- Find the (imperative) verbs in the recipe. (Using highlighter pens)
- Add the adverbs in the recipe. (Cloze procedure)
- Which words are used that link with time e.g. 'next', 'then'? (Replacing the temporal connectives)
- How is the recipe organised? (Sequencing a cut up recipe)

From investigating published recipes children can then move on to being supported in writing their own recipes, initially as a shared writing exercise. At this point an enlarged writing frame can be used as a model. A writing frame gives a series of prompts specific to the genre so a writing frame for a recipe might look like this:

- How to make . . .
- Ingredients . . .
- Equipment . . .
- Method . . .
    First
    Next
    Next
    Finally

With this support, the children could either go on to individual work with frames or they could write their own recipes independently. For a child who needs more support additional information can be inserted into the writing frame (e.g. some of the ingredients with quantities); for the more experienced child you could delete prompts under 'Method' shown here. (Full examples of a variety of frames are outlined more fully in the books by Lewis and Wray.) When the child is using the frame with confidence, recipes can be written independently. Such scaffolded teaching is powered by and is a clear demonstration of Vygotsky's (1978) theory of the zone of proximal development (see Chapter 1).

Many teachers in Key Stage One also teach the procedural genre through the use of recipes after children have been cooking. At this age the work might focus on broader aspects of layout, particularly how the ingredients appear as a list (*National Curriculum*, p. 9). Preliminary activities to 'warm' the genre could include reading and sharing recipes, and sequencing cut-up recipes. With an enlarged version of a favourite recipe a shared text session could be used to identify and label the different 'sections' in the recipe. After shared work on an enlarged frame the children could proceed to individual work, this time with a modified version of the one on page 71. For instance, the stages in the method could be numbered.

In summary we have seen children in the examples above:

- clarifying the audience and purpose;
- exploring and discussing different texts, in an interesting and structured way;
- writing the genre alongside the teacher;
- using a frame to support their own writing, either alone or with a partner;
- writing the genre independently.

In the next example a group of Year 5 children use the procedural genre to write an instruction book for a school camera. The handbook had been lost and the class was asked to write new handbooks for different people in the school. This gave the children real audiences and a purpose for doing the writing. One group wrote a handbook for the nursery children and staff, another group for children of their own age, and another wrote (Figure 4.6) for the staff of the school. The teachers had instructed them to make the text simple, straightforward and understandable! As it was Christmas, the children included 'Snappy the Reindeer' to act as guide for the book – an ingenious play on words. The manual was word-processed.

```
                    PREPARATIONS


     To take a photo takes a lot of
preparation.
  First of all you have to buy a film.
  To load it you pull a catch on the
bottom of the camera on the right hand
side.That will open the back.
  Pull up a little switch (called the
rewind button)on the top of the right
of the camera .With the little knob on
the bottom of the film slot it into
the chanell on the left hand side
inside the camera.Push the rewind
button home again and pull about four
inches of film, across from the reel
and put the holes of the film on the
sprockets which are on two cogs.Slot
the bit of the film that gets narrower
into the take up spool on the right
side of the camera and turn it slowly
clockwise until the film catches.Close
the back of the camera and wind on the
film until the numbers on the top of
the camera reach 0.You are now ready
to position your aspect,ready for the
photo.
```

Figure 4.6

The text makes some use of imperatives, such as 'pull', 'slot' and 'push'. Although laid out in one block, it takes the reader clearly through the sequence of steps required to take a photograph. It might have been more appropriate for the instructions to be laid out in numbered or lettered bullet points which would help the reader follow the instructions. Such support could have been introduced through the use of a writing frame.

The last example shows how an equally purposeful context, this time personal understanding of her pet guinea pig, motivates the Year 5 writer to take on board the features, including layout, competently.

How to Look After a Guinea-Pig
You will need:

- A guinea-pig
- A hutch
- An old tooth-brush
- A run
- Some grass
- Guinea pig food
- Some straw
- Water

1. Gently pick up your guinea-pig.
2. Get an adult to set up the run on a patch of grass.
3. Now gently put the guinea-pig inside the run. DO NOT drop the guinea-pig. If it starts kicking gently put it down inside the run.
4. Get inside the run. Get your old tooth-brush and gently pick up your guinea-pig and place it on your lap.
5. Gently brush your guinea-pig's fur like this.
6. Put some straw in your Guinea-pig hutch, some food and water. (Ask an adult to help.)
7. DO NOT leave your guinea-pig alone, because a cat could kill it or it could escape.
8. Pick up your guinea-pig and put it in the hutch.

Taking notes

In many non-narrative writing activities, both across the curriculum and within the Literacy Hour, children need to research specific pieces of information. Such pre-writing activity and research may involve reading information books, searching CD-ROMs, or exploring the Internet. In such research children need to make notes and this is something they need support with, particularly in overcoming the problem of verbatim copying of facts. The *NLS* states that children need to know the purpose and use of the note taking (Year 5.1). Wray and Lewis (1997: 37) remind us that 'to neglect the link between purpose and recording is to risk leaving children feeling that they have to note down all the information they read, even if it is only slightly relevant'.

As with other forms of writing the teacher can model note taking in shared writing with the class or guided writing with a group. Such modelling could use a CD-ROM or television screen as well as written text and could be reinforced in guided reading and writing sessions. Another way of helping children is through the use of a frame or grid which will help them consider what they already know and what they want to find out. Here is one example of a 'Know, Want, Learn' (KWL) grid with the third column allowing for note taking:

What do I know? What do I want to find out? What did I learn?
(Ogle 1989, in Wray and Lewis 1997: 47)

When reading information texts, children can be shown how to identify words and phrases that are significant. Teacher modelling can illustrate how this can be achieved, using an OHP. After this children can work on their own photocopy, highlighting key words and writing notes in the margin. A further suggestion might be for children to read a piece of information writing and then retell it to a partner in their own words. This oral rehearsal allows children to articulate what they want to write down and thus gives clarity to their thoughts. The important thing in all of this is to keep the link between purpose and recording very clear for the children.

Layout

Children know quite a lot about how texts are laid out from their experiences of writing outside school. Rules for playing games, instructions for assembling Lego models, catalogue pages and video packaging are all very much part of their reading lives. We can build on this implicit knowledge to help children explicitly reflect on the role of organisation and layout in non-fiction writing.

Different types of writing require different layouts and, even though writers may not attend to this aspect in the early stages, knowing about layouts and ultimately using them can aid the organisation of the composition. In your discussions and modelling of layout with children you will of course look at the layout of some narrative texts such as play scripts and poetry where layout plays such an important part; there are also some layouts such as those used for letters which relate to both narrative and non-narrative texts. Some are specific to non-narrative: lists, rules, instructions and so on. Some layouts are very familiar in our society and children will use them with ease; others are not so visible and children will need more inducting into their conventions.

As we saw in the examples above, layout is an important aspect of some genres, governing, as it does, the reader's expectations. For instance, look back at Figure 4.5 ('Preparations') and consider how much the use of headings and sub-headings and the use of bullet points would have helped the reader. Writing on screen enables layout aspects to be worked on easily.

Writing in Role: narrative and non-narrative

One further area to explore, in this chapter, is writing in role. This allows children to explore imaginary situations and can give them encouragement and support in writing in a range of genres. Writing in role allows young writers to feel a real need and purpose for writing; it gives them a strong context for writing and empowers them to write for a real (albeit imaginary) audience. Taking on writing in another role is a possible follow-up from reading or from drama.

Writing after reading

One of the most productive contexts for working on non-narrative is, paradoxically, the context of a story. A text such as *Mrs Plug the Plumber* (Allan Ahlberg and Joe Wright) could stimulate writing activities such as:

• a catalogue of a plumber's equipment, labelled and in alphabetical order;
• safety notices for certain pieces of equipment e.g. the blowlamp;
• a leaflet to advertise Mrs Plug's services;
• tickets for the world cruise and luggage labels;

Figure 4.7

- a note to cancel the milk;
- a postcard home from the Plugs.

Figure 4.7 is an example of the postcard which Elloa has written using the information that she gained from the story. (The address was clearly scribed on the reverse of the card.) She is writing in role as Mrs Plug although she does not completely sustain it as we see when she switches into her own name as she signs off.

The story has enabled Elloa to write in a generic form, in this case a recount which is quite a comfortable genre for children as it is often personal and about people and events familiar to them (see Chapter 2). She uses 'I' and 'we' and the past tense, all generic features of recount, and not difficult to manage because of the clear links with writing in the first person narrative.

All stories can give opportunities for genuinely contextualised writing in non-narrative genres. At Key Stage Two, a novel such as *The Runaways* (Ruth Thomas) could give rise to writing a missing persons' poster, a newspaper article about the missing children and a police report on progress in the investigation so far. A historical novel such as *The Wreck of the Zanzibar* (Michael Morpurgo) gives opportunities for persuasive writing, promoting the grandmother's and Laura's view that the turtle should not be eaten, and procedural writing in the form of instructions on how to reach the Scilly Isles. Within this context children not only have a real purpose for writing but also develop and extend their understanding of the narrative. This has clearly been outlined in the research by Barrs and Cork (2001) described in *The Reader in the Writer* in which Year 5 children learnt, and developed their writing through the opportunities given to compose in role.

> Under some circumstances children do seem able to write in the kinds of genres that genre theorists regard as socially important. It is observable, for instance, that children writing in role, either as part of a drama or in what might be termed 'drama on paper' can take on voices that they never usually use, and write as politicians, scientists or news reporters. (Barrs 1994: 255–6)

The Volcano, Learning through Drama (ILEA 1985) is a drama resource pack that places children on an island with an active volcano. Although this pack was devised many years ago the ideas are still relevant in the primary classrooms of the twentyfirst century. Through the drama each child takes on the persona of a character who lives on an isolated volcanic island. A crisis occurs as the volcano starts to erupt; the islanders all decide to leave except for one who stays to look after the animals. Usually the class teacher or drama teacher will take on this character and carry out a hot seating activity with the class in order to identify who this person is and why they have decided to stay on the island. After carrying out the initial drama, a class of Year 5 children, with total involvement and commitment to the drama, wrote in a variety of styles and forms. The first example (Figure 4.8), a flier from the tourist office, is a piece of writing that had been written before the eruption, intended to encourage eco-tourists to visit the island.

This is another example of the persuasion genre, here organised in the form of an advertisement. The piece is written for tourists who want a quiet environmentally friendly place to visit and the flier suggests the island has 'no pollution' and 'a wide range of wild life'. Such a piece could have been developed further by reading travel brochures to understand the language and structure that are often used to encourage tourists.

The next example is a word-processed newspaper report from *The Daily Scoop*:

> The islanders of Passamquddy fled in terror from the volcano, Mississippi. The Mississippi last erupted in 1928, over 60 years ago. The Mayor held a meeting on the subject last Monday. It was decided that the island should be evacuated but a 16 year old girl named Geraldine Harris said she would not be forced to leave Passamquddy. Geraldine is now living on Passamquddy alone. On leaving Passamquddy a boat went down off the coast of South America. Geraldine is quite sure that Mississippi will not erupt so she will be quite safe.

Finally a child in role as Bert Robinson, the butcher, wrote to the only islander who remained on the island. His letter, Figure 4.9, is a mixture of persuasion and recount genres.

There were many more examples written after just one morning's drama. The children were stimulated and eager to write as the project allowed them to explore writing within an imaginative framework that gives them a real purpose and audience. Although such lengthy drama work cannot be attempted within the structure of the Literacy Hour, the follow-up writing can be. Other such drama contexts can be developed in order to encourage a range of writing such as: a proposed development of a piece of land in order to build an office block; the closing of a youth club or the banning of all ball games in the playground.

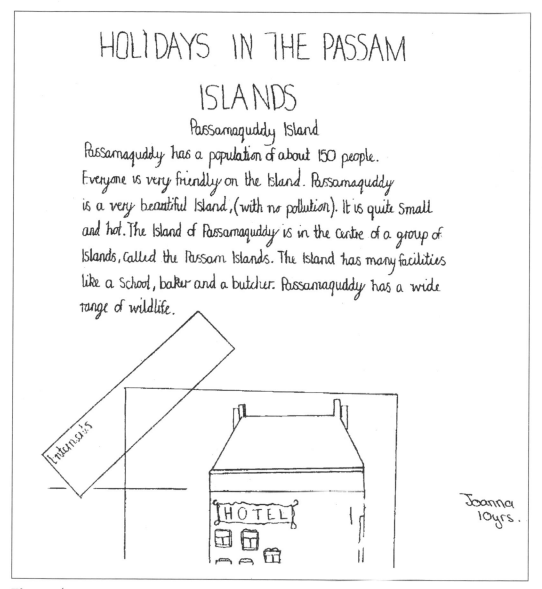

Figure 4.8

It is important that young writers of non-fiction understand the links between reading and writing, and from this they will begin to understand the structure and form of different types of writing. With appropriate support, children will move on to writing the genres independently for themselves. When children come to understand the purpose of the task, they will appreciate and enjoy the craft of non-narrative writing.

Many of the ideas in this chapter intended to aid children's composition in narrative, poetry and non-narrative writing are explored because young writers need encouragement to produce and shape writing, especially in new forms and especially when the transcription elements in the writing process have not yet become automatic. The role of the teacher is clear: she keeps the composition process going from

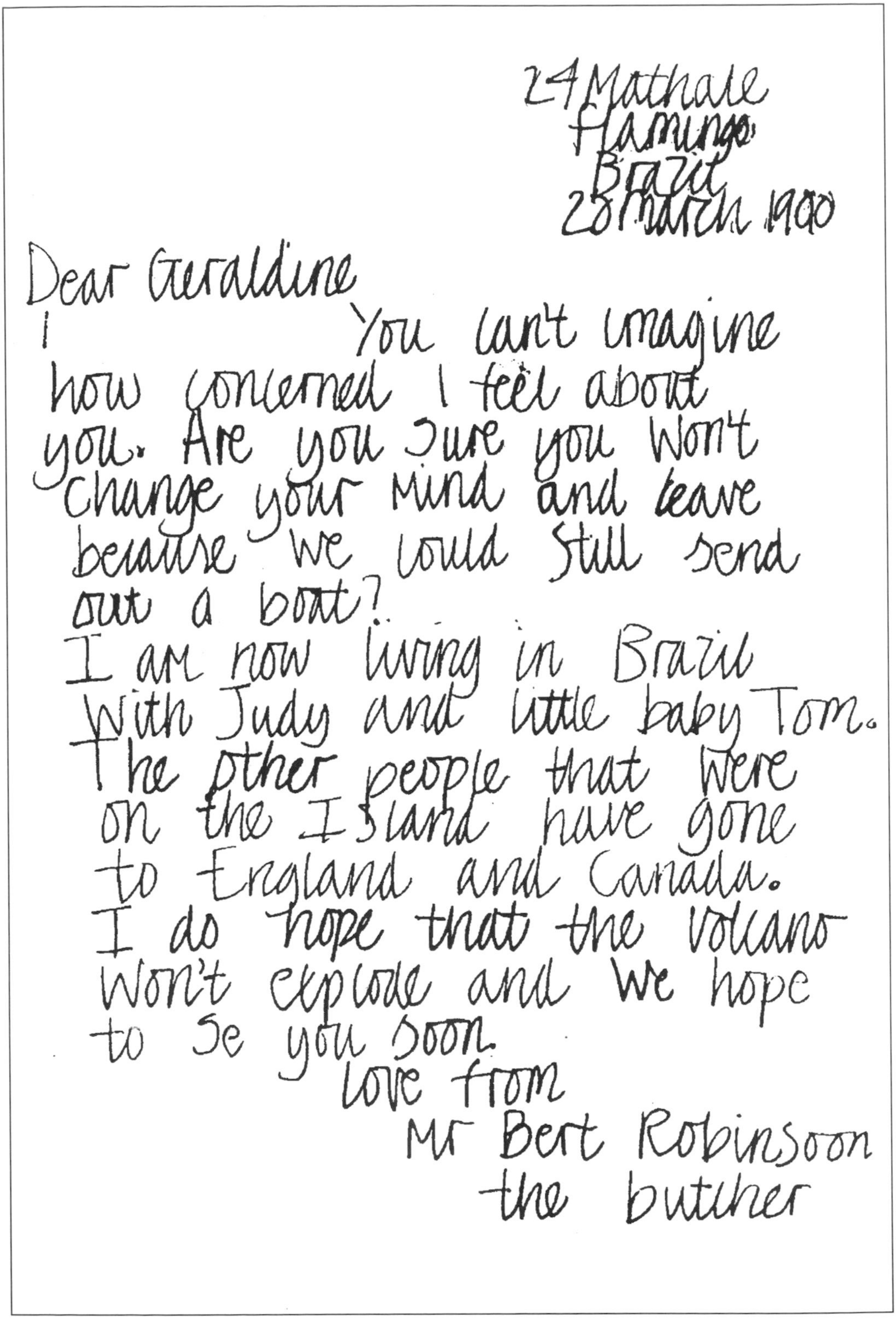

24 Mathale
Flamingo,
Brazil
28 March 1900

Dear Geraldine
I   You can't imagine
how concerned I feel about
you. Are you sure you won't
change your mind and leave
because we could still send
out a boat?
I am now living in Brazil
with Judy and little baby Tom.
The other people that were
on the Island have gone
to England and Canada.
I do hope that the volcano
won't explode and we hope
to se you soon.
             love from
                  Mr Bert Robinsoon
                  the butcher

Figure 4.9

'warm-ups', through discussion, sharing of information and key words; she helps with clarifying form, purpose and audience; she provides prompts and interest during the writing; she helps with revision; she shows respect and pleasure when the work is finished. As Margaret Meek explains in the introduction to *The Reader in the Writer* 'When young writers believe that their teacher is interested, really interested, in what they want to communicate, they will do their best to get their meaning across' (2001). Composition is at the heart of writing and the creative process is at the root of many of the most important activities that humans engage in. We need to nurture these impulses and ensure our writers leave the primary school as eager to compose in writing in every sphere as they normally are in their speaking.

Further reading

DfES (2001) *Teaching Writing: support materials for text level objectives*. London: DfES.

Goodwin, P. (1999) *The Literate Classroom*, Chapter 12. London: David Fulton Publishers.

Merchant, G. and Thomas, H. (2001) *Non-Fiction for the Literacy Hour*, London: David Fulton Publishers.

Palmer, S. (2001) *How to Teach Writing Across the Curriculum at Key Stage Two*. London: David Fulton Publishers.

Wellington, J. and Osborne, J. (2001) *Language and Literacy in Science Education*, Chapter 5. Buckingham: OUP.

See also Scholastic *Writing Guides* for Non-Fiction and Nelson Thornes *Primary ICT Handbooks* series.

CHAPTER 5

Transcription: Spelling, Punctuation and Handwriting

Alison Kelly

> My earliest memories of writing, and the only thoughts that still remain from my primary
> school days, are of continually repeating letters and words in set spaces, making sure that all
> the letters were the same size...
> (Year 1 undergraduate on BA [Primary Education] course)

This is the experience of many children – that 'writing' means the physical aspects of spelling, handwriting and punctuation. You will remember that Chapter 2 introduced the distinction between 'composition' and 'transcription' and that in Chapter 4 we took a careful look at supporting composition. These earlier chapters discussed the importance of ensuring that children have a balanced view of the writing process and are aware of the importance of the content of their writing as well as its 'presentation' as the *National Curriculum* describes it. But now we turn to the secretarial aspects of writing: spelling, handwriting and punctuation, which are, of course, very important.

SPELLING

In order to teach spelling effectively, teachers need to have a clear personal grasp of some of the principles and difficulties of the English spelling system; these are the focus of the first section. With this underpinning, we go on to examine effective spelling strategies, recent concerns about the teaching of spelling and what is known about how children learn to spell. The final section provides practical suggestions for effective teaching.

What do teachers need to know about spelling?

In this section we look at the spelling lessons we have to give ourselves in order to teach children effectively.

The English Language

> I take it you already know
> Of tough and bough and cough and dough?
> Others may stumble but not you,
> On hiccough, thorough, laugh and through.
> (in Rosen 1995: 36)

English has an alphabet of 26 letters but a spoken language which uses at least 44 single sounds (phonemes). So, as the anonymous extract above shows, the 26 letters have to work hard to represent such a multitude of sounds!

One difficulty lies with the alphabet used for English, which is not one that was intended to fit English sounds. Its history can be traced back over thousands of years and thousands of miles to 1700 BC in the Middle East, where a North Semitic language, very similar to Hebrew, was spoken. This alphabet was passed from the Phoenicians to the Greeks, whose model influenced the Etruscans, who, in turn, influenced the Romans. Christian missionaries arrived in this country in the sixth century and brought the Roman alphabet with them (Crystal 1995).

In addition, as you will see in the section below on Etymology, our language has also been profoundly influenced by the many different groups of people who have settled here over the centuries all bringing with them their own languages. So an alphabet ill-matched to the sounds of the English language and a history of repeated invasion have contributed to a rich and sometimes bewildering linguistic pot-pourri.

Etymology

Etymology, the history of words, is full of stories about language. It is a fascinating and rich area that can engage children's interest and stimulate their curiosity. It is an area of study that demands we know a little about the history of the English language itself. This history is about the many different groups of people who arrived and settled here across the centuries. They brought their own languages and we can find traces of these in English today. The chart in Figure 5.1 provides you with an overview of these influences.

Etymology explains connections between words: for instance 'telephone', 'television', 'telepathy' and 'telegraph' all share the same prefix, 'tele-', which comes from Greek meaning 'at a distance'; 'centigrade', 'per cent' and 'centipede' come from the Latin root 'cent' meaning 'one hundred'. Etymology accounts for oddities such as silent 'k' (as in 'know') which used to be sounded: in Saxon times, the Old English word for 'knife' was 'kanif', and it was only when the word became shortened to 'knif' that sounding the 'k' was dropped. The study of etymology also reveals how word meanings have changed over time. For example, David Crystal (1995) shows how the word 'silly' started life in Old English some thirteen hundred years ago as meaning 'happy' or 'blessed' and moved through several shades of meaning such as 'innocent' (Middle English) to its current definition of 'foolish'.

Morphology

Morphology, the structure of words, provides one way of overcoming some of the difficulties created by the nature of the English language.

It is an area that teachers need to know about explicitly because it enables them to help children see unchanging patterns in spelling. Take the word 'teach' which is the root (or stem) of '*teach*er', '*teach*ing' and 'un*teach*able'. The bits that come before and after word roots are called affixes. There are two sorts of affix: prefixes which come before the root and suffixes which come after the root. So in the word 'unteachable', 'un-' is a prefix and '-able' is a suffix. (It helps to know that 'pre' comes from Latin and means 'before' and the 'su' in suffix comes from the Latin 'sub' meaning 'under'.)

Affixes work in two ways: inflectionally and derivationally. Inflectional suffixes (and they are always suffixes) show changes in meaning and mark grammatical contrasts. The main inflectional endings in English are as follows:

- plural: e.g. dog*s*
- to mark possession: e.g. the dog's collar, the dogs' collars

DATE	INFLUENCES	WORDS STILL IN USE
500 BC	Celtic tribes speaking different languages	crag, torr
43 AD–410 AD	Romans invade and settle. Latin becomes official language of government. Celtic languages persist.	
350–600	Angles, Saxons and Jutes invade. Old English (OE) develops from their Germanic dialects.	under, in, skirt, mother, farm, love
597	Arrival of first Christian missionaries (Roman). Latin becomes more influential.	altar, wine, candle
500 – 800	OE written down using Latin alphabet which did not have symbols for some sounds e.g. 'th'. OE spoken in different dialects. Celtic and Latin also spoken.	
Late 700s	Viking invasions (from Scandinavia) and settlements begin bringing Old Norse with them.	sky, egg, Thursday, sister
871–899	Alfred defends Wessex against the Vikings. Develops use of English to promote national identity. Records, literature written in English. Some Latin works translated.	
1066	Norman invasion: French becomes the language of the court, ruling classes, government; Latin still used in church; OE still spoken. Norman scribes import French conventions e.g 'qu' for 'cw'.	beef, court, castle, prison, tax
1100–1450s	'Middle' English develops from French influence.	
1362	King's speech at opening of parliament made in English.	
1387	Chaucer's *Canterbury Tales* written in English.	
1300–1600	Standard English develops out of East Midlands dialect (used by universities, court, government). First grammar books written.	
1476	Caxton's printing press contributes to standardisation.	Introduction of 'gh' for hard 'g' sound e.g. 'ghost'.
Renaissance	Renewed importation of Greek and Latin words with revival of interest in classical languages.	'dette' becomes 'debt' (to show its Latin source: 'debitum').
1755	Samuel Johnson's dictionary stabilises spelling conventions still further.	

Figure 5.1

- regular verbs:
    the past tense: e.g. I walk*ed*
    past participle: e.g. I have walk*ed*
    present tense, 3rd person singular: e.g. she walk*s*
    present participle: e.g. walk*ing*
- comparatives and superlatives: e.g. bright, bright*er*, bright*est.*

There are exceptions to all of these and you will find that children's errors frequently demonstrate their over-generalisation of such endings; for instance, they may write 'mouses' instead of the irregular plural 'mice'. Another difficulty that children may encounter with inflectional endings is the fact that they sound different; try saying 'ripped', 'pinned' and 'plodded' and you will hear the same '-ed' ending sounding as '-t', '-d' and '-id' respectively. Plurals can be heard differently too as you can see in a child's spelling of 'dogz'. There is more consistency between the look of words than there is between their sounds. The '-ed' remains constant in writing despite changes in pronunciation. The important thing for children to know is that it is the meaning that is privileged over and above the sound of the word.

'Derivational affixes' are used to create new words; they both add and change meaning. Adding the prefix 'un-' and the suffix '-able' to 'teach' makes for a total change of meaning! It is interesting for you (and older children) to note that a derivational suffix changes the word class of the root it is added to, but a derivational prefix does not. So the addition of the suffix '-er' to 'teach' changes the verb 'teach' into the noun 'teacher'. On the other hand, while the prefix 'un-' changes the meaning of 'happy', it has not changed the word class: 'happy' and 'unhappy' are both adjectives.

Affixes and roots are morphemes – 'the elements out of which words can be constructed' (Crystal 1995: 198). These are the smallest chunks of words that make meaning and cannot be broken down further. There are two types: 'free morphemes', which are just that, free to stand on their own ('teach', 'dog', 'talk'), and 'bound morphemes', which have to be bound or tied to another morpheme to make sense. Inflectional suffixes such as the 's' in 'dogs' and the 'ed' in 'talked' are bound morphemes as are the prefix and suffix in '*un*teach*able*'.

Two free morphemes may be combined to form a compound word such as 'earthquake', 'seaside', 'goosebump' and 'goldfish'. These are usually nouns and the spelling of the two morphemes remains the same in the compound as it did when they stood alone. Sometimes though the morphemes are blended together as in 'channel' and 'tunnel', which come together as 'chunnel'.

Language change

As this last example shows, one of the most interesting aspects of any kind of word study is what it reveals about the dynamic nature of language: it never sits still, as the addition in the 1990s of 'Teletubbies' to the stock of 'tele-' words demonstrates.

Prefixes move in and out of fashion too. The prefix 'mega' (from Greek meaning 'big' as in 'megaphone') was reborn in the late twentieth century and is used to kick off any number of phrases ('mega-hungry/sad'). Melvyn Bragg (*Roots of English*, BBC) provided a wonderful example of the merging of old and new when he reported on the use of the word 'megashant' by youth in one Cumbrian village. Here the prefix 'mega' is combined with 'shant', an old Cumbrian dialect word meaning 'shamed'.

Our language is rich in borrowed (loan) words like 'cafe' (French), 'bungalow' (Hindi) and tycoon (Japanese). We add new words (neologisms) such as 'internet' and 'website'; the Oxford English Dictionary has an 'Addenda' section for these. After a while, of course, these either become so commonplace that they are no longer neologisms or they slip out of usage completely. Crystal (1995) cites the examples of 'blurb' (coined in 1907) which has stayed with us, whereas 'gubble' (to indulge in meaningless conversation) did not find a niche for itself! Then there are acronyms like AIDS (Acquired Immune Deficiency Syndrome), INSET (In-service Training) and SCUBA (Self-Contained Underwater Breathing Apparatus).

Spelling rules

Morphology, informed by etymology provides a rather more reliable way of understanding the regularities and constants in our complex spelling system than looking at what were traditionally known as the 'rules' of spelling. Following such rules is not straightforward, partly because of the inconsistencies in our language and partly because the rules are sometimes just very hard to understand. This one seems simple enough: 'there will be a double "l", "f" or "s" after a single vowel at the end of a short word (e.g. tell, sniff, fuss)', but then there are the exceptions – 'us', 'bus', 'gas', 'if', 'of', 'this', 'yes' – to name a few. Others rules are more extended and, therefore, harder for young children to get their heads round: 'Words ending in both a single vowel and a single consonant always double the last consonant before adding an ending beginning with a vowel (e.g. stop, stopped, stopping)' (rules taken from Bannatyne and Cotterell 1966).

Rules are only useful when they apply to a large number of words, when there are few exceptions and when they are easily understood. Mike Torbe (1995) suggests that the following might be helpful; he calls them 'descriptions' rather than 'rules':

1. 'q' is always followed by 'u' and another vowel always follows the 'u';
2. 'i' (pronounced 'eye') at the end of words is spelled 'y' or (less often) 'igh';
3. words that sound as if they have an 'o' in them generally spell it with 'oa' in the middle of the word and 'ow' at the end;
4. words that sound as if they have an 'a' in them generally spell it 'ai' in the middle and 'ay' at the end;
5. English words do not end with 'i', 'o', 'u', 'j' or 'v'. Instead they follow these patterns: i = ie or y, o = ow, u = ue, j = ge or dge, v = ve;
6. the 'er' sound at the end of words is generally spelled 'er';
7. when you add 'full' to the end of a word, it drops one 'l' and becomes 'ful'.
(Torbe 1995: 77–8).

Spelling strategies

So how are spellers to contend with the complexities of the English language? This classroom snapshot demonstrates the range of strategies that we call on as we spell.

I am watching five-year-old Billy writing a story. His first sentence reads: 'the likl dog hd a spotid tale' (*the little dog had a spotted tail*).

He starts with 'the', which is, of course, spelt correctly – it is part of his repertoire of known words, his 'sight vocabulary'.

We can imagine the effort that has gone into his encoding of 'little': he has segmented (separated out) each phoneme and made a valiant attempt to represent each one as he hears it. And it is a very good approximation: 'little' splits into four phonemes – /l/ /i/ /tt/ /le/ – and Billy has tried to represent these – /l/ /i/ /k/ /l/. The American researcher, Treiman (1993) has shown just how complex the cognitive processes are when a child engages in such an apparently simple task. First the child has to segment the word into its spoken elements, then remember the order of these and then choose the appropriate graphological fit for each unit. It is only on the third stage that Billy has stumbled as he assigns inappropriate graphemes for the phonemes /tt/ and /le/. And it is a very logical assignation for /k/ is the way Billy pronounces /tt/ in this word. A more mature speller who pronounced the word in the same way as Billy would know that this pronunciation is not echoed in the spelling.

Billy started with the opening consonant phoneme /d/ for 'dog', but then he hesitated before completing the word in one confident move with its rime '– og'. He has been reading about the adventures of *Meg and Mog* and it is highly likely that he has made a link (or analogy) between the rime that 'dog' and 'Mog' share. He is not so successful with 'hd' where, again, he picks up the dominant consonant phonemes but uses the 'd' to stand for the whole of the rime, omitting the vowel completely.

Billy goes about spelling 'spotted' just as he did 'little' by segmenting the phonemes and trying to represent them with graphemes. But 'spotted' holds an additional challenge: its two morphemes (spott/ed). If Billy had picked up the inflectional suffix 'ed', he might have had more success. Again, Treiman's insights are helpful here as she shows us that not only do children have to analyse a word into its spoken, phonemic, units but they need to detect the morphemic units as well.

Billy's use of the homophone 'tale' for 'tail' shows him using graphic (visual) strategies. 'Tale' is part of his repertoire of sight words and is a perfect match in terms of sound but not meaning.

Billy's efforts reveal what a complex and multi-faceted process spelling is. This young writer is already orchestrating different types of knowledge from different sources. What follows is a summary of these sources which some writers describe as the 'cue-systems' of spelling. Like reading, we need to draw on all of these and there is no particular hierarchy or order in which these can be learnt. The point is that some words will yield more easily to being encoded by one strategy and others by another.

Phonemic strategies: segmenting

Segmenting is the process of picking out the separate phonemes and representing these graphically. It is closely linked to blending, the corresponding process in reading, whereby a child comes to a new word and sounds out, or blends its phonemes in order to decode it. In the case of segmenting (before writing) the child already holds the whole word (e.g. 'duck') in her head that is to be encoded (/d/u/ck/) whereas in blending (when she is reading) she has to amalgamate the sounds to create a 'new' whole word (/d/u/ck/ – 'duck').

Phonemic strategies: onset and rime

Recent research has given us another, more child-friendly way of splitting words up: into their 'onsets' and 'rimes'. Many words, such as 'bread' and 'tread', can be broken down into an onset (the opening consonant or consonant cluster i.e. 'br', 'tr') and rime (the vowel sound and any other consonants, the unit which rhymes i.e. 'ead'). Several researchers (Bryant and Bradley 1985; Goswami and Bryant 1991; Goswami 1995) have investigated the importance of children's early phonemic awareness and the impact this has later on their ability to use phonic strategies. These researchers show that early experience of rhyme (through nursery rhymes, rhyming books etc.) lays important foundations for phonemic awareness. These foundations are established as children draw on their experience of rhyme to make rime analogies which draw their attention

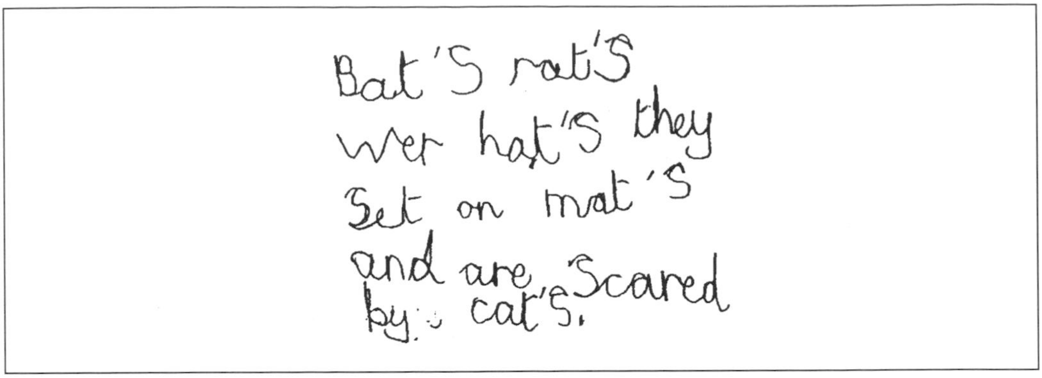

Bat's rat's
wer hat's they
set on mat's
and are scared
by cat's.

Figure 5.2

to phonemes. So a child may be able to link the words 'man', 'van', 'pan' and 'can' because she can hear the shared rime ('-an'). In Figure 5.2 a five-year-old enjoys the power of onset swapping!

Onsets and rimes provide a way of seeing regularities between words that are more reliable than sound strategies. Goswami (1995) tells us that there are 90 words that share the 'ight' rime, while common rimes such as 'en' (in 'ten') and 'an' (in 'fan') have a staggering 904 and 750 respectively!

Morphemic strategies

As we saw above, in the section on 'Morphology', understanding the morphemic make-up of words provides stable information about spelling patterns. A more mature or experienced speller than Billy would have recognised the inflectional suffix '-ed' in 'spotted'. Morphemic understanding is enhanced by etymological knowledge. So the child who has learnt about the Latin prefix 'bi', meaning 'two', will avoid starting a spelling of 'bicycle' with either 'by' or 'buy'.

Graphic strategies

We also use visual, or graphic strategies when we spell. This means we may remember whole words (as part of a sight vocabulary) or parts of words (significant letter strings maybe as in 'banana'). You will realise that none of these strategies operates independently or discretely of one another. A child may aurally split a word into its onset and rime but will also bring graphic strategies into play when making an analogy (as Billy did with 'dog').

High interest words

Even spelling has an affective dimension, and there are some words that are highly significant for children that they can spell with ease. Consider how effortlessly a dinosaur-obsessed child will spell 'tyrannosaurus', 'stegosaurus' and other challenging polysyllabic words.

In summary we have to draw from a range of features when we spell. These are listed below with an indication of where they appear in the *National Curriculum* Programmes of Study for Writing:

- the look of the word (Key Stages One and Two);
- the phonemes in the word (Key Stages One and Two);
- common letter strings (Key Stage One) e.g. -ough...;
- knowing that groups of words are linked by meaning (Key Stage Two) e.g. fact, factual, finite, definite, infinite;
- inflectional endings (Key Stage Two) e.g. flapped, glided, soared;
- rime analogies e.g. m*ight*, f*ight*, l*ight*, c*at*, b*at*, r*at*;
- etymology (Key Stage Two) e.g. *volvere* (Greek – to roll): *revolve, revolver* (pistol with a revolving mechanism), *Volvo*
- prefixes and suffixes (Key Stages One and Two) e.g. im-, bi, -ed, -ing.

Concerns about the teaching of spelling

As the Introduction and Chapter 1 in this book show, early approaches to writing focused exclusively on transcriptional aspects at the expense of composition. Rote learning and copying were the order of the day. By the 1960s, the pendulum had swung back with the 'creative writing' movement, where all the focus seemed to be on the production of imaginative writing. A teacher from that era was quoted as saying that 'spelling is learned naturally by the children and, from the reading, punctuation becomes increasingly familiar' (quoted in Clegg 1964: 40). This idea that, for some children, spelling can be learned 'naturally' is one that recurs from time to time and Margaret Peters' research into spelling (first published in 1967, revised edition 1985) gave us a neat soundbite for this with the title of her book *Spelling: Caught or Taught?* Peters cites evidence of challenges (and counter-challenges) to the systematic teaching of spelling from the very beginnings of this century, and the more recent writing 'process' movement and 'developmental' or 'emergent' approaches to writing have been criticised for marginalising the teaching of the presentational skills of writing.

Writing process approaches

Let us start with the writing process movement (see Chapter 2) which drew teachers' attention to the composition/transcription distinction and suggested that it was necessary for children to be clear about that separation too. A teacher's prompting that children should, in the first instance, concentrate on getting the ideas down without worrying about the spellings is indeed a worrying one if that is all that is going on. But for many, such advice was seen only as the first step in the process of writing and the children would go on to 'edit' their work, paying proper attention to the spelling and other surface skills of writing. It could be that the separation of composition and transcription, with the apparent relegation of transcription to second place, led to some misunderstandings about the importance teachers were placing upon it. This may have been the case for some teachers, but many carefully attended to the teaching of spelling and handwriting.

'Developmental/emergent' approaches

The tension between composition and transcription is possibly most visible for a very young writer when the strain of forming letters and spelling words can seriously inhibit the fluency of writing. This is why routines such as dictated writing (see Chapter 3), which allow a focus on composition, are so important in the early years.

As we showed in Chapter 2, research into children's early moves into literacy

Figure 5.3

revealed how they can make active and creative hypotheses about ways in which all of the writing system works. Remind yourself by looking at Figure 5.3, Madeleine's representation of her first day at play group.

As well as drawing the teacher and children, she has 'written' their names underneath. She knows that drawing and writing are different: that they look different and that they have different functions. Arriving alongside insights about composition and transcription, such findings had exciting potential for work in the early years. It became clear that encouraging children to make unaided spelling guesses not only showed teachers what the children knew and understood about writing but it also freed children from the transcriptional strain of 'getting it right' at the first attempt. They were enabled to focus on what it was they wanted to say. So the suggestion that children should 'have a go' at their spellings stems from a concern to free up composition.

At about the same time, interesting research was being published about the nature of the children's invented spellings. For instance, the work of Ferreiro and Teberosky (1979), two researchers who were influenced by Piaget's work, suggested that children pass through stages in their writing and that it is possible to describe a developmental progression. *The Beginnings of Writing* (Temple *et al.* 1982) was read by many teachers and reinforced the idea of spelling stages. We will return to the idea of spelling stages below but the important point is that the idea of stages can be interpreted as suggesting that there is a natural progression and this can marginalise the teacher's role. The danger with labels like 'developmental' or 'emergent' is that they might suggest that the teacher can simply let it all happen and does not need to do any specific teaching. The notion of stages also suggests a rigidity and uniformity in children's learning and that all children will pass through the same stages in the same way. Teachers know that this is not the case!

How do children learn to spell?

What do we know about how children learn to spell? This is an area that has inspired some fascinating research over the last 30 years which has had a significant impact on classroom practice.

Some children appear to learn to spell quite easily without any apparent spelling lessons and one source of anxiety for teachers about their role could rest with an implicit view that somehow we are born as 'good' or 'bad' spellers. Such a view can leave the teacher feeling uneasy about the effectiveness of her teaching so it is helpful to know what does contribute to the success of some children. This is what Margaret Peters (1985) looked at in her study of children who appeared to have 'caught' spelling. She found that verbal ability and interest in words, good visual perception and what she terms 'carefulness' in handwriting were important factors in the children's success (p. 21). Such research provides helpful classroom pointers and we shall look at practical activities which support the development of these factors in the sections below on teaching spelling and handwriting.

Spelling development

Another area we know much more about now concerns spelling development. New knowledge about spelling development has enabled teachers to identify what counts as spelling progress. Research into early literacy (e.g. Clay 1975; Bissex 1980; Goodman 1984) has yielded fascinating insights into the very beginnings of spelling development, and knowing about these early stages can inform our teaching considerably. One commonly used model of spelling development comes from Richard Gentry (1982), who identifies five possible stages. His work is based on the case study of a single child (Bissex 1980), which means that we do need to approach it with some caution. The labels he uses for the different stages describe what the child is doing, not the teacher. As we said above, the notion of stages can be a very beguiling one and it is most important that we use this understanding flexibly and do not treat the stages as neat milestones through which every child will pass in just the same way. Here is a brief summary of some of the features of Gentry's stages:

1. *Pre-communicative*
- knows that symbols can be used to say something;
- uses a range of symbols (invented, numbers, letters – upper and lower case);
- does not make sound–symbol connections.
2. *Semi-phonetic*
- is beginning to make sound–symbol connections;
- knows about word boundaries, how writing is arranged on a page;
- may shorten some words.
3. *Phonetic*
- uses sound–symbol connections consistently;
- uses known words (sight vocabulary).

4. *Transitional*
- uses visual strategies;
- uses most conventions of spelling system.

5. *Correct*
- has basic knowledge of spelling system and rules;
- knows about word structure (morphology);
- has a large sight vocabulary.

Uta Frith (1985) offers another model of spelling development. This is a more fluid, flexible model with 'phases' rather than 'stages' but, like Gentry's model, Frith's analysis provides teachers with helpful ways of understanding children's spelling efforts and focusing teaching appropriately. She shows how children progress from reading whole words (the logographic phase) to a phase where they start analysing parts of words (through onset and rime or at the level of the phoneme). Finally, they move from this analytic phase to the orthographic one, where whole words are read and can then be spelt. The model is neatly summarised by O'Sullivan and Thomas (2000): 'what Frith describes is a movement from whole words to parts of words, and back to an attention to whole word structure' (p. 16).

Another strength of this model lies in the way Frith clarifies how spelling and reading connect. Essentially, what she shows is a shifting in the balance of power between reading and writing. At first, it is reading that powers the process as children recognise whole words in context. But the balance shifts to spelling as children's analytic skills develop through their early efforts to segment and analyse words into onsets and rimes. Reading takes over again as the primary site for the development of children's orthographic skills.

The two models are complementary as Figure 5.4 shows. What is important is that we use these models to inform our understanding and appreciation of the children's efforts.

The progress of one child across her first year in school illustrates aspects of these models. First, a word about the context of these pieces. They were written by Kelly when she was five years old and attending a primary school in South-East London. She was a confident and outgoing child, neither an over- nor an under-achiever. It was part of the school's assessment policy that samples of children's writing would be kept regularly and be passed from teacher to teacher in a portfolio (see Chapter 6). The samples were to be unaided (i.e. containing the children's own spelling attempts) so that both composition and presentation could be monitored. Such unaided writing was only one part of the writing curriculum in this reception class. Shared writing, copying, dictated writing, spelling and handwriting were all regular classroom routines and it is important to remember this when looking at the examples below, as such development came about as part of well structured and carefully focused teaching. There is much to be said about the composition of Kelly's pieces but the focus of this chapter is spelling. The reminder about content is important though and in this classroom the teacher was most rigorous in responding to the content of the pieces as well as to the presentational aspects. Finally, the intention of presenting these pieces here is to illustrate spelling development; I will look at practical issues concerning the nature of our responses to such early attempts in a later section.

In her first week at school Kelly (age 5.3) wrote the story in Figure 5.5.

The fox in the wood. What can he see? Some ducks playing in the pond. A little boy called Sean came along. The little boy said 'Get away you nasty fox.' The fox ran away and the boy said to the ducks 'Don't be afraid, I am only a little boy.'
(as dictated to her teacher).

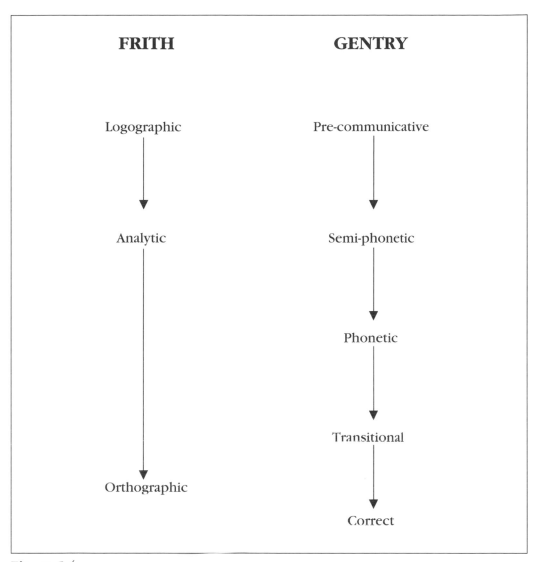

FRITH

GENTRY

Logographic

Pre-communicative

Analytic

Semi-phonetic

Phonetic

Transitional

Orthographic

Correct

Figure 5.4

This is an example of Gentry's 'pre-communicative writing' in that there is no apparent evidence of sound–symbol correlation. The label 'pre-communicative' is slightly misleading as she clearly is communicating meaning but remember that 'pre-communicative' is a label for the spelling. (You might find 'pre-phonemic', as used by Temple *et al.* 1982, a more useful label.) However, she already knows quite a lot about the presentational aspects of spelling: she knows writing runs from left to right and is arranged on the page in lines; she knows that writing consists of strings of letters (but not that these are divided up into units – words – yet) and that the same letters can be used in different combinations. In common with many young writers she draws heavily on the most familiar of all strings of letters at this point – her name.

As an important aside, compare Kelly's work with that of a bilingual child, Shirin, in the same class, as seen in Figure 5.6. This was Shirin's response to her teacher's request to write something about her holiday. A fluent Urdu speaker, the writing shows

Figure 5.5

Figure 5.6

what a remarkable amount Shirin has already grasped about two quite separate writing systems. She started with the top line which ran from right to left and includes distinctive characters influenced by the Urdu alphabet. When she went on to write 'Allah' on the next line she used the characters of the English alphabet written from left to right. Such early attempts need to be recognised, applauded and built upon. In this case, the teacher went on to make a book with Shirin who dictated what she wanted it to say to the teacher and then her father was enlisted to translate it into Urdu. These two versions allowed the teacher to build on the child's mother tongue while supporting her development in reading and writing English.

Back to Kelly who, a month later, wrote the caption in Figure 5.7 for a picture: 'I am in the garden and my friend is in the garden and we found a frog. The frog hopped away.'

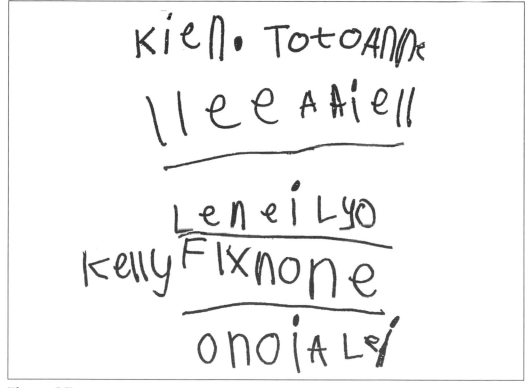

Figure 5.7

Although this is still 'pre-communicative', you will see that Kelly has made considerable progress in her understanding. Most importantly she seems to be moving towards the concept of words, as the underlining and the relished full stop after 'kien' suggest. There are words she can spell, 'To', 'to' and 'Anne' (her friend's name), and she is using a greater range of letters. Still in the early stages of reading, her identification of a few whole words and her recognition of words in the environment are typical features of Frith's logographic stage.

In December she makes a most significant leap with the reply in Figure 5.8 to her teacher's 'post-it' on a message board enquiring about Kelly's weekend plans. She replies: 'My friend's coming tomorrow and we are going to play with each other.'

We see here the beginnings of sound-symbol correspondence as Kelly starts to map her graphological knowledge onto her phonological knowledge. She has moved into

Figure 5.8

Frith's 'analytic' phase, and what Gentry terms 'semi-phonetic' writing. Look, for instance, at her partially successful segmentation of the phonemes in 'tomorrow'. There are sight words in use too: 'to' and 'we'. The use of 're' for 'are' is characteristic of this stage where the child draws on the name of the letter – 'R' (for that is what she hears). Importantly though, the 'e' at the end of 're' shows that she is not only making use of phonemic strategies but also using the look of the word; we cannot hear the 'e' on the end of 'are', we see it on the page. In Frith's model, this is where the balance of power between reading and writing has shifted to writing: as children begin to segment the phonemes in their writing with such intent concentration so their attention will be drawn to the phonemes in their early blending efforts in reading. Goswami (1995) shows how children's attempts at writing words help crystallise the concept of the phoneme, thus enhancing phonemic awareness, an important underpinning for effective use of phonic strategies in reading.

   The next piece, written in February, is a caption for a drawing: 'I like this flower because it smells nice and it is lovely.' There is a real attempt here to spell each word

Figure 5.9

relying mostly on the phonemes, especially initial ones. She is no longer using letter names. Apart from the omission of 'is' in the last line, there is one-to-one correspondence (i.e. matching of spoken and written units), there is more evidence of sight words and, in the brave attempt at 'because', evidence of sight strategies – she knows there is a 'u' in there somewhere! She is on the way to the 'phonetic' stage where there is an attempt to represent each sound.

The final sample from this year is the first page of a story (Figure 5.10) written in June, which shows Kelly continuing to progress: 'One day there was a little boy who wanted a little bear but his mummy wouldn't let him have one. "Then I'll be upset", said the little boy.'

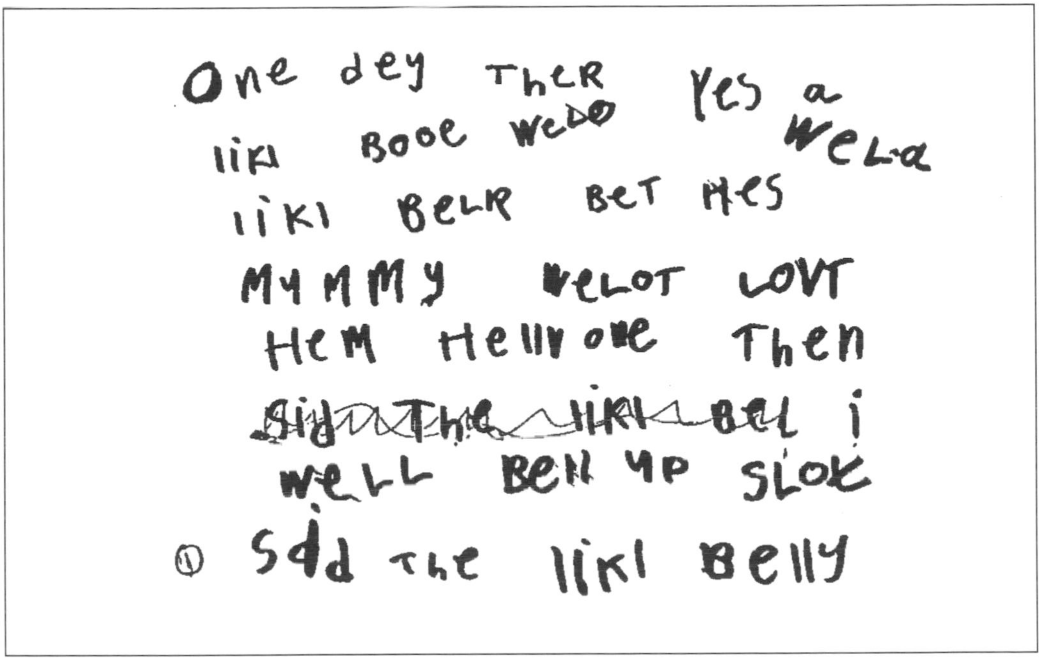

Figure 5.10

She continues to use phonic strategies ('likl booe'), graphic strategies ('sid' for 'said') and known words. The fact that she resorts to the earlier strategy of using her name when really stuck – see her last attempt at 'boy' ('belly') – is a useful reminder of the fluidity of these early writing stages and the fact that children do move backwards as well as forwards! The important thing is to be able to recognise the strategies being used so that you can respond appropriately.

Gentry's final stages are 'transitional' and 'correct'. A transitional speller will be using vowels in each syllable and beginning to develop visual strategies. We have evidence of Kelly doing the latter but not the former. In Figure 5.11 a Year 2 child is showing a confident grasp of aspects of the transitional stage.

Note the spellings of polysyllabic words such as 'beautifulest', 'keeper' and 'expensive' (Two other points of interest are the circled words being the ones that she has identified as needing help with and the use of the initials 'ct' for 'Christmas tree' which stems from class discussion about drafting techniques.)

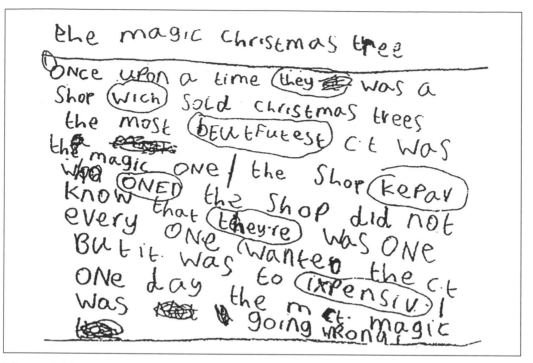

Figure 5.11

Learning styles

It is clear from looking at the transcripts and tone of Kelly's work that she is a confident young writer; this is not the case for all children and we do need to take account of what we know about children's different learning styles when we plan our teaching. A longitudinal study by Bussis *et al.* (summarised in Barrs and Thomas 1991) has illuminated our understanding about this. Focusing mainly on reading, it revealed that some children favoured the so-called 'big shapes' (the pattern and language of the texts) whereas others went for 'smaller units' (words and sounds). The former group tended to be risk takers as they went for the overall meaning and fluency of a text, sometimes at the expense of word for word accuracy. Those who went for the smaller units were not such confident risk takers preferring a step by step approach as they tackled individual words and letters. Bussis' findings suggested that such learning styles were not restricted to reading and extended to other curriculum areas and it seems highly likely that the same findings will apply to the confidence with which children approach spelling tasks.

In the section on spelling strategies we look at ways of developing children's confidence. More recent research (Dombey and Moustafa 1998) suggests that difference in learning styles also extends to whether the children initially draw from visual or aural data. The important issue here is to take on board these different learning styles and to be mindful of Bussis' finding that, provided the teacher was offering a balanced teaching 'mix' which addressed all aspects of reading, then the children were not disadvantaged by their learning style. So when we come to think about planning for spelling, it is most important that we structure it to include a balance of strategies.

Teaching spelling

When?

You will need to plan opportunities for teaching spelling into your regular routines such as shared reading and writing (see Chapter 3). As well as using these to introduce new work (for instance looking at inflectional 'ed' endings in a story), these routines provide ideal opportunities for consolidating and reinforcing previous work. Some of your teaching will arise more incidentally from ongoing pieces of writing as the children work on editing, and you may identify a number of common difficulties that you choose to tackle in a specially planned whole-class or group session. Spelling also lends itself well to short sharp bursts of teaching; maybe a quick five minutes focusing on a word many children are finding hard – 'because' is always a good contender! Draw the class together to look closely at the word, identify its particular difficulties, highlight these, maybe make up a class mnemonic ('bears eat cakes and unpack suitcases early'), and draw analogies with another word – 'cause'. Regular slots like these, taken at a good pace, can tackle individual difficulties and generally raise the children's interest in words.

How? Four more 'rules'

How do we go about teaching spelling? The first rule is – positively! Spelling is an area of enormous anxiety for many children so the quality and tone of our response to their attempts is important. Look back to Figure 5.11 and the child's guesses for 'which'/'wich', 'beautifulest'/'beutfutest' and 'expensive'/'ixpensiv'. In each case she has got more of the word right than wrong; children will be most encouraged when this is pointed out to them. As well as engendering a more positive attitude this also focuses the children's attention on the different parts of the word; having identified what they have got right, they are then encouraged to look with care at the part of the word that is wrong.

Closely tied to this comes the second rule: encourage the children's interest and curiosity in words. Enthusiastic teaching can offer the children a model of spelling as a topic that is fascinating, not fearful. Many of the activities below encourage the children to find out about words, their history and their make-up. Activities that focus on the regular features of language such as prefixes and suffixes (see teaching ideas on these below) will be most supportive in enabling children to see regularities and consistencies and increase their curiosity and confidence.

Thirdly, make sure the children can attend to spelling in a focused way. Previous chapters have emphasised the importance of ensuring that transcriptional strains do not stifle the children's compositional powers and it is, of course, just as important that children should be similarly free to attend to transcription. So discrete sessions are needed as is an emphasis on attending to spelling in the editing stage. Occasionally a compositional context, rewriting a known story for example, will be fairly undemanding so a focus on spelling would be manageable and appropriate.

The fourth rule, and it is one that holds good for all aspects of presentation, is to do with context and the importance of reminding children that such work belongs to the realms of real life reading and writing. A cautionary tale comes from my early years of teaching when I worked hard to teach my eight-year-olds how to do cursive (joined up) writing. After a few weeks I realised that they were doing beautiful joined up writing in their handwriting books but nowhere else! Try to ensure, as this Year 2 teacher does, that work on discrete aspects of spelling is grounded in shared texts work. The class were learning about the prefix 'un-'. After some shared writing about an unhappy caterpillar the teacher goes on to make a shared list of words with the children that take the 'un-' prefix. Later in the week this is revisited with the whole class, whose attention is drawn to this page in an enlarged version of *Six Dinner Sid* by Inga Moore: 'Unlike Aristotle Street, the people who lived in Pythagoras Place talked with their neighbours.' In independent group work the children work as 'word detectives' hunting out their own examples from a range of carefully chosen picture books and pages from comics and newspapers.

What?

As very young children make early moves into writing teachers can begin to alert their attention to letters and words. The child's own name is a significant first source of information as is the environmental print he or she sees all around on packets, signs and notices. You need to ensure that your classroom is print-rich and exploits these early understandings by providing many opportunities for children to write (e.g. shopping lists pads in the role-play area, a noticeboard with examples of environmental print, children's names prominently displayed). Shared reading and shared writing provide ideal contexts for making links with letters that the children already know. As well as a rich range of literature and non-fiction you will need a selection of alphabet friezes and books and lots of rhyming texts. As you know from an earlier section in this chapter, there is important work to be done with such texts in the early years in developing phonemic awareness. We cannot start work on individual sounds if children are unable to single them out, and plenty of reading aloud as well as sharing nursery rhymes and finger rhymes will all feed such awareness. For the Foundation stage the *CGFS* provides a number of stepping stones (p. 60–1) which focus on developing children's early rhyming skills and tuning young children into the rhythm and sounds of English.

The *NC* provides a list of what should be covered in Key Stages One and Two, and the *NLS* provides a more detailed breakdown in the form of its Word level objectives. There are two additional publications to support you with teaching ideas: *Progression in Phonics* for the Foundation Stage and Key Stage One, and *Spelling Bank* for Key Stage Two. *Progression in Phonics (PIPs)* offers games and activities to develop children's blending and segmenting skills. As we saw above, reading and writing development are closely linked so, although this appears to be rather more of a reading document, there is much to help with spelling. *Spelling Bank* promotes an investigative approach to the teaching of spelling at Key Stage Two and provides activities for all the spelling objectives.

The suggestions that follow are grouped around broad strands from the *NLS*. Some are particularly appropriate for the early years or later Key Stage Two work but many can be differentiated according to the needs and abilities of the children you work with. They complement the activities offered in *Progression in Phonics* and *Spelling Bank*. There is not room in a book like this to include detailed activities so some books are recommended that have full details of useful activities. They are all included in the booklist at the end of the chapter.

Alphabetic knowledge

- Have a good range of books and friezes (on the wall and on the tables).
- Sing and chant the alphabet.
- Make alphabets for younger classses.

- Make address/phone books.
- Encourage multi-sensory learning by providing different materials with which to form letters (paint, sand, magnetic letters, plasticine, felt tips, chalk, crayons).
- Play 'I spy...'
- Use software such as *abc-CD: the talking animated alphabet* (Sherston).

Names

- Make name cards for the children.
- Make personalised (laminated!) placemats for use at lunch time in the nursery.
- Spot letters, letter strings from names in other words (especially environmental print with young children).
- Make books featuring children's names.
- Play with names e.g. make up alliterative phrases.

Rhyme and word play

- Make regular use of songs and finger rhymes.
- Read nursery rhymes and rhyming texts aloud regularly.
- Collect jingles.
- Encourage children to participate in shared reading of rhyming texts.
- Make lists of words that rhyme from texts you have read together.
- Make up games e.g. rhyming snap.
- Make up alliterative phrases and sentences. Spot examples of alliteration in poetry.
- Older children can look for rhyming patterns in poetry and try writing their own e.g. limericks.
- Use a CD-ROM such as *Ridiculous Rhymes* (Sherston) which gives the children the opportunity to listen and/or sing along.

Homographs and homophones

- Build on word play ideas to look at words that are spelled the same but mean different things (homographs), as in 'Follow my lead, drop the lead, use unleaded petrol', and to look at words like 'bare' and 'bear' that sound the same but are spelled differently (homophones).
- Make books to illustrate these differences.

Onset and rime

- See 'Rhyme' above.
- Read books like *Mig the Pig* (Colin and Jacqui Hawkins) where the changing onsets are made very clear through the use of split pages; go on to make one like it using a different rime.
- Set up activities where children can physically change the onsets of words, e.g. with cards, magnetic letters.
- *The Starspell* (2001) software package includes onset and rime.
- *Rhyme and Analogy Activity Software* complements the *Oxford Reading Tree* but can be used independently of this.

Learning words

Children need to develop a sight vocabulary of known words and the *NLS* contains lists of words to be learnt from Reception through to Year 5. Try to vary the ways in which you teach these:

- Point them out in shared reading and writing.
- Use 'look-cover-write-check'.
- Play games, e.g. snap.
- Focus on one a day ('word of the day').
- Include them in wordsearches and crossword puzzles.
- Group them, e.g. by initial sounds, meaning, letter strings...
- Have children keep personal lists ('my spelling targets for the week'). There are numerous software packages that include onscreen word banks (e.g. *Write Away*; *Clicker 4*).
- Make a shared list with the children of ways of remembering spelling (see list under Spelling Strategies above).
- Find out about software that allows children to practise spelling, e.g. *I Love Spelling* (Dorling Kindersley) for older children has an intergalactic setting in which children travel to different planets to meet spelling challenges. *Starspell* uses 'Look-cover-write-check' strategies and speaks the words for the children (in an English accent). *Focus on Spelling* (HarperCollins) complements the *NLS* objectives and provides a range of activities, investigations as well as diagnostic tests.
- Use talking books software on the computer, e.g. Talking stories *Oxford Reading Tree* is now available in this form. You can highlight particular words by clicking on them.

See Hackman and Trickett (1996) for a useful selection of activities on 'How to Learn a Spelling'.

Developing graphic strategies

As well as learning whole words children need to develop visual (or graphic) strategies to remember strings of letters. All of the suggestions above will help these as will the following:

- Play 'Shannon's Game', which is like 'Hangman' but you have to guess the letters in order, which encourages the children to predict common letter strings.
- Teach and encourage the use of analogy e.g. by collecting words that share the same rimes such as '-ight' or '-an'.

Work on phonemes, clusters and digraphs to support segmenting and blending:

- Find examples in shared reading and writing.
- Find examples in the children's names.
- Make up tongue twisters and alliterative sentences.
- Make word wheels.
- Make a *br*ick wall of words that start with the 'br' cluster, a *tr*ain of 'tr' words and so on!
- Make a display of objects and pictures starting with the phoneme/cluster/digraph.
- Make a shared list of words that children can add to during the week.
- Play 'I spy'; children could make 'I spy...' quiz cards for a particular sound e.g. '...something beginning with "ch"'.

Work on roots, prefixes and suffixes:

- Look at roots of words and see how many different ways you can make them 'grow' using prefixes and suffixes e.g. 'eat': 'uneatable', 'eating', 'eater'.
- Use shared reading and shared writing to demonstrate fixed inflectional endings such as '-ed' and '-s'.
- Make shared lists of prefixes, find out where they come from (Latin or Greek) and what they mean e.g. 'photo-' is from Greek and means 'light'; 'bi-' is from Latin and means 'two'. See Pratley (1988) for useful lists.
- Collect verbs that take the regular '-ed' suffix and sort them according to the different sounds these endings make e.g. ripped, pinned, rushed, robbed, saved, plodded, laughed . . . .
- Make collections of words that share prefixes e.g. 'un-'. Take a theme such as 'giants' and use this as a starting point for drawing and/or writing about the unwell, unhappy, unwise, unreasonable . . . giant.
- Investigate the ways in which derivational suffixes change the word class e.g. 'eat', a verb, becomes a noun with the addition of '-er': 'eater'.

Compound words

- Collect examples.
- Make up new ones.
- Make a set of cards for Pelmanism consisting of different elements of compound words (e.g. wind/mill, white/board etc).
- Enjoy the literal meanings of some compounds (babysitter, heartbroken); children could illustrate these.
- Allan Ahlberg's book *The Clothes Horse* is a whole exploration of compound words and the poet Roger McGough is clearly intrigued by compounds as so many of his poems play with them.

Using dictionaries and word banks

- Have a good range of dictionaries in all classes.
- Use word level slots or short class/group sessions to demonstrate dictionary skills.
- Turn class word banks into mini-dictionaries. A word bank for your work about Victorian England can become a Victorian dictionary.
- Make topic related word banks (e.g. for Hogwarts School).
- Multimedia information sources now include dictionaries e.g. *Concise Oxford Dictionary* (OUP on CD for WINPC) and see Hackman and Trickett (1996) for an excellent range of dictionary activities.

Finding out about words: etymology, loan words and word families

- Encourage curiosity in words.
- Show children how to use an etymological dictionary (which will always list the abbreviations used e.g. 'L' for Latin).
- Look at lists of loan words and research their origins e.g. judo (Japanese), zebra (Bantu), pyjamas (Persian), yacht (Dutch).
- Categorise words into families e.g. centigrade, centurion, centipede . . .
- Make collections of acronyms (LASER etc.) and neologisms.
- Find out about the stories of words e.g. the silent 'b' in 'debt' came about in the

sixteenth century when scholars wanted to show off their knowledge of Latin, so changed 'dette' (Middle English word) to 'debt' to show they knew it came from the Latin 'debitum'. Look for other examples of these in Chapter 4 of Liz Laycock's book *Spelling and Vocabulary*.

- Use CDs such as the *Oxford Thesaurus* (OUP on CD for WINPC).
- Enjoy Terry Deary's *Wicked Words* in the *Horrible Histories* series (Scholastic).

Independence and risk taking

While some children will happily 'have a go' at spellings others are much more reluctant. We have already talked about the importance of focusing on the bits of the word that the child has got right. Here are a few more ways to boost confidence:

- Give them 'have a go' books or encourage them to have a go on a separate piece of paper.
- Encourage them to write as much or as little of the word as they can even if this is just the first letter.
- Suggest they draw a 'magic line' where the spelling should be if they are really stuck (but be careful about this one; some children latch on to this too readily and their writing becomes a mass of magic lines!)
- Make sure that you demonstrate that crossing out is acceptable when drafting; do this ostentatiously during shared writing.
- Encourage the child to work on a word processer right from the start (it is not just for the final product!) and to use the spell-check function. Alert children to the aspects computers do not check, e.g. grammar, so that 'She gave them there dinner' would not be picked up because 'there' is correctly spelt.
- Use a spell-check package like *Co-Writer* (Don Johnston for Mac and PC) which allows you to type a few letters and then shows possible words which the child can click on to choose. *Write: Out Loud* includes a checker which interprets early spellings beyond the first two letters (which is all that conventional checkers respond to).
- Use a hand held spell-checker where the child types in a word and it gives alternatives.
- Use speech support on the computer; most new PCs come with this option whereby each word is spoken as the child writes (or it can be set to read back after each sentence or as you prompt).
- Discuss spelling strategies with the whole class thus reminding them of the many different ways they can tackle spellings (see section above on Spelling Strategies).
- Make class lists of relevant spellings for a topic, e.g. on a word mobile.
- Make a class list of different ways the children can find out how to spell a word without asking you, e.g. from notices on the wall, from books, from a word bank, from a writing partner...

Glossary

ACRONYM:	a word made up from the first letters of words e.g. LASER (Light Amplification by the Stimulated Emission of Radiation)
AFFIX:	prefixes and suffixes joined to base words, e.g. 'un-' and '-ing'

ALLITERATION:	where words start with the same phoneme, e.g. 'six sizzling sausages'
BLEND:	In its noun form a 'blend' used to mean what is now called a 'cluster' (see below). Its more contemporary use is as a verb referring to the process of sounding out phonemes in an unknown word while reading.
CLUSTER:	phonemes which run together, e.g. 'br', 'spl'. Note that each phoneme can be heard.
BOUND MORPHEME:	a morpheme (see below) that has to be attached to another morpheme in order to make sense, e.g. 's' on the end of 'dogs'
COMPOUND WORD:	the combination of two free morphemes, e.g. 'whiteboard'
DERIVATIONAL AFFIXES:	create new words, e.g. 'teach' changes meaning with the addition of the suffix '-er' to become 'teacher'
DIGRAPH:	two letters which make one phoneme, e.g. 'ch', 'ee'
ETYMOLOGY:	the history of words
FREE MORPHEME:	a morpheme (see below) which can stand on its own, e.g. 'dog'
GRAPHEME:	You may find different definitions of a grapheme. The *NLS* describes it as the smallest unit of sound represented as a written symbol. The twenty-six letters of the alphabet are graphemes and so are groups of letters which emerge as one sound, e.g. 'ow' in 'hollow'. David Crystal, however, provides a rather broader definition: 'the smallest unit in the writing system capable of causing a contrast in meaning' (p. 257). Because they affect meaning, punctuation marks and symbols such as '&' would count as graphemes.
HOMOGRAPH:	words that look the same but mean something different, e.g. 'font' (as in church and on the computer)
HOMOPHONE:	words that sound the same but mean different things, e.g. 'bear'/'bare'
INFLECTIONAL AFFIXES:	suffixes which mark grammatical contrasts. In English these are to mark plurals, possession, subject–verb agreement and comparatives and superlatives
LOAN WORD:	words that have been 'borrowed' from other languages, e.g. 'bungalow' from Hindi
MORPHEME:	units of meaning that cannot be broken down any more, e.g. 'dog'
MORPHOLOGY:	the study of the structure of words
NEOLOGISM:	new word
ORTHOGRAPHY:	a language's writing system (i.e. letters, spelling and punctuation conventions)
ONSET AND RIME:	'onset' is the consonant or cluster of consonants at the beginning of a word or syllable which precede the vowel, e.g. 'str(-ing)'. 'Rime' is the rest of the word or syllable, including the vowel, which enables the word to rhyme with other words, e.g. '(str-)ing'.

PHONEME:	the smallest unit of sound that can be spoken or heard such as 'b' in 'bat'. Meaning changes with the replacement of the phoneme, e.g. 'cat' or 'bag'. Over forty-four vowel and consonant sounds have been identified in English.
PHONEMIC AWARENESS:	is the ability to detect phoneme distinctions
PHONOLOGICAL AWARENESS:	the ability to hear and detect difference in the sounds of a language
PREFIX:	an affix at the beginning of a word, e.g. '*dis*appear' or '*un*pleasant'
ROOT:	the 'base' or 'stem' of a word to which prefixes and suffixes can be added, e.g. 'teach'
SEGMENT:	separating out the phonemes in a word for encoding. Note that this complements 'blending' (see above), the difference being that the child already holds the word, ready for segmentation whilst writing. In contrast, blending involves sounding out and reassembling the phonemes of an unknown word.
SUFFIX:	an affix at the end of a word, e.g. 'count*ed*', 'help*ful*'
SYLLABLE:	segment of a word that always includes a vowel (with 'y' counting as a vowel in this case)

Further reading

Hackman, S. and Trickett, L. (1996) *Spelling 9–13*. London: Hodder and Stoughton.
Hunt, G. (1999) 'Working with words: vocabulary development in the primary school' in Goodwin, P. (ed.) *The Literate Classroom*. London: David Fulton Publishers.
Latham, D (2002) *How Children Learn to Write*, Chapter 5. London: PCP.
Laycock, L. (2001) *Pocket Guides to the Primary Curriculum: Spelling and Vocabulary*. Leamington Spa: Scholastic.
Palmer, S. (2000) *A Little Alphabet Book*. Oxford: OUP/TES.
Ramsden, M. (1993) *Rescuing Spelling*. Devon: Southgate Publishers.
Torbe, M. (1995) *Teaching and Learning Spelling*, 3rd edn. East Grinstead: Ward Lock.

Useful websites

Suppliers:

www.cricksoft.com
www.donjohnston.com
www2.sherston.com
www.collinseducation.com

For up to date information about software go to teachers' reviews of CD-ROMs on www.becta.org.uk/technology/software/index.html

PUNCTUATION

   ...it breaks it up; otherwise it would just make a lot of nonsense...
   ...annoying little things that make you stop writing...
   (Two six-year-olds on punctuation)

Despite the second child's misgivings in the above, punctuation is crucial to coherence, clarity and meaning in writing but it is a more elusive and low profile aspect of presentation than spelling or handwriting. Why is this? At a glance it seems to be rather straightforward, with a relatively small number of punctuation 'marks' whose functions seem quite clear (see the Glossary at the end of this section to check those functions). Its elusiveness is partly because there is relatively little research evidence about punctuation compared to the wealth that has been amassed about other areas of writing. It is also because understanding punctuation is part of a larger web of complex understanding that the child has to grapple with: namely the differences between spoken and written language and, in particular, the concept of a sentence.

The inclusion of punctuation in a chapter on transcription is itself questionable because of the central role it plays in determining meaning. Michael Rosen (1995) gives us these examples – which Key Stage Two children enjoy – and which make a telling point:

> The butler stood by the door and called the guests' names.
> The butler stood by the door and called the guests names. (p. 40)

Indeed, the first version of the English *National Curriculum* included punctuation in Attainment Target 1 (Composition) because 'it helps the reader to identify the units of structure and meaning that the writer has constructed' (Cox 1991: 148). Interestingly, and maybe reinforcing the earlier point about scant research in this area, this is the only reference to punctuation in Cox's chapter on Writing. In this book we have chosen to discuss punctuation alongside spelling and handwriting as we believe it is more easily understood and tackled as part of the secretarial aspect of writing. As the well crafted little story in Figure 5.12 by a six-year-old shows, an insistence on correct punctuation in the first draft of a piece of writing could be as stifling to the child's compositional confidence as could a similar insistence on correct spellings (as we discussed in the section on Spelling).

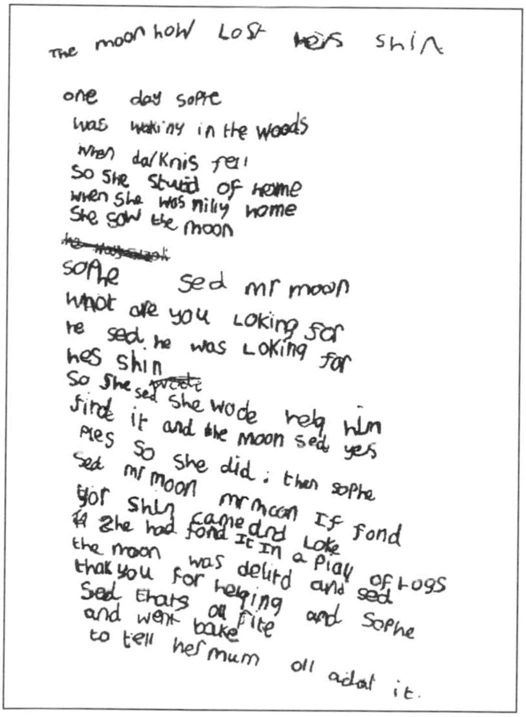

The Moon Who Lost His Shine
One day Sophie
was walking in the woods
when darkness fell,
so she started off home.
When she was nearly home
she saw the moon.
Sophie said 'Mr Moon,
what are you looking for?'
He said he was looking for
his shine.
So she said she would help him
find it and the moon said 'Yes
please' so she did. Then Sophie
said 'Mr Moon, Mr Moon, I've found
your shine, come and look.'
She had found it in a pile of logs.
The moon was delighted and said
'Thank you for helping' and Sophie
said 'That's all right'
and went back
to tell her mum all about it.
(corrected version)

Figure 5.12

In this section I will look at what punctuation does, at some of the problems it presents and at what is known about how children learn to punctuate. The final section provides teaching suggestions.

What is punctuation?

Martens and Goodman (1996) give us the following definition:

> Punctuation is the conventionalised means by which an author shares with a reader necessary information about meaning or language structure not contained in the words of the text. Grammatical divisions such as sentences, clauses, phrases and words, along with marks signifying meaning, such as exclamations, support, clarify and enhance written messages for the reader.
> (p. 37)

In spoken language we use a range of linguistic and paralinguistic devices to make our meaning clear. These devices include intonation, stress, gestures and pauses. None of these is available to the writer who has to turn to the orthographic device of punctuation to do this work. If you think of the way your voice rises at the end of a question you can see how a question mark provides a written equivalent. Now try the same with exclamation marks: 'Get me some honey or I'll hit you with my bommy knocker!' shouts the giant in *The Hungry Giant* (Story Chest 1980). Take away the exclamation mark and see how much calmer his demand becomes. You could even try replacing the exclamation mark with a question mark (which may feel clumsy but bear with the activity) and see what a difference that makes to the way you read the piece. So question marks and exclamation marks contribute towards stress (or emphasis) and intonation.

Other punctuation marks act as boundary markers. They differentiate between different structural units: phrases, clauses, sentences and direct speech. Look at the sentence I have just written and note the colon between the main clause and the list (which is a phrase), the comma separating elements of the phrase, and the full stop marking the end of the sentence. If you feel unsure about these conventions the best way to reinforce understanding (and this works very well with children) is to seek out examples in literature.

Punctuation problems

So far so good, but it is not all quite so easy. For a start, the rules of punctuation are a convention and not very stable; they have been and continue to be subject to much change. Secondly, hearing and identifying the structural units mentioned above is not something children find easy. I will take each of these problems in turn.

Changing rules

Like spelling, the conventions surrounding punctuation have changed over time. Crystal (1995) tells us that the very earliest texts did not even have gaps between words, let alone any punctuation marks. It seems that punctuation was first introduced as a way of indicating how the text should be read aloud, as reading aloud – 'oratory' as it was called – used to be a high status activity. In fact Parkes (in Hall and Robinson 1996) found that, in Roman times, it was the *reader* who inserted the punctuation. In England, it was not until the seventeenth century that punctuation began to be used to mark grammatical distinctions. The notoriously problematic and misused apostrophe for possession (as in 'the dog's tail' or 'the dogs' tails') was not introduced until the second half of the seventeenth century and speech marks were not used for direct speech until the eighteenth. Commas and full stops are two of the oldest marks, whereas the question mark is a relative newcomer on the scene (Clark 1996). Some marks are no longer used: for instance, Crystal describes an ivy leaf shaped 'hedera' which was used in Anglo-Saxon writing to mark the end of a piece of writing. Maybe its descendant is the small, black square that some magazines use to indicate to readers that they really have reached the end of an article scattered over several pages.

Caxton's printing press (1476) was a major stabiliser for different aspects of language, particularly for the development of a standard English (the East Midlands dialect) and spelling. Spelling conventions were further consolidated in 1755 with Samuel Johnson's dictionary, which was not the first but was certainly a most significant early dictionary. Therefore, although the printing press did bring some stability to punctuation conventions, they have not been subject to the same degree of standardisation as spelling and remain quite flexible. As I write, there are renewed calls for the apostrophe that marks possession to be abolished.

Authors seem to vary in the status they give to punctuation. Crystal tells us that, although Charles Dickens was punctilious in his use of punctuation, William Wordsworth left his to the publisher. The authors of *Writing Under Control* had no such options! The publisher's notes on the final presentation tell us that 'Although the book will be professionally copy-edited and proofread, the author is responsible for correct spelling and punctuation' (Fulton 1998: 1).

Older children will enjoy knowing something of punctuation's evolution and it will help them think about the functions of contemporary punctuation marks. You will find ideas below which will encourage this.

Spoken and written language

We look now at punctuation's function as a boundary marker in writing. One major difference between speech and writing is that speech occurs in 'utterances' – chains of clauses which are rarely completely formed sentences. Typically these clauses will be joined by conjunctions such as 'and' and there will be many pauses, false starts and 'vague completers' (i.e. implied appeals to the listener such as 'isn't it/innit' and 'you know'). Look back at Chapter 2 for more detail about these differences.

Writing, on the other hand, uses the sentence as its basic unit, so a prerequisite for placing full stops, question marks and exclamation marks appropriately is an understanding of what a sentence is. The *NLS* says that 'a sentence is a unit of written language which makes sense on its own'. The authors go on to identify four types of sentence, to describe the punctuation required and to say that most sentences will have a subject and predicate (see next paragraph). As teachers, it is important that we have a clear definition but, as you will appreciate, explaining this to children is not so straightforward.

Hall (Hall and Robinson 1996) gives us a clear overview of some of the difficulties children can experience with grasping such definitions of a sentence. It is important to say here that Hall was writing before the advent of the *NLS*, so was not criticising its definition, but his comments do cast critical light on it. He points out that young children find grammatical definitions abstract and hard; we ourselves may grapple with the notions of 'subject' and 'predicate' so it is harder still for a child. He also suggests that the idea of a sentence 'making sense' is problematic: 'Does a word have complete sense? Does a sentence have complete sense if it is part of a paragraph, or a chapter or a book?' (Hall and Robinson 1996: 15). You will see children in school finding their own ways of tackling these difficulties, maybe by imposing physical boundaries and putting capital letters at the beginning of a line and full stops at the end, regardless of meaning. One such example is illustrated in Figure 5.13.

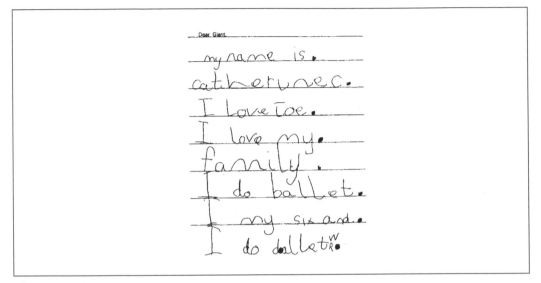

Figure 5.13

All of this is not intended to deter you from helping children to understand sentences. There are practical ideas included in the final section which are informed by what we now go on to look at: the experiences and understanding that children do bring to learning about sentences and using punctuation.

How do children learn to punctuate?

Despite the lack of research in this area it is possible to draw on our understandings about children's moves into writing in order to illuminate some key aspects of learning about punctuation.

Learning about sentences

Unless children have experienced some kind of language delay, they generally come to school as competent speakers of their mother tongue. This means that they have a fund of implicit knowledge about how language works syntactically (such as the order in which words occur) in spoken language but they will not be so attuned to the concept of a sentence, which belongs to written language. You will remember from Chapter 2 that Kress (1982) showed how children's difficulties in learning about sentences are best understood when seen as part of the child's moves from spoken to written mode.

However, many children will have made a start in securing understanding of written language, particularly if they have been read to from an early age. Studies of children's early reading behaviour (Holdaway 1979) and of their dictated stories (Fox 1993, and see Chapter 3 of this book) show children using structures from written language in oral retellings. As a child retells a story or dictates one, he or she will pause or add appropriate emphasis in ways that suggest an understanding, again implicit, of the sentence as a unit. Here is a dictated story by a four-year-old; obviously you cannot hear him tell it but if you read it aloud you will see how sure his understanding is of sentence boundaries and other punctuation conventions such as exclamation marks. Included in Matthew's story is a favourite video character, Captain Planet, and two characters, Mr Wiggle and Mr Waggle, who featured in a story he was told at school:

> Captain Planet was flying about looking for his friend the Planeteer. He saw Mr Wiggle and Mr Waggle. He said, 'You can play in my spaceship but you don't touch any of the buttons.' But the naughty pair touched a big red button which sent them flying off to the moon in one hour. Captain Planet flew to the moon and told them not to press any more buttons. The next day they went exploring and Captain Planet got them some flying pizzas. Captain Planet said 'You can fly home now and tell your friend Matthew what happened.' When they woke up they thought it was a dream but then they heard 'Look out!' (child asked for this to be written 'big') and Captain Planet swooped down from the ceiling and said 'Do you think it was a dream? No such thing as dreams.'

Now look back at Figure 5.12, the six-year-old's story called *How the Moon Lost His Shine*. If you read it through, you will find that it is syntactically very accurate and that you can infer the punctuation quite easily even though she has only used a full stop twice. Take the opening: 'One day Sophie was walking in the woods when darkness fell so she hurried off home.' This complex sentence has three clauses and the child has organised the units on separate lines showing an awareness of them as different from each other. If you look at the rest of the story you will see that, although she does not make consistent use of such a device throughout, she does seem to be making some use of layout as a substitute for punctuation.

It is reassuring then to have evidence like this that shows children do develop implicit early understandings about sentences. The stronger these implicit understandings are, the more potential there is for making children's knowledge explicit, and it is for this reason that we include reading aloud, shared reading and shared writing in the section on teaching punctuation. The latter two routines can both provide opportunities to teach about specific aspects of punctuation, but joint readings and composition will also develop more explicit understanding about sentence structure. The practice of encouraging children to read their written work aloud works in the same way, encouraging them to draw on implicit knowledge about word order and the flow of language.

Learning about punctuation: the marks and the system

Environmental print is a rich source of information about writing, and it is not hard to find examples of question marks and exclamation marks scattered liberally around the supermarket and television screen. However, some aspects of punctuation are more visible and accessible than others. Exclamation marks and question marks are high profile and easily observed, so children can relish detecting and using them. The same cannot be said for apostrophes, especially as there are so many public misuses of them ('lunche's' being just one example spotted recently). There are implications here when considering the order in which punctuation marks should be taught; these are addressed in the teaching sections below.

Research mentioned in other parts of this book shows the discoveries very young children make about the form and functions of writing and examples of children's earliest writing attempts will often include punctuation-like marks. Figure 5.14 shows

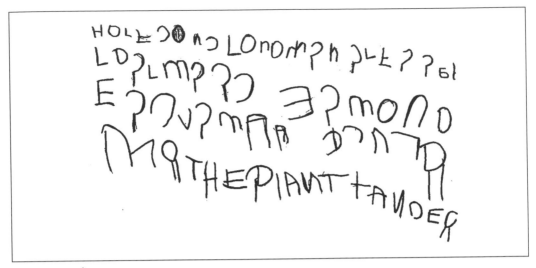

Figure 5.14

writing by a Reception age child who told her teacher 'It's the story of *Knock, knock, who's there?*' The writing arose from a Shared Reading session where one focus was on question marks. She has gone on to incorporate them into her own writing but not with a clear understanding of the function of the symbols themselves. Her use of a range of different writing-like symbols is typical of the earliest stages of writing. Such symbols may include up and down lines (as in Figure 5.3), letters, numbers, letter-like shapes, letters from different orthographies (see Figure 5.6), mathematical symbols and punctuation marks. A key element of early writing is the enjoyment children experience in playing with and organising these different symbols. There is something graphically satisfying about punctuation and you will all have favourite examples of children of all ages relishing the use (and often overuse) of a newly learned mark. Figure 5.15 shows a Year 2 child making accurate and enthusiastic use of the full stop.

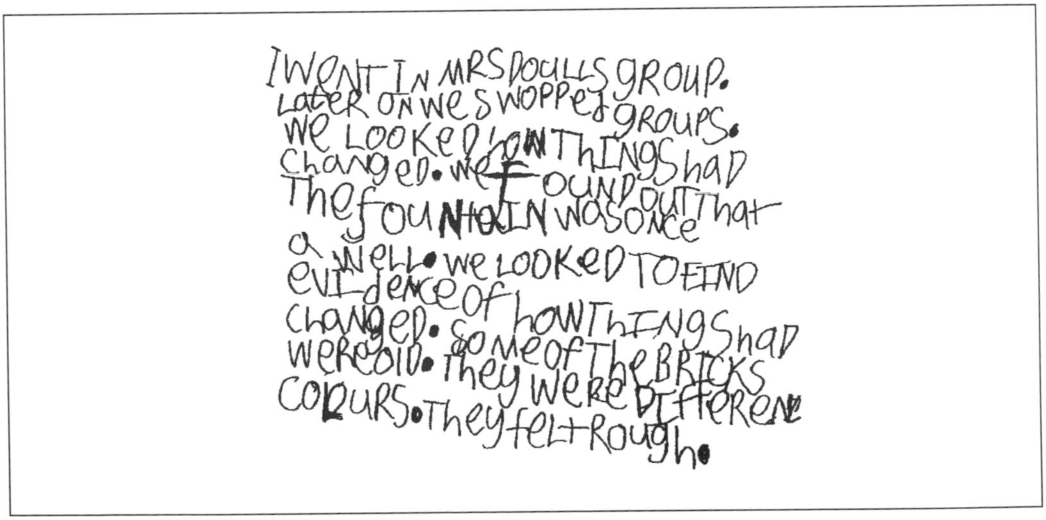

Figure 5.15

There is, of course, an important difference between using a symbol and understanding its significance and as children's understanding develops, so their use of symbols becomes increasingly differentiated. Martens and Goodman (in Hall and Robinson 1996) looked at young children's use of punctuation and found examples of children working with punctuation in specific ways that reflect the nature of the system. Some examples show invented punctuation symbols which added meaning to writing and they give a wonderful example of an eight-year-old's invention of a 'sadlamation' mark:

> I've invented a new punctuation mark. A mark for something sad. It is used in a sentence like this. I had a dog. It died (*mark inserted – a v with a small circle attached to top of left side*). It does look funny but it will get better looking soon, just like all of the others.
> (p. 38)

Nigel Hall's overview of research into children's learning about punctuation suggests that it is a complex process and not 'a passive process in which children simply learn a set of rules and can then punctuate accurately' (p. 33). What the studies did show is that, in common with other aspects of the writing process, children work actively in trying to build up an understanding of the system. Look back again at Ben's apostrophes (Figure 5.2): he knows they are used with the letter 's' when it occurs at the end of a word but has not yet grasped the possessive principle.

A sense of audience

A factor that contributes to children's understanding of the punctuation system is their developing sense of writing for an audience, which was discussed in the chapter on composition. The point here is that, as children write for a range of audiences and purposes, they become increasingly aware of the fact that we write with a reader in mind and that punctuation is there to help that reader (and this is included in the Programme of Study for Key Stage One). This was Brian Cox's (1991) reason for including punctuation with composition, and you can see how vital it is that children keep in touch with the idea of an audience, a reader for their writing. So work on punctuation needs to be grounded in a rich writing environment. Although the *NLS* document does not use the term 'audience' until Key Stage Two in the Text level requirements, you will find many different forms of writing specified where a sense of audience is crucial. Take playing with and using lists, menus and cards (Reception), making storybooks (Year 1.1), and writing labels and diagrams (Year 1.2 and 1.3). At Key Stage Two the stipulation to write book reviews for different audiences (3.3) offers some rich possibilities. The stronger the sense of audience the greater the imperative to punctuate correctly.

Teaching punctuation

When?

As with spelling you will need to plan opportunities to teach punctuation both through the Literacy Hour framework (Sentence level work) and through routines – and especially shared reading and writing – that may go on at other times. The *NLS* specifies that the second time slot be shared between Sentence and Word level work at Key Stage Two, but that Sentence level work at Key Stage One 'should be covered in the context of shared reading and writing'.

How?

Again, you need to look back to the 'How?' section in 'Teaching spelling'. Working positively with what the children already know and use continues to be important. As the section above on 'Changing rules' showed, punctuation, like spelling, is an area that can be a source of interest for children, so make sure you include activities (such as inventing new punctuation marks) that will foster their curiosity. Keep your work contextualised, and make sure that children really are free to focus on the particular aspect of punctuation you are trying to teach and are not trying to contend with too many different things at once. Be ready for some overgeneralisation as children start to adopt new conventions in their writing; we have seen Ben's vigorous use of apostrophes (Figure 5.2) and Figure 5.16 shows an energetic over-use of exclamation marks.

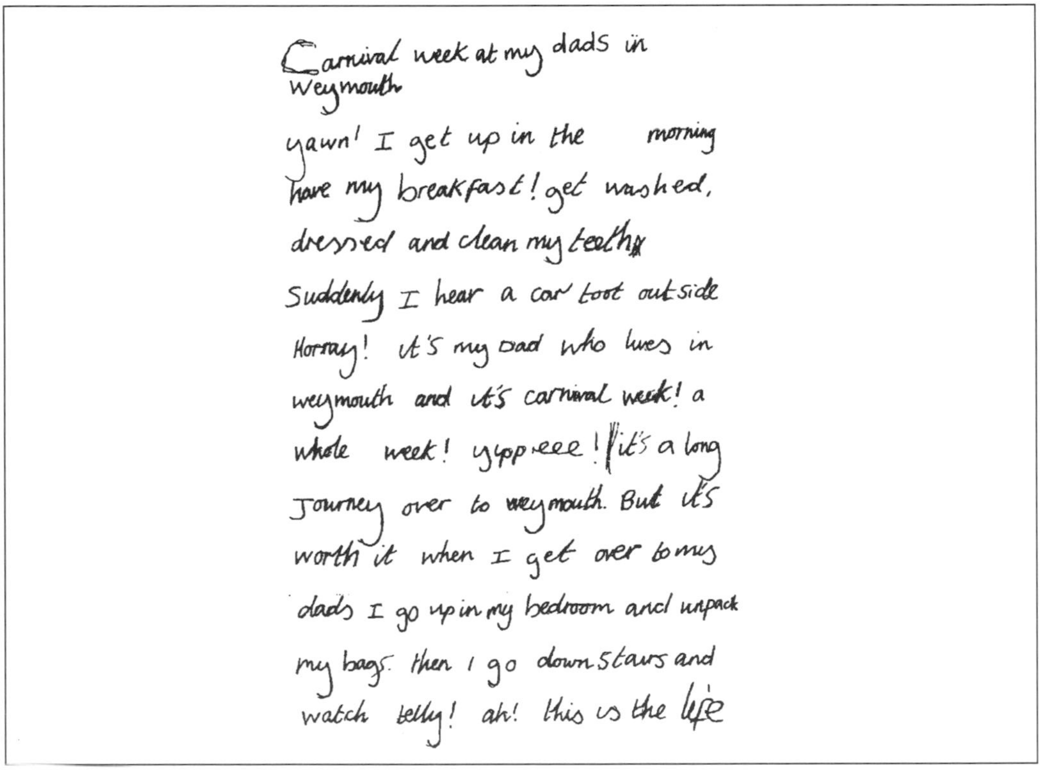

Carnival week at my dads in Weymouth

yawn! I get up in the   morning have my breakfast! get washed, dressed and clean my teeth Suddenly I hear a car toot outside Horray! it's my Dad who lives in weymouth and it's carnival week! a whole week! yippeee ! it's a long Journey over to weymouth. But it's worth it when I get over to my dads I go up in my bedroom and unpack my bags. then I go downstairs and watch telly! ah! this is the life

Figure 5.16

This nine-year-old is using exclamation marks to inject expression into a lively piece, which is quite close to spoken language. You could refine her use of them by looking at examples in books and demonstrating their use in shared reading and writing.

What?

The *National Curriculum* gives broad guidelines for what is to be covered and the *NLS* gives a term by term progression. This starts with using capitals in Reception right through to secure use of the semi-colon in Year 6. Given what we have said about the visibility and impact of some marks – especially question and exclamation marks – you might want to explore children's understandings of these a little earlier than the *NLS* suggests (Year 1.1 and 1.2). The *NLS* publication, *Grammar for Writing*, provides many activities for punctuation work at Key Stage 2.

We have looked at the use very young children may be making of marks in their early writing and those of you working in nurseries will need to observe such use and make sure that shared reading and writing opportunities include some reference to marks that children have picked up on. Your displays of environmental print should also include examples that you can draw on.

Developing a sense of audience

- Provide writing opportunities for a range of audiences, e.g. books for each other (see Chapter 4) and other classes, invitations to class assemblies, notices and so on.
- Support these opportunities through the provision of a range of writing contexts, e.g. class cafe, shop . . .
- Shared reading and writing sessions where you omit punctuation will help children understand and develop a sense of audience.
- Encourage children to read their work aloud, either to themselves or to a writing partner.

Developing an understanding of sentences

- Remember that a sentence has to have a subject and a finite verb.
- Children read their work aloud (as above).
- Read aloud to the children.
- Use the children's own writing corrections – 'How did you know it wasn't right?'
- Brainstorm with the children what they think a sentence is, discuss examples of non-sentences and sentences, encourage the children to generate definitions and rules.
- Focus on a particular type of sentence, e.g. interrogatives (questions), look for and make up examples.
- Focus on particular parts of speech, e.g. verbs as another context for discussing sentences.
- Use shared reading and writing to talk about sentences.
  Give children an assortment of sentences split up into their subjects and predicates (e.g. The pirate/brandished his cutlass; The fairy/flapped her wings; The boy/wanted mum.) Let the children reassemble these, making the silliest sentences possible. Go on to give them strips of paper to make up their own examples for others to try out.
- Use *Breakthrough to Literacy* sentence makers to demonstrate sentence building.

Teaching specific aspects of punctuation

- Model during shared reading/writing.
  Give the children punctuation fans (*Grammar for Writing* CD has a template for these). They can use these to indicate omitted or concealed marks in Shared Reading/Writing. Alternatively, they can write their suggestions on whiteboards.
- Use the children's own work to target specific aspects.
- Punctuate text with the aspect you want to teach omitted.

- Use comic strips and speech bubbles to teach about speech marks.
- Get children to make up their own punctuation marks, e.g. different 'hedera' (Crystal on p. 107) for different genres of writing, or tell them about the 'sadlamation' mark and make up marks for different emotions.
- Write style guides for younger children, e.g. how to use an exclamation mark!
- Find out about the history of the mark you are teaching (e.g. question mark: 'Q' is for 'quaere', Latin word for question. Originally the whole word 'quaere' was written after a question, then shortened to 'Q', before being replaced by the mark we now use (Jarman 1979). You may also have noticed that in Spanish the question mark is used upside down at the start of sentences as well as in its normal position at the end.
- Find examples from favourite classroom books, make lists and see if the children can start to make rules.
- Use a CD-ROM such as *The Punctuation Show* (Sherston). This provides four different sporting contexts (football, grand prix, etc) in which children can practise and reinforce their knowledge of different punctuation marks.
- Older children could seek out examples of punctuation misuse in the environment. Start a 'Punctuation Howlers' board.

Play with punctuation and graphic effects

One way of helping children to understand the way punctuation functions is to 'play' with its effects.

- Exchange exclamation marks and question marks and see what the effect is on reading aloud.
- Collect examples of exaggerated and attention-grabbing uses of punctuation e.g. from advertisements and cartoon characters 'Aargh!!!'
- Give children cards with ambiguous sentences that rely on punctuation for their meaning (such as the example on p. 105, or 'The man's computer knows its boss.'/ 'The man's computer knows it's boss.') They should read these aloud in pairs considering the effect on meaning the different punctuation evokes.
- Use ideas from Michael Rosen's lively chapter in *Did I Hear You Write?* where he suggests ways that children can represent different effects in their writing, e.g. a word or phrase said loudly, or a single word said very slowly, as we do when we call out for mum (!)
  (1989: 41)

Glossary

APOSTROPHE ('):   Apostrophes have two uses. They can be used to show where a letter or letters have been omitted (contraction): *'Don' you worry Harry. You'll learn fast enough.'* (*Harry Potter and the Philosopher's Stone*, p. 66) An apostrophe placed at the end of a noun and before the 's' indicates possession (*wizard's hat*). Where the noun is plural, then the apostrophe goes after the final 's' (*wizards' hats*). Note that the possessive pronoun 'its' does not follow this rule: *it's* <u>always</u> indicates *it is* or *it has*.

BRACKETS ( ):	Brackets contain extra material within a sentence: *He could hear (though he had no idea what Black's voice might sound like) a low, excited mutter.* (*Harry Potter and the Prisoner of Azkaban*, p. 158)
CAPITAL LETTERS:	Capital letters are used at the beginning of sentences, for 'I' and at the start of names, places, titles, days and months.
COLON (:):	A colon is used to precede a list or a quote. It may also be used in a sentence where the second half of the sentence explains or unfolds from the first. *He was striking to look at: he was no taller than Lord Asriel's hand span, and as slender as a dragonfly.* (*The Amber Spyglass*, p.60)
COMMA (,):	They may be used to separate units in a sentence which could be words, phrases or clauses. *Every time they passed the third-floor corridor, Harry, Ron and Hermione would press their ears to the door to check that Fluffy was still growling inside.* (*Harry Potter and the Philosopher's Stone*, p. 167) They may also be used to separate items in a list comprising single words (*She saw lions, tigers, penguins and cheetahs.*)
DASH (–):	A dash may be used like brackets – but not for full sentences – or else preceding a final comment.
ELLIPSIS (. . .)	Ellipsis denotes omission of words or an interruption.
EXCLAMATION MARK (!):	An exclamation mark is used at the end of a sentence to add force and emphasis. It is used for a range of emotions, e.g. anger, happiness, surprise.
FULL STOP (.):	A full stop is used to mark the end of a sentence.
HYPHEN (-):	A hyphen is used for a word break at the end of a line and for compounds such as '*tail-ender*'.
QUESTION MARK (?):	A question mark is used at the end of a question.
SEMI-COLON (;):	Semi-colons are used to separate items in a list that contains lengthy items. *The basket contained a strange array of foods: fresh, brown, enormous eggs; seven squashy, mouldy bananas; chocolates that had seen better days and a pork pie.* They are also used to punctuate sentences with two main clauses that could stand as separate sentences but where the ideas are closely linked and benefit from closer linkage than a full stop allows. *Harry didn't speak at all as they walked down the road; he didn't even notice how much people were gawping at them on the Underground.* (*Harry Potter and the Philosopher's Stone*, p. 66) Note that a full stop or connective ('and' would work here) could be used in place of the semi-colon, but not a comma which is insufficiently strong. (Misuse of a comma between two main clauses is known as a 'comma splice' and is a very common error.)

SPEECH MARKS (" " or ' '):   Speech marks (sometimes known as 'quotation marks') are used to demarcate direct speech. Punctuation that belongs with the direct speech is kept within the speech marks:
'Where are you going?' the child asked. 'I hope it's not far.'

Further reading

Allen, R. (2002) *One Step Ahead: Punctuation*. Oxford: Oxford University Press.
Hackman, S. and Trickett, L. (1996) *Punctuation 9–13*. London: Hodder and Stoughton.
Hunt, G. (2000) *Pocket Guides to the National Curriculum: Grammar and Punctuation*. Leamington Spa: Scholastic.

HANDWRITING

At Standard 1 children should be able to form on the blackboard or slate from dictation, letters capital and small manuscript.
(1862 Standards for Writing (in Aldrich 1982: 81))

The ability to write easily, quickly and legibly affects the quality of a child's written output, for difficulty with handwriting can hamper his [sic] flow of thoughts and limit his fluency.
(Bullock 1975: 184)

The teaching of writing used to consist almost entirely of handwriting exercises. The logbook from an Oxfordshire village school records younger children copying letters onto slates while the older ones were still copying but had graduated onto 'moral' sentences to be written in copybooks (Wendlebury, Oxon – private copy). We have a richer and more balanced writing curriculum now, but Bullock reminds us, nearly one hundred years later, that handwriting remains as a most important secretarial aspect of the writing process and so it does today despite the advent of word-processing.

Aims of handwriting

The *National Curriculum* requires that we teach children a legible and fluent style, and Rosemary Sassoon (1983), author of many practical and useful books about handwriting, suggests that there are three aims we should have when teaching handwriting. These are: that it is legible; that it can be speedy; and that teaching allows for development of an individual style of writing.

You might find the following activity a useful way of illuminating these aims and helping you to reflect on what is involved in handwriting. Find someone to work with and copy a passage of prose at speed for five minutes. When the time is up, look at your two pieces of handwriting and discuss them using the following prompts:

- Who was able to write the fastest?
- Is the handwriting always legible?
- Were you both comfortable, i.e. could you have continued to write at speed for some time?
- Are there features which might interrupt the flow of the handwriting? Are any of these solely decorative?
- How do you both feel about your handwriting?

- Do you use different styles at times e.g. in exams, for an important letter?
- Is either of you left-handed?
- Do you have any 'favourite' writing implements?

You might also like to compare the way you positioned yourselves, held the writing implement and placed the paper. You should have found that the process of observing closely was revealing and, of course, the same holds good for our work with children. We will return to the practical implications of these observations later in the section.

Issues in the teaching of handwriting

A Motor skill

Handwriting is a physical activity that requires very specific teaching in order to develop the fine motor skills that it involves. Although watching a fluent writer as she writes is important, ample practice with writing implements and guidance is necessary for children to become skilful handwriters.

This is why providing the right equipment and seating arrangements (see Checklists 1 and 2 below) are so important. You will find suggested ways of developing very young children's manipulative skills in Checklist 3 (and see Chapter 3 on Copying and Tracing routines). You may also find some of these suggestions useful when supporting children with handwriting difficulties (see Checklist 5).

A personal style

As well as developing the appropriate motor skills, we also have to foster each child's individual writing style. When I look back through examples of writing from children I taught over twenty years ago, their handwriting still evokes each individual child, as vividly as ever. Perhaps you have childhood memories of experimenting with different styles, implements and ink colours. Handwriting is part of our identity, our own particular hallmark, and this could be why the tradition of collecting autographs persists. You might feel that the idea of a personal style is becoming less relevant with the ever-increasing use of word processors but in word-processing personal styles also develop. We realised, as we began to edit first drafts for this book, that our colleagues had distinctive word-processing styles. They had preferred fonts, made different choices about spacing, layout and whether to print in 'draft' or not. I have childhood memories of trying to copy the handwriting style of a friend as I thought it would mean I would write with her fluency and ease. It is the notion of individuality in handwriting that brings us back to a strand that has been running through this chapter concerning the development of children's curiosity about different aspects of writing. Such curiosity can and should extend to handwriting and you will find some ideas for this in the section on teaching handwriting.

Audience and purpose: making presentational choices

Ellen and Nicola (Year 2) have been asked to make a notice for the book corner reminding the class to keep the books tidy. The notice has been planned and checked for correct spelling so now they have started on the final version. Halfway through I find Ellen standing at one end of the book corner holding the notice while Nicola is reading it from the other side of the classroom. 'We just want to make sure people can read it, miss', they tell me.

While the notions of audience and purpose are not directly linked with the physical formation of writing, they do need reaffirming with regard to handwriting. One of the prompts in the opening activity concerned the choices we make about legibility, size, and perhaps style, which will depend on the audience and purpose of the piece of writing. You will find that the *NLS* specifies the need for 'special forms' (Year 4) of writing such as print script for posters, and the appropriate use of capitals. This ties in closely with points made in Chapter 4 regarding the different types of presentation that accompany different genres of writing. Secure understanding of both writing process and product will also enable children to make confident use of a more informal script for note taking than they would for the scribing of a favourite poem for a class anthology in their 'best' handwriting.

Cursive writing

The handwriting exercises that the children at Wendlebury Village School carried out a hundred years ago would have been written in copperplate – a cursive hand. Jarman (1979) tells us that this joined up handwriting style developed in the eighteenth century at a time when more handwriting was needed for commercial purposes and book-keeping than ever before. (Its name derives from the traditional use of a plate of copper on which a printing design would be engraved.)

This changed after 1913 when a scholar called Edward Johnston gave a lecture to London teachers in which he suggested that children's reading would be improved by the adoption of a print script, sometimes called the 'ball and stick' method.

Jarman (1979) points out that, while this did provide a clear model for reading, the 'system of building up letters from separate parts' was not conducive to a fluent and speedy hand.

There was a return to cursive writing for many children with the publication of Marian Richardson's copybooks in the 1930s. However, this return was not wholesale and different handwriting schemes have been published since then. Many of these offer a compromise between print and cursive with letters given entry and exit strokes (ligatures) in readiness for joining up.

Recently though, there has been a rather more persistent move to revive the idea of teaching children a cursive hand from the start.

The argument is that it is better to start as you mean to continue, rather than learning one way and then having to relearn (as I expected my class to in the example given in the Spelling section). Penni Cotton (1992) cites the French model where children are taught 'l'ecriture anglaise' (cursive!) right from the start. In the nurseries classroom labelling, letters that go home and early reading texts are in cursive script. This early exposure is reinforced outside school where many books (like Brunhoff's *Babar*), comics and displays also use cursive. Most French teachers – now and in the past – use a very similar form, so children are also likely to meet this in their parents' handwriting.

While there are issues here about the extent to which such an approach might suppress the development of an individual hand, there are also persuasive arguments about a joined up script following on more naturally from children's first writing attempts (as in Figure 5.3). It is claimed that it is easier for the children to detect separate words because they do not get muddled by spaces between letters and between words. It allows for useful links to be made with spelling, as strings of letters can be seen as a whole unit and handwriting practice can be used to reinforce such strings. Charles Cripps, in a recent lecture (date unknown), argues that such an approach sets up a motor pattern for common letter strings (e.g. -ing, -tion) and that this acts as a back-up for the visual pattern.

Some schools report enthusiastically on the benefits of this approach; others remain more sceptical, arguing that very young children's cursive attempts are poorly controlled and do not offer the clear graphic information needed in spelling. The *NLS* recommends that a print script be taught 'that will be easy to join later' (Year 1), and that joins should be taught from Year 2. Whatever the pros and cons, the outcome needs to be a system that allows the child to concentrate on composition so that letter formation does not 'hamper his flow of thoughts and limit his fluency' (Bullock 1975).

Teaching handwriting

When?

The best time to show a child how to hold a pencil and form letters is when she or he first shows an interest in writing implements and writing. Young children are likely to hold pencils and other writing implements long before they know about letters, so helping to establish a good grip may come before demonstrating letter formation. In the nursery, this means ensuring the provision of a range of writing materials and implements as well as the kinds of enticing writing contexts we have discussed elsewhere in this book. In addition to this, young children need opportunities to develop the fine motor skills they will need for handwriting (see Checklist 3). So you will need not only to think about overall provision (see below) but also, through your observations, to be responsive to individual children's needs.

Handwriting can be taught during the Word level slots during the Literacy Hour. In common with other aspects of transcription you will also want to plan other opportunities to demonstrate and reinforce work through regular routines. Shared writing is a good context to remind children about correct letter formation and, for younger children, copying and tracing activities provide valuable extra practice (see Chapter 3). There are some television programmes that provide well contextualised opportunities for handwriting practice (e.g. *Words and Pictures*, *Look and Read*). Look back too at the IT suggestions in the spelling section; many of the software packages there offer spelling and handwriting practice.

How?

Again, it is important to remember that your teaching should be positive and well contextualised. Make the most of the links between spelling, phonics and handwriting and use handwriting sessions as an opportunity to reinforce and revisit spelling patterns or sound work that you have taught earlier. On the whole handwriting is best taught either as a whole-class session or during teacher focused group work, as it is most important that you are able to observe the children so that you can check an uncomfortable grip, awkward posture or inaccurate letter formation. There will be times however, when children are working independently (as in the earlier example of writing out a favourite poem for a class anthology).

Your own handwriting is important: you should adopt the school's style and use it when you write on the board, in children's books, on worksheets and in shared writing.

What?

Most schools will have a policy for handwriting with regard to letter formation – not every school will want to teach entry strokes as well as exit strokes – and when to start joining. This may be backed up by a published scheme, such as *New Nelson Handwriting* (Smith and Inglis 1984) or the *Jarman Handwriting Scheme* (Jarman 1982), which provide graded exercises and copybooks. If you should find yourself without such support then you will find Rosemary Sassoon's (1990) book, *Handwriting: the way to teach it* provides useful guidance on possible models. The *NLS* offers a progression through from Reception to Year 4 with specific guidance as to when and how to start joining letters (e.g. Year 2, diagonal joins to letters without ascenders e.g. 'ai', 'ar', 'un'). Their publication, *Developing Early Writing*, provides specific guidance on letter formation.

You will also need to find out if there is a school policy with regard to the use of lined or unlined paper and the types of writing implements that are available (and whether these are specific to particular age groups). See the section on Provision below for more ideas on this. As the opening activity of this section demonstrated, teaching handwriting is about more than just forming letters; the way we sit and the way we hold our pens are just two other aspects we have to think about. Checklist 1 gives some guidance on these preliminaries. The rest of this section has been organised as a series of checklists, mostly for you, but there is also one for children. You will find much more detail in the books listed at the end.

CHECKLIST 1: Preliminaries

- Are the children sitting comfortably, looking ahead and leaning forward a bit?
- Are the tables or desks at a suitable height?
- Is the lighting sufficient? Left-handers will need it directed over their left shoulder.
- Is the child holding the writing implement with a comfortable and usable grip?*
- Is the paper positioned well (i.e. to the right of the body for right-handers and left for left-handers, top of page slanted to the left for right-handers, either way and at a greater angle for left-handers)?
- Can the children all see the board/copybook they are using?
- Have the children all the appropriate equipment (good quality paper and implements; you cannot form letters with care using coarse paper or soft unsharpened pencils)? Are the paper and implements the right size? Rosemary Sassoon (1983) says small children need small bits of paper so that their writing arms are neither stretched nor cramped.
- Can you observe all the children?

* The question of grip is problematic. Traditionally children were taught to use the so-called 'triangular grip' but this is not comfortable for everyone. You will need to observe the child's grip 'in use' in order to ascertain whether it is allowing for fluency and legibility. The older the child the harder it is to undo an unwieldy grip! Left-handers might find it easier if they hold the implement further up than right-handers so that they can see what they are writing.

CHECKLIST 2: Provision

Early years:

- Material to encourage experimentation and early mark making e.g. range of colours, sizes and types of paper, pencils, crayon, felt tips, paint, sand, plasticine.
- Examples of environmental print, frequent use of children's names (which will

probably be the first word they try to write and your first opportunity to show them how to hold the implement and form the letters).

As children get older set up a handwriting area.

- Include many different writing implements. Talk about using different ones for different purposes; discuss children's favourites; try Rosemary Sassoon's idea of getting the children to try out different implements and record their findings, e.g. 'the pen because it's comfortable to hold…and I can grip it better' (Sassoon 1990).
- Include lined and unlined paper, line guides, rough and best paper. Again, talk with the children about the most appropriate uses for these, e.g. rough for notes, unlined with line guide for writing for classroom wall.
- Include examples of different types of printing and writing, e.g. James Berry and Louise Brierley's (1994) beautifully presented *Celebration Song* which has a cursively written text.
- Include different alphabet posters (English and in other scripts too, e.g. Urdu, Bengali, Turkish).
- Include examples of illuminated letters which children can use to enhance presentation of special pieces of work, e.g. postcards from the *Book of Kells* and from manuscripts in the British Museum, Jan Pienkowski's (1984) *Christmas*.
- Include examples of books with striking borders, e.g. Antonia Barber and Nicola Bayley's (1990) *The Mousehole Cat*, Selina Hastings and Juan Wijngaard's (1985) *Sir Gawain and the Loathly Lady*.

Establishing an area like this is best done with the children, so that you can discuss the different materials and involve them in decisions about what type of implement or paper might be best suited for a particular purpose. Sassoon (1990) suggests the children could survey all the different material and draw up 'dos and don'ts for handwriting lists'. She includes some lovely drawings by children showing good and bad positioning for writing (p. 41).

CHECKLIST 3: Developing fine motor skills

- Give children practice in copying and tracing shapes before progressing on to patterns (see any of the publications under 'What' above, for guidance on these).
- Provide activities that develop children's manipulative skills e.g. jigsaws, bead-threading, cutting and model making.
- Ensure there are ample opportunities to develop children's graphic skills through painting, chalking as well as drawing, colouring and mark making.
- Let the children manipulate letter shapes in sand, with playdough and with wooden and magnetic letters.

CHECKLIST 4: Promoting an interest in handwriting

As well as including the range of scripts, books and letters mentioned above there are other ways of fostering children's curiosity about handwriting. You could:

- find out about the work of graphologists: people who analyse handwriting and tell us about the psychological significance of the way we form letters. Did you know, for instance, that a 'd' written with loops suggests that you are vain? (Crystal 1995: 269).
- collect pictures and photos of children writing; there are many images of Victorian schools to be found;

- collect examples of handwriting from famous people; discuss autographs;
- find out about calligraphy as a craft, e.g. writing implements through the ages – Jarman gives instructions as to how to make a quill pen (1979: 134–5).

CHECKLIST 5: Possible problems

- Are the letters being formed correctly, completely, and consistently? (Watch out for the starting point, stroke direction, poor joins, closure of letters such as 'a' which if not closed looks like 'ci'). Look at the inconsistencies evident with the child's joins in Figure 5.16 and the trouble Kelly has with 'p' in Figure 5.8.
- Are children waiting – as they should – until they have completed words in cursive script before dotting the 'i' and the 'j' and crossing the 't'? In other words, check that they are not lifting their hands unnecessarily from the page.
- Is spacing between letters and words accurate? Note the difficulties the child in Figure 5.15 has with spacing.
- Are ascenders and descenders (see below) the right height and length (i.e. no more than twice the length of lower case letters)? Look at the difficulties the child has with this in Figure 5.15.
- Are all the downstrokes parallel?
- Is the writing too big or too small?
- Is the writing sitting on the line? Note how lined paper would have supported the child's efforts in Figure 5.12.
- Are bits of letters being taken out or put in (and does it matter)?

And for left-handers:

- Is the paper to the left of the child's body?
- Is s/he too close to a right-hander? Rosemary Sassoon recounts this useful little rule devised by a child for when left- and right-handers are sitting next to each other: 'Don't knock funny bones.' (1990: 33).
- Is the child holding the implement comfortably? (see Checklist 1 on grip.)
- LDA publish useful guidance on letter formation for left-handers.
  There is a mail order service for left-handed equipment: the Left-Handed Company, PO Box 52, South DO, Manchester M20 2PJ.
- For those of you who are right-handed: the best way to understand the difficulties left-handers have is to try writing left-handed yourself. One thing you will find is that left-handers will be pushing the writing implement rather than pulling it which makes for a less smooth action and has the effect of covering (rather than uncovering) the writing.

(Some of these ideas come from John Foggin's (1992) *Real Writing* and some from Jarman.)

Finally, here is a checklist that children could use. You would probably want to adapt it depending on the age and experience of the children you work with.

CHECKLIST 6: My handwriting checklist

As you get organised to do some writing ask yourself these questions:

- Are my pens and pencils in good condition?
- Have I cleared my table so that I've got room to write?
- Am I comfortable and do I have my writing paper in a good position?

Before you start writing ask yourself these questions:

- Is there anything I need to think about to improve my handwriting?
  - the formation of letters that I find difficult to write;
  - joining my letters up;
  - making my writing sit on the line;
  - making my writing bigger or smaller;
- What sort of writing do I need to do?
  - drafting;   – my neatest writing;
  - note taking;   – word-processing.

When you finish writing ask these questions:

- Can I read my writing?
- Can other people read my writing?
- Is my writing tidy enough?
- Did I use the right kind of handwriting for the job I was doing?
- Next time, what could I improve on?

Glossary

ASCENDERS:	occur in b, l, d, f, h, k, t; the part of the letter above the midpoint
CURSIVE:	joined up writing
DESCENDERS:	occur in g, j, p, q, y; the part of the letter below the line
DIAGONAL JOIN:	all letters in cursive script join to their next letter with a diagonal join except o, v, w and, in some cursives, b
ENTRY STROKE:	join or line going into the letter (ligature)
EXIT STROKE:	join or line leaving the letter (ligature)
HORIZONTAL JOIN:	o, v, w and, in some cursives, b join to their next letters with a horizontal join
LIGATURE:	joining strokes
LOWER CASE:	small letters a, b, c . . . ,
PRINT:	writing that is not joined up
UPPER CASE:	capital letters A, B, C . . . ,

Further reading

DfEE (2001) *The National Literacy Strategy, Developing Early Writing*. London: Heinemann.

Sassoon, R. (1990) *Handwriting: the way to teach it*. Cheltenham: Stanley Thornes.

Taylor, J. (2001) *Handwriting, A Teacher's Guide*. London: David Fulton Publishers.

CHAPTER 6

Monitoring and Assessing Writing

Liz Laycock

> The marking at my Primary school was not very helpful. The teachers wrote comments at
> the end like 'Good' or 'See me' or something like that. I used to get really annoyed when
> they wrote something like 'Good' and left you wondering what good really meant.
> (Year 7 pupil in National Writing Project 1989)

INTRODUCTION

In this chapter I shall consider what is involved in responding to, monitoring and
assessing children's writing.

Children are expected to write in every area of the curriculum, so teachers have a
great deal of reading and assessing to do. Sometimes the writing will be a way of
assessing a child's knowledge of another subject or a way of checking the child's recall
of the details of an observation or a visit. In most cases, whatever the subject, the
teacher will 'mark' errors in spelling, punctuation or grammar and may make a general
comment about the content or the quality of the work. The proper marking of written
work is one of the ways in which those who do not see what goes on in the classroom
(e.g. parents) feel they can judge a teacher's effectiveness. It is the outward and visible
sign that the teacher is doing her job well.

But we need to reflect on this marking activity; it is all too often a proofreading
exercise, with the teacher correcting errors of various kinds. Given the amount of time
devoted to marking, we need to consider whether this is the most productive way of
helping children to improve their writing skills. Not many children take our corrections
so seriously that they never make errors again. Qualitative judgements such as 'good'
or even 'excellent' rarely give pupils an indication of what was considered in making
the judgement.

It is most probable that the teachers' 'good' assessments of the pupil quoted at the
beginning of this chapter. were influenced by accurate spelling, legible handwriting and
correct punctuation. When a teacher looks at a piece of writing by a child, it is easy to
spot the mistakes; however competent the writer, there will generally be some spelling
and punctuation errors to be corrected. Paying attention to these surface features can
often prevent the teacher-reader from seeing beyond them to the content or message
which was the purpose of the writing. The teacher will generally be making an assessment *of* the child's completed learning, rather than seeking to make an assessment *for*
the child's further learning, with feedback which will help move him/her forward.

The whole question of 'assessment for learning' has been much discussed in recent
years (see references at the end of this chapter), since it has been appreciated that
children make better progress when teachers' assessments focus on supporting future
learning, rather than concentrating on assessing summatively.

You may need to think in terms of 'feedback' and 'response' to writing rather than
'marking' and 'correction', and to consider the ways in which this might be achieved.
One starting point might be to ensure that young writers themselves understand the

criteria by which writing will be assessed. These should be made clear to pupils before they begin to write and they should understand the purpose and audience for the writing, as well as the form it should take. You might initially restrict oral or written feedback to a response to the content or to the writer's use of a particular form, offering guidance on how these could be improved, before moving on to correction of transcriptional errors. The need to separate the compositional from the transcriptional aspects of writing has been identified throughout this book, but nowhere is this more important than in the process of assessment. This is not to suggest that the mechanics of writing are unimportant; indeed, precisely because the surface features are so rapidly judged, it is vital that teachers help children to get them right. But we need to regard errors in a more positive light, seeing them as evidence of learning, as efforts to master the conventions, rather than as failure.

One of the purposes of this chapter, therefore, is to help you to get the assessment of writing under control and to offer formative assessment frameworks and procedures which allow teachers to monitor progress. Formative assessments allow you to identify the aspects of writing the pupil needs to work on and thus inform the plans you make for further teaching about writing. The teacher's cumulative record of formative assessments will provide the evidence for summative assessments, which record what the child now knows and is able to do. Summative assessments are needed at the end of a school year or Key Stage. Both types of teacher assessments are needed to provide fuller information than will be gained from tests or *National Curriculum* assessment (previously known as SATs) scores alone.

You need both to observe writers at work and to look closely at samples of writing in order to analyse the children's writing strategies, their level of 'independence and confidence' as writers and their current 'knowledge and understanding' of writing. (See Barrs *et al.* (1990) for full descriptions of these 'strands of learning'.)

TEACHER ASSESSMENT OF WRITING – FORMATIVE ASSESSMENT

Observation and sampling in the Foundation Stage

However young the child, it is possible, through observation of the writer at work and through analysis of the product, to identify the child's current knowledge about the purposes for writing and the kind of writing, as well as his/her hypotheses about the conventions of writing in English.

In Figure 6.1, which is by a child in a Reception class, much is visible. The inspiration for this story was a toy mouse (Freddie) in the classroom, about whom the children had composed a story through shared writing. Many then wanted to write their own stories about the mouse. Hanife told her teacher that it said: 'Freddie the mouse came out of the cupboard. Freddie the mouse came out of the door to see if it was safe. Then Freddie had a terrible fright. It was Jade's cat.'

The telling of this short story shows that she has a good sense of the characteristics of the narrative form: it has a series of events leading to a climax. She was also clear about the purpose for the writing – she wanted to contribute another story about Freddie, in booklet form. The child approached the writing task with absolute confidence; she knew she could write a story and that her efforts would receive a positive response from her teacher. The picture was drawn first, on the left-hand side of the page (following the convention of many picture-story books), and represents the startled mouse meeting the cat. The writing was then fitted into the space on the right-hand side. The first three lines were written from left to right but she then

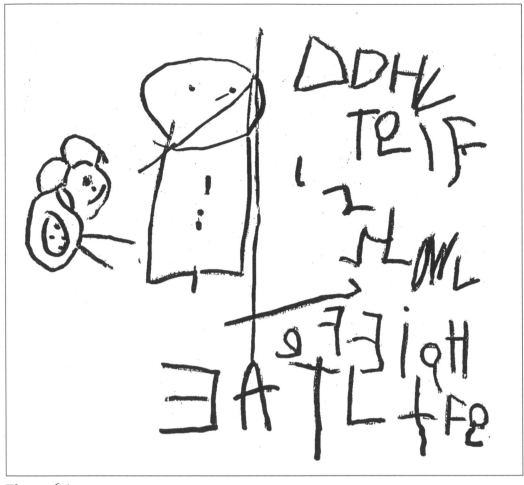

Figure 6.1

completed the page writing from right to left. The text is a mixture of real letter shapes, many of which are the letters in her name, 'Hanife', alongside letter-like shapes. There is some evidence that she is grouping letters together as in words, but there is no attempt to match the letters to the sounds of the words she is writing nor of one-to-one correspondence. The writing has a mixture of upper and lower case letters and many of them were formed in an unconventional way. (See Gentry's 'pre-communicative' stage in Chapter 5.)

Much of this information was available because the teacher had observed the writing in progress and had heard Hanife's running commentary as she completed the task. For example, Hanife had told the teacher what was in the picture and the teacher had been able to observe the shift in directionality as the child wrote. She was also able to see the way in which she formed the letters. The teacher had not intervened because she wanted to observe the child's current knowledge and understanding about writing; this was not an occasion for teaching, but for assessing before teaching. As we saw in Chapter 5, the use of known letters, most commonly from a child's name, to generate new writing is typically observed in young children's early writing and indicates that the child understands that writing is made up of letters. It is important, when samples like this are being collected, to ensure that full annotations of the context, of the child's intentions and approach, confidence and independence, are recorded, so that the evidence in the sample can be drawn upon in planning further teaching.

This teacher now knows that she will need to work on directionality of writing in English and on handwriting, as well as alphabet and letter sound knowledge. She also knows that Hanife has a basic understanding of how stories are structured which can be built on by encouraging her to write more and possibly by inviting her to dictate stories (see Chapter 3). She may also give her opportunities to experiment with other forms of writing (e.g. letters, lists).

Sampling at Year 2

Although formal assessments (e.g. *National Curriculum* assessments) are based on single pieces of writing, teacher assessments, related to the Level descriptions of the *National Curriculum*, should be made with reference to a range of samples, which reflect different purposes and genres.

In Figures 6.2 to 6.4, three pieces of writing from a Year 2 child, Martin, have been selected, though more of his output would certainly be taken into consideration by the child's teacher. The examples selected are three different genres.

The scientific investigation in Figure 6.2 approximates to what we would normally call a recount, as it is a retelling of the experiments Martin did. As we discussed in Chapter 4, the recount genre is one that young writers feel quite comfortable with. In fact, scientific writing such as this would typically be written as a report or a piece of procedural writing. However, unless the teacher has specified and supported the type of writing expected, it is not surprising that Martin has written a recount. Many teachers will recognise this as a transitional stage. Martin has described three different activities and has indicated this by separating the writing into three sections. His spelling is largely based upon phonic analysis of words e.g. 'lite', 'werkt', though he shows some awareness of conventional letter strings e.g. 'ends', 'line'. (See Gentry's 'phonetic stage' in Chapter 5.) He demarcates sentences with capital letters and full stops. His handwriting shows generally correct letter formation and clear ascenders and descenders.

From the evidence in this writing, the teacher can obtain a clear idea of what she needs to teach to move the child forward. For instance, he might benefit from working with a writing frame, perhaps with the use of chronological linking words (e.g. 'First...', 'Next...', 'Then...'). Teaching the correct spellings of words he needed to use (e.g. 'light', 'buzzer', 'battery') and the correct terminology for 'wire', 'crocodile clip', would also help.

The story in Figure 6.3, written three months later, is incomplete, but shows some features of a narrative with a sequence of events in the 'adventures of...' manner, on an ambitious canvas (the world!). There is not, however, a series of events moving towards a conclusion, which is fairly typical of stories when the child has not thought through ideas first and thus rambles fairly aimlessly from one event to another (see Chapter 4). His teacher had praised Martin's use of 'describing words' (though she has not given him an example of what she means), and he has the confidence to experiment with new vocabulary (e.g. 'route' spelt as 'rot').

Since the previous sample, his spelling has progressed. There are now many high frequency words spelt correctly; some of the incorrectly spelt words show evidence of graphic awareness of conventional letter strings (e.g. 'poler') while others show spelling at the transitional stage (e.g. 'bera' for 'bear' and 'how' for 'who') with correct letters in the wrong order. He is still using phonic analysis as a strategy for tackling

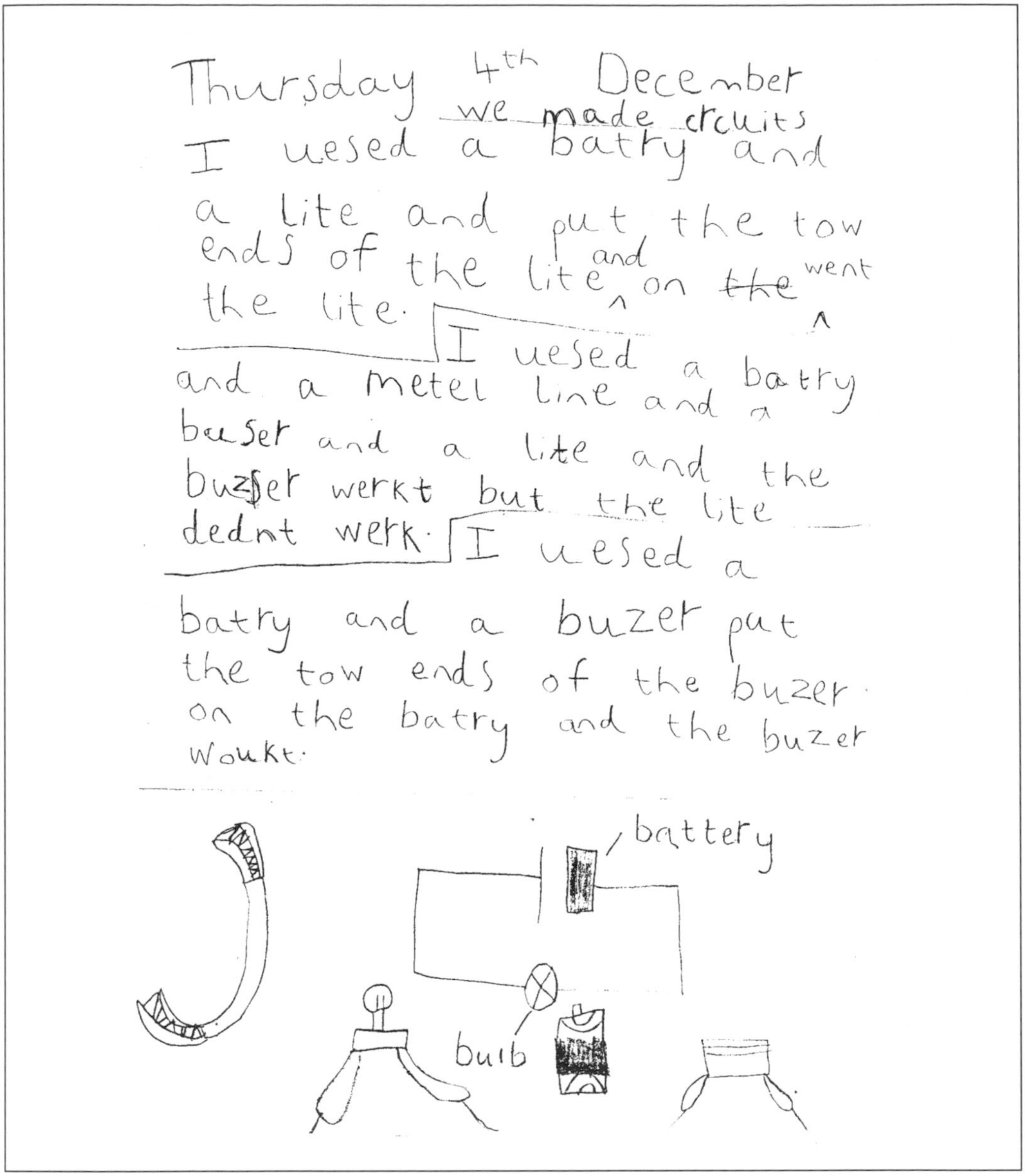

Thursday 4th December
we made circuits
I uesed a batry and
a lite and put the tow
ends of the lite and on the went
the lite. I uesed a batry
and a metel line and a
buser and a lite and the
buzzer werkt but the lite
dednt werk. I uesed a
batry and a buzer put
the tow ends of the buzer
on the batry and the buzer
woukt.

battery

bulb

Figure 6.2

unknown words in some instances (e.g. 'ostralyer' for 'Australia', 'miyls' for 'miles' and 'tiyed' for 'tired'). He still spells the inflectional '-ed' ending with a 't' ('bumpt') as he did in his first sample – 'werkt' for 'worked'. Sentences are sometimes demarcated with a full stop, but these are not always followed by a capital letter; there is no attempt to use inverted commas to mark direct speech. He uses the apostrophe correctly in the contraction 'didn't' but not in 'wasnt'; he does not use the possessive apostrophe in 'dragons'.

Martin needs guidance to develop his control of narrative form, so a way forward might include: encouragement to plan stories, so that he has a sense of where he is

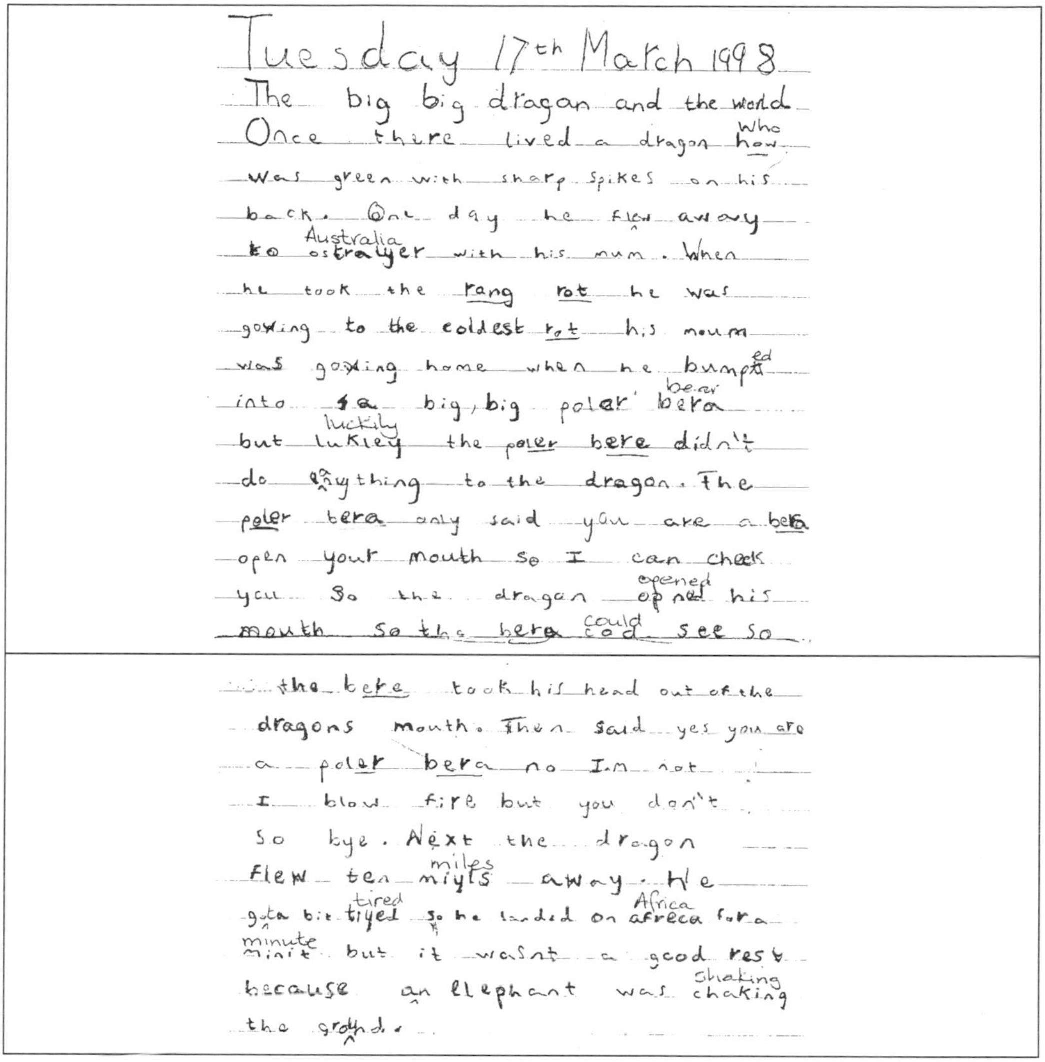

Tuesday 17th March 1998
The big big dragan and the world
Once there lived a dragon how (who) was green with sharp spikes on his back. One day he flew away to ostrayer (Australia) with his mum. When he took the rang rot he was going to the coldest rot his mum was going home when he bumpt (bumped) into a big, big poler bera (bear) but lukiey (luckily) the poler bere didn't do anything to the dragon. The poler bera only said you are a bera open your mouth so I can check you. So the dragon opned (opened) his mouth so the bera cod (could) see so the bere took his head out of the dragons mouth. Then said yes you are a poler bera no I.m not I blow fire but you don't so bye. Next the dragon flew ten miyts (miles) away. He got a bit tiyed (tired) so he landed on afreca (Africa) for a minit (minute) but it wasnt a good rest because an elephant was chaking (shaking) the grond.

Figure 6.3

proceeding; talking with him about the structure of stories and clear demonstrations of these structures. (See Chapter 4.) After praising his correct spelling, the teacher should help him to learn those words that he has misspelt but which are near to correct forms, using the 'Look, cover, write, check' routine. You will notice on Martin's writing that the teacher helped him to learn the unchanging suffix '-ed', used in words such as 'bumped' (see Chapter 5). He should be invited to edit his own writing: he could, for instance, be encouraged to underline or circle for himself those words whose spelling he feels he might need to check. As we have emphasised in other places, he will need to know how to find those words from the classroom resources. You will see that there are other errors in Martin's writing (e.g. absence of inverted commas) but you need to be aware that he will not be able to take this all on board at the same time.

The third example, Figure 6.4, was written two weeks later. It is included because it shows progress in Martin's recount writing. It is chronologically organised and the

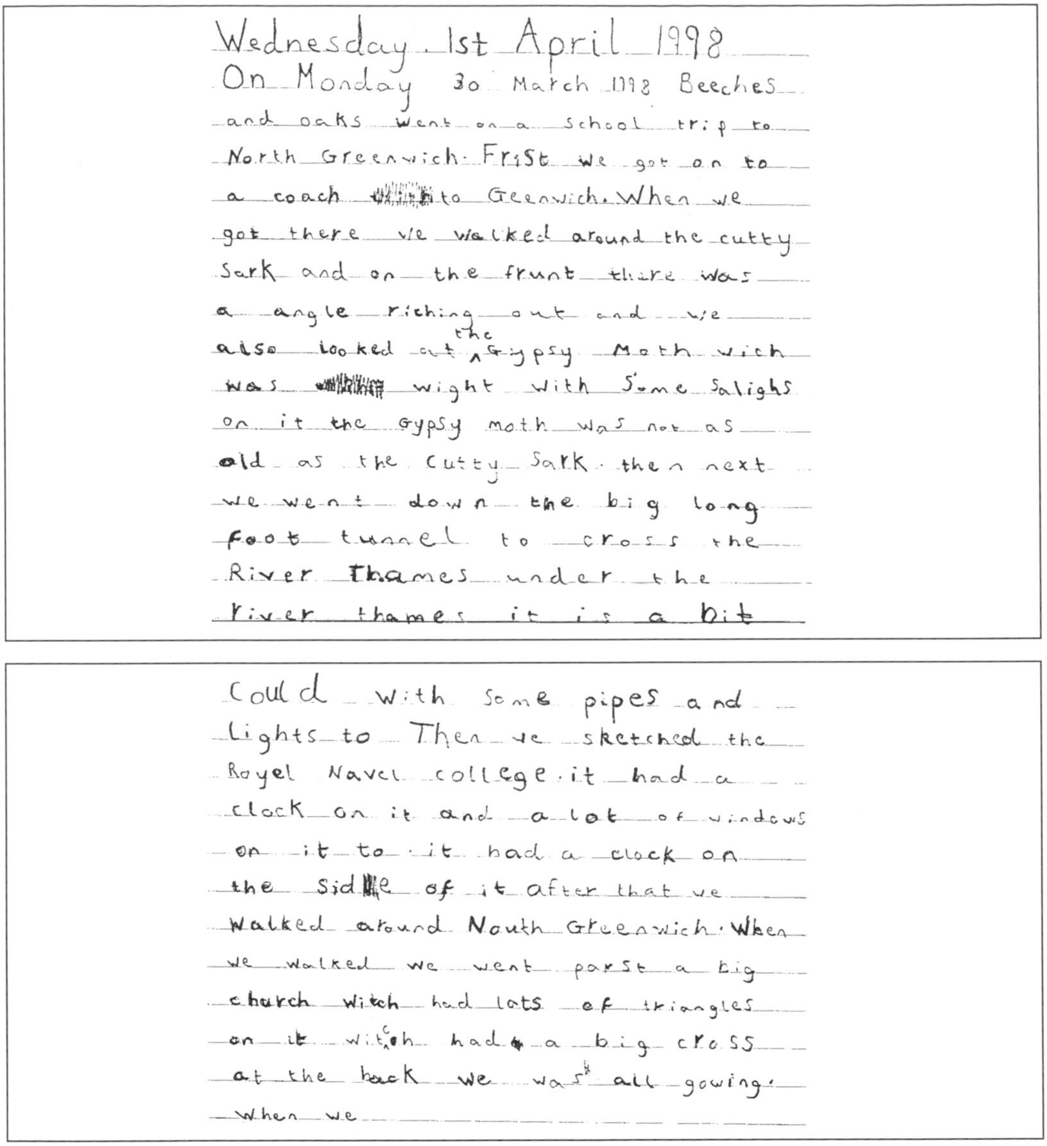

Wednesday 1st April 1998
On Monday 30 March 1998 Beeches
and oaks went on a school trip to
North Greenwich. Frist we got on to
a coach to Geenwich. When we
got there we walked around the cutty
Sark and on the frunt there was
a angle riching out and we
also looked at the gypsy Moth wich
was wight with Some Salighs
on it the Gypsy moth was not as
old as the Cutty Sark. then next
we went down the big long
foot tunnel to cross the
River Thames under the
river thames it is a bit

Could with some pipes and
Lights to Then we sketched the
Royel Navel college. it had a
clock on it and a lot of windows
on it to it had a clock on
the sidlle of it after that we
walked around Nouth Greenwich. When
we walked we went parst a big
church witch had lots of triangles
on it witch had a big cross
at the back we was all gowing.
when we

Figure 6.4

sentences are linked with appropriate connectives – 'first', 'then', 'when', and 'next'. He writes in discernible sentences although they are not all correctly punctuated (see Chapter 5). One indicator of his spelling progress is the way he has taken on his teacher's help with the '-ed' ending, making no errors with 'walked', 'looked', and 'sketched'.

These three samples of writing show progress over time in several areas: control of genre; spelling strategies; handwriting.

Using the Level descriptions

The *National Curriculum* provides statements describing the expectations for children at different stages. These are formally applied at the end of Key Stages One and Two.

As Martin is approaching the end of Year 2/Key Stage 1, it is appropriate to look at the Level descriptions and to decide which description best fits his current achievement. These samples of writing (formative assessments), together with information gathered by his teacher during the year, will provide evidence for this summative assessment. The description for Level 2 reads:

> Pupils' writing communicates meaning in both narrative and non-narrative forms, using appropriate and interesting vocabulary, and showing some awareness of the reader. Ideas are developed in a sequence of sentences, sometimes demarcated by capital letters and full stops. Simple, monosyllabic words are usually spelt correctly, and where there are inaccuracies the alternative is phonetically plausible. In handwriting letters are accurately formed and consistent in size.

The description for Level 3 reads:

> Pupils' writing is often organised, imaginative and clear. The main features of different forms of writing are used appropriately, beginning to be adapted to different readers. Sequences of sentences extend ideas logically and words are chosen for variety and interest. The basic grammatical structure of sentences is usually correct. Spelling is usually accurate, including that of common, polysyllabic words. Punctuation to mark sentences – full stops, capital letters and question marks – is accurately used. Handwriting is joined and legible.

Looking at these two alongside each other, it is clear that Martin has met all the criteria at Level 2 so consideration must also be given to Level 3. He is well on the way to meeting many of these criteria, certainly those which relate to the structure and content of the writing. But he does not yet meet the transcriptional criteria. We must, therefore, conclude that Level 2 is the best fit.

Another set of descriptions has been provided by the Centre for Language in Primary Education in the shape of writing scales (Barrs *et al.* 1996). These scales map fine distinctions in children's writing achievements and may help you in amplifying the Level descriptions in the *National Curriculum*. Those teachers taking part in the piloting of the scales reported how useful they found the group moderation sessions:

> As well as providing a basis for quality assurance in assessment, moderation has other bene-fits. It encourages teachers to justify their judgements and to be more explicit about their approach to assessment . . . Moderation focuses attention on the evidence for teachers' assess-ments, and helps to demonstrate the kinds of evidence that can be most informative in arriving at agreed judgements. In this way it can influence work on record-keeping in schools.
> (Barrs *et al.* 1996)

Having collected samples of your children's writing you would find it valuable to discuss your own evaluations of these with a group of colleagues. You will find some guidance on this in the SCAA (1995a) publication *Consistency in Teacher Assessment: Exemplification of Standards.*

Sampling at Year 4

The samples of writing in Figures 6.5 to 6.9 cover a period of six months and a range of different kinds of writing in different curriculum areas. The writer, Jatinder, is a boy in Year 4. He was born in England – his mother is a monolingual English speaker and father speaks both English and Panjabi. Jatinder is a fluent speaker, reader and writer of English and, although a speaker of Panjabi, he is not literate in it. The pieces include a book review, some scientific writing, a letter of invitation, a story and a diary. If we view these samples as a collection made by the class teacher over time, we can see that they reflect a range of purposes and forms. In every case the teacher had given clear guidance about what was expected in the particular form and, in some cases, had provided a writing framework (not, generally, a writing frame) for guidance. Some of these samples are presented as marked by the teacher, so that her responses to the writing can be seen. In this class, books are used so that there is a blank page alongside the child's writing where the teacher can write comments, suggestions and sometimes corrections and where the child can actually redraft sections of the writing. Thus, when appropriate, the writer is given guidance about redrafting content as well as indications of where spellings need to be checked. It is obviously helpful if there is an agreed school policy on marking and correction, which children know and understand. In the absence of an existing policy, you might feel it would be worthwhile drawing up a set of marking symbols which would be explained to the children and, certainly initially, displayed in the classroom. These would need to make a distinction between the marking of transcriptional errors and ways of indicating redrafting suggestions. Once established, these could be used by children in editing their own work, and in responding to each other's work, as well as by the teacher. (See Chapter 3 on writing partnerships.)

If we look across these samples we can gather a good deal of information about Jatinder's writing.

Figure 6.5, a book review of a title selected by the writer, is succinct, includes relevant information about the book, a brief résumé and personal evaluation.

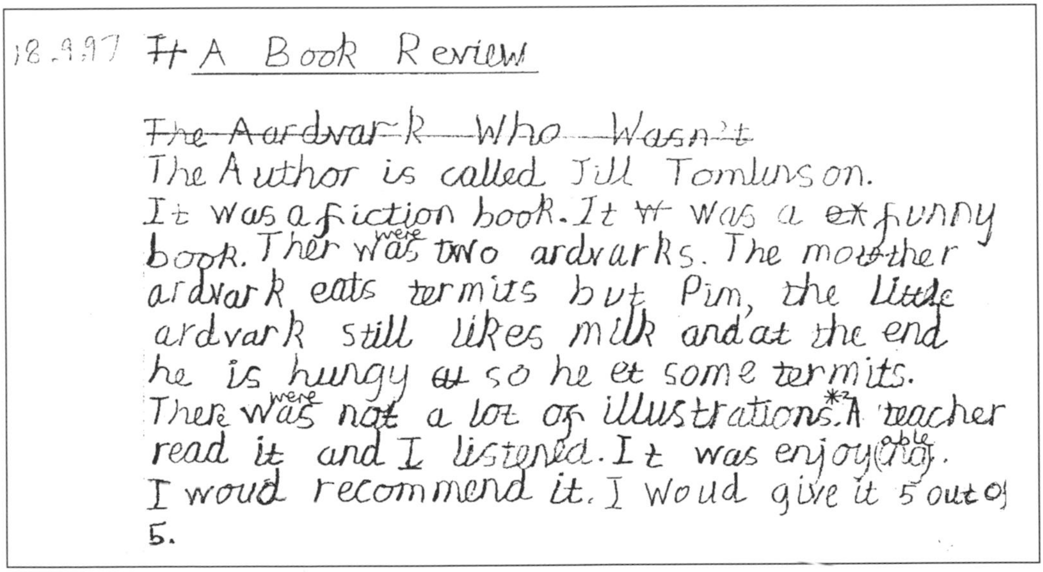
18.9.97 ~~It~~ A Book Review

~~The Aardvark Who Wasn't~~

The Author is called Jill Tomlinson.
It was a fiction book. It ~~w~~ was a ~~ex~~ funny
book. Ther was (were) two ardvarks. The mo~~th~~ther
ardvark eats termits but Pim, the little
ardvark still likes milk and at the end
he is hungy ~~at~~ so he et some termits.
Ther was (were) not a lot of illustrations.*2 A teacher
read it and I listened. It was enjoy(~~ing~~)able.
I woud recommend it. I woud give it 5 out of
5.

Figure 6.5

Figure 6.6 is about an experiment to find out which material best reflects light. It starts with a step by step (procedural genre) account of how they went about the experiment and then records the findings. Jatinder has clearly separated the procedure (on the left) from the findings (on the right). Vocabulary is used accurately throughout but the voice of the writer, which is appropriately impersonal in the clearly expressed instructions, takes on an understandably personal tone when describing the results.

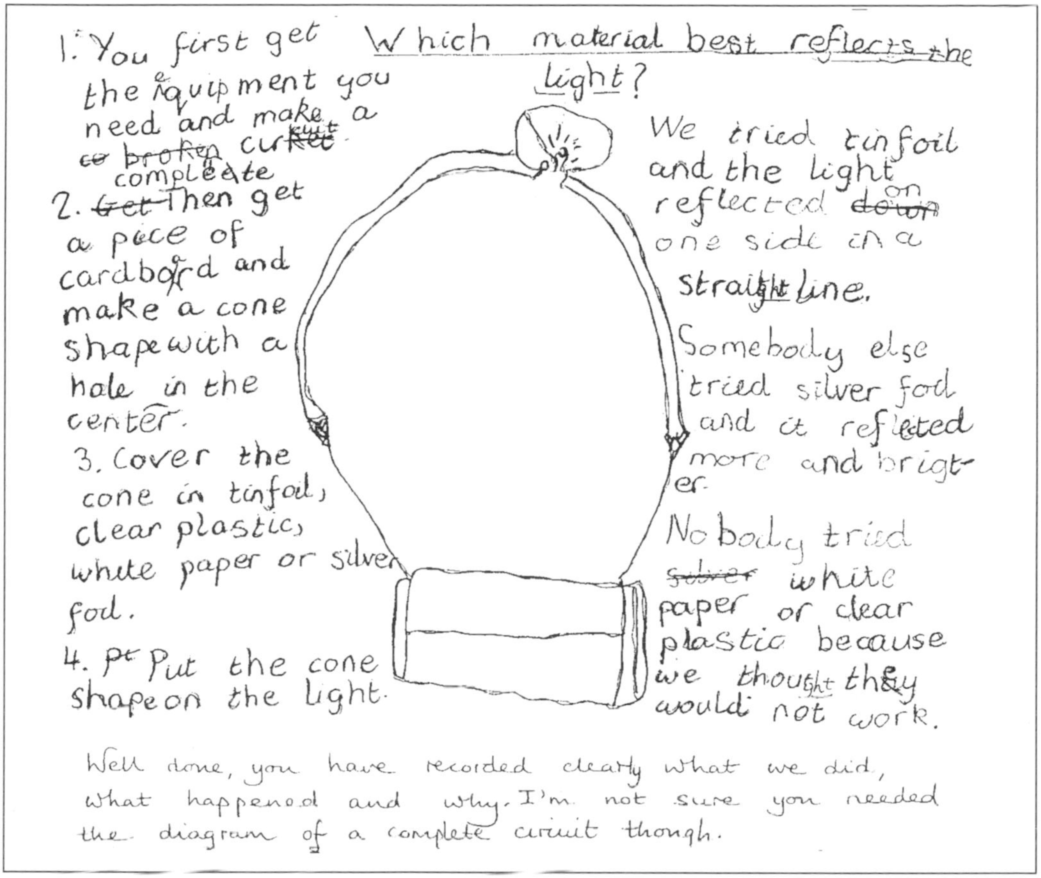

1. You first get the equipment you need and make a compleate broken curket.
2. Then get a piece of cardbord and make a cone shape with a hole in the center.
3. Cover the cone in tinfoil, clear plastic, white paper or silver foil.
4. Put the cone shape on the light.

Which material best reflects the light?

We tried tinfoil and the light reflected on one side in a straight line.

Somebody else tried silver foil and it reflected more and brigter.

Nobody tried white paper or clear plastic because we thought they would not work.

Well done, you have recorded clearly what we did, what happened and why. I'm not sure you needed the diagram of a complete circuit though.

Figure 6.6

In Figure 6.7, the address, which has been erased, was correctly laid out. This letter of invitation shows good knowledge of the letter format and tone. Writing in role to a fictitious character with an invitation to an imaginary party has provided the writer with a purposeful context and shows his command over a chronologically organised piece of writing.

In Figure 6.8, the story plan at the top allows Jatinder to decide on the setting, characters and opening line. He begins dramatically with speech without any preamble or scene setting. The content of this story derives from characteristic interests of boys of this age (see Chapters 4 and 7). The structure of the story is that of a true narrative, with a series of events, leading to a resolution (his escape), and with a most effective ending in the capture of the dog! He sustains the third person narrative throughout. There is some characterisation of the hero, Alex, in his cynicism about the letter. There is also some descriptive detail – 'wet grass', 'gigantic spaceship', 'wooden cage', 'thin stick', and 'in a dash'.

The diary entry in Figure 6.9 arose from the study of the Tudors in history. After finding out about the destruction of the Spanish Armada, the children were asked to write an account of the event in diary format. This required them to adopt a personal voice. The final version was published as a diary for display. It is written in the first person and conveys real feeling (the heat of the fire and his fear and then relief). The

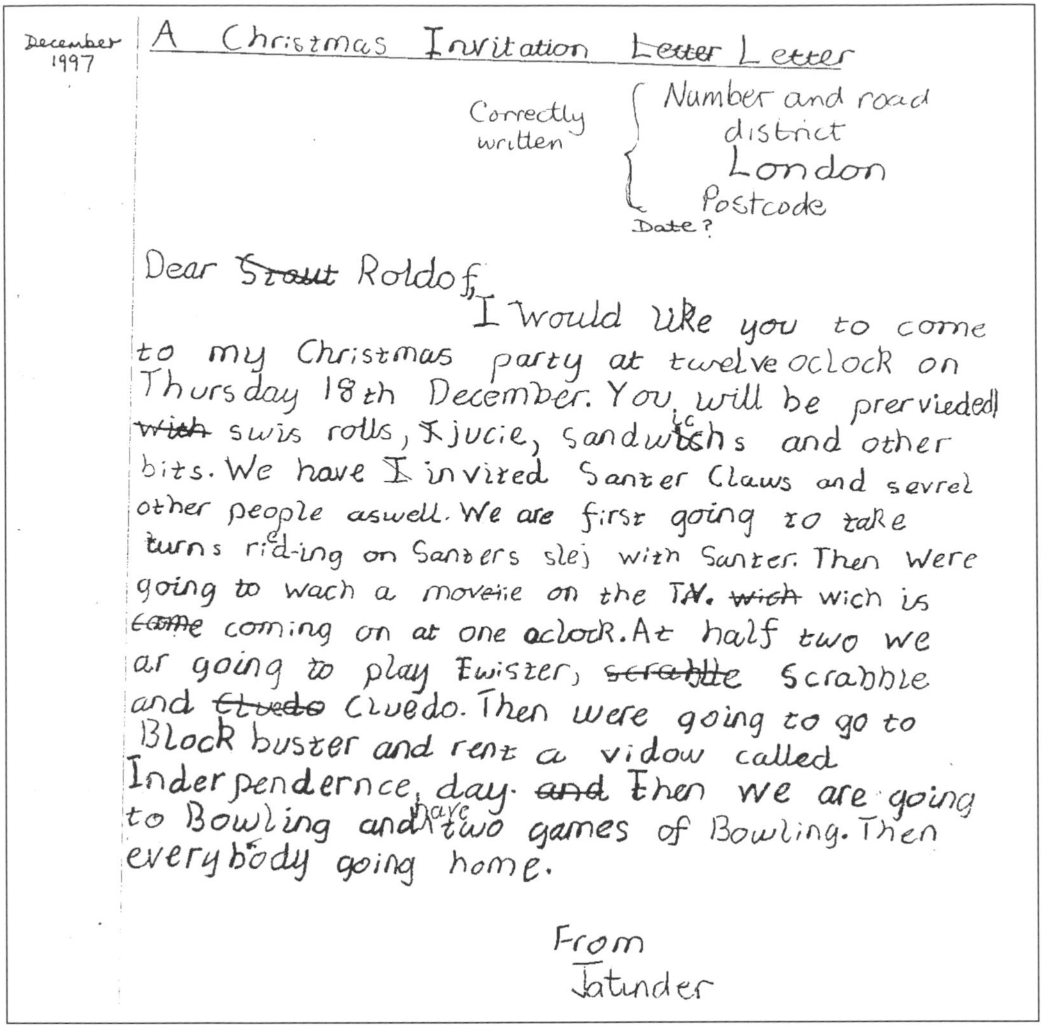

A Christmas Invitation ~~Letter~~ Letter

December 1997

Correctly written ⎧ Number and road
                  ⎨   district
                  ⎩   London
                        Postcode
                  ~~Date~~?

Dear ~~Staut~~ Roldof,
            I would like you to come
to my Christmas party at twelve oclock on
Thursday 18th December. You will be prervieded
~~with~~ swis rolls, Xjucie, sandwitchs and other
bits. We have I invited Santer Claws and sevrel
other people aswell. We are first going to take
turns riding on Sanders slej with Santer. Then were
going to wach a movetie on the T.V. ~~wich~~ wich is
~~come~~ coming on at one oclock. At half two we
ar going to play Twister, ~~scrabble~~ Scrabble
and ~~cluedo~~ Cluedo. Then were going to go to
Block buster and rent a vidow called
Inderpendernce, day. ~~and~~ Then we are going
to Bowling and have two games of Bowling. Then
everybody going home.

                    From
                    Jatinder

Figure 6.7

teacher also kept the first draft of this piece of writing in which she had responded enthusiastically to his use of similes. It is important that your collection of samples includes drafts as these can reveal the whole of the writing process and not just the final, polished version.

With these samples in front of her the teacher is in a strong position to review Jatinder's progress. As you will have seen from the comments above, this is a confident, independent writer who is able to adjust his writing to different purposes and for different genres. His teacher has already provided models and guidance for these different genres, and, on the basis of this evidence, she is able to note areas where he needs more experience. She will be able to plan a range of opportunities to meet his needs, perhaps encouraging writing for a wider range of audiences beyond the classroom.

In all except the earliest sample, where he writes the spoken London dialect form in 'there was two . . .', 'there was not many', he uses Standard written English. He shows increasing control over complex sentence structure ('I am just reminding myself what I

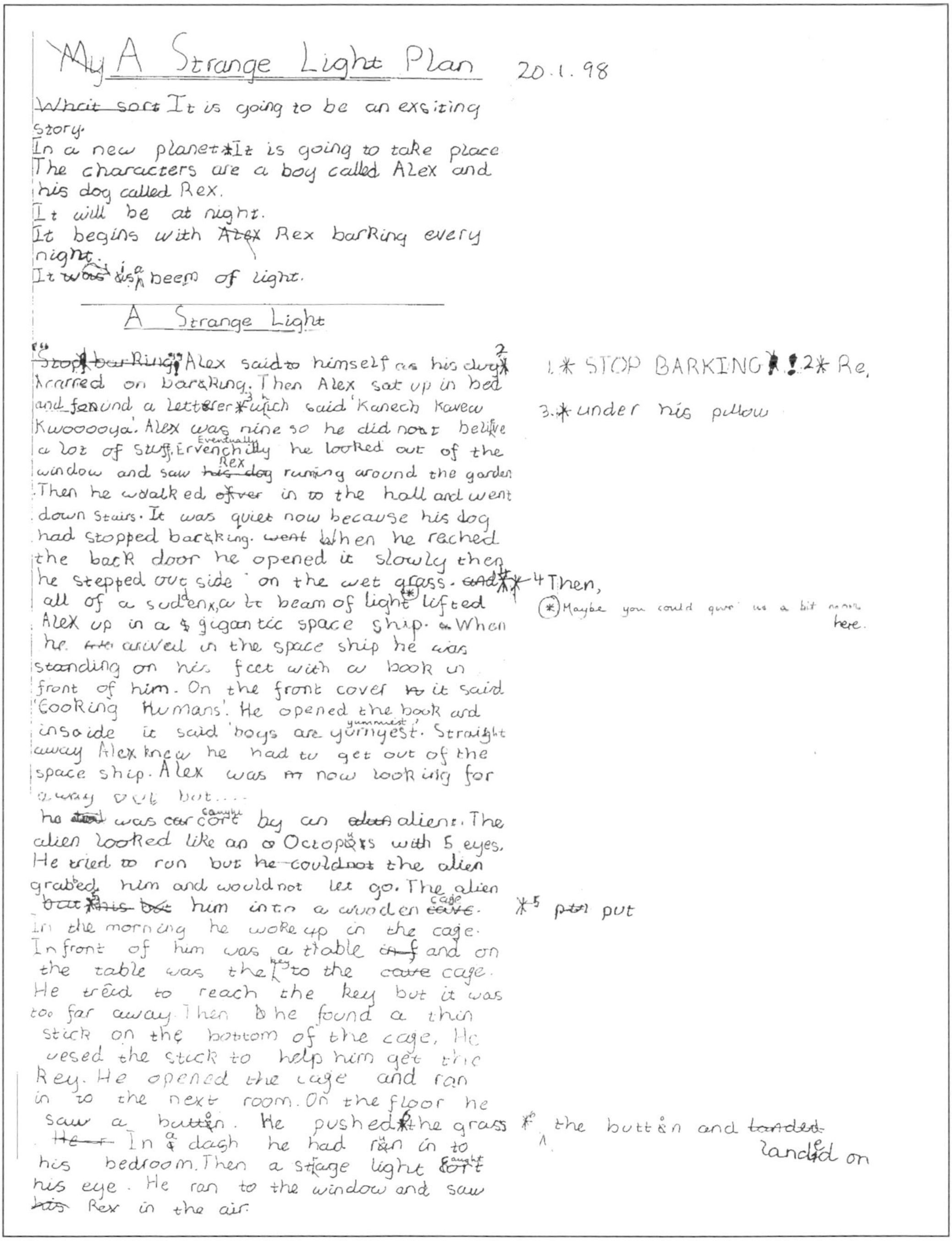

My A Strange Light Plan   20.1.98

What sort It is going to be an exsiting story.

In a new planet It is going to take place

The characters are a boy called Alex and his dog called Rex.

It will be at night.

It begins with Alex Rex barking every night.

It was is a beem of light.

A Strange Light

'Stop barking' Alex said to himself as his dog carried on barking. Then Alex sat up in bed and found a letter which said 'Kaneeh Kavew Kwooooya'. Alex was nine so he did not belive a lot of stuff. Eventually he looked out of the window and saw his dog Rex runing around the garden. Then he walked over in to the hall and went down stairs. It was quiet now because his dog had stopped barking. When he reached the back door he opened it slowly then he stepped outside on the wet grass. and Then, all of a sudden, a bt beam of light lifted Alex up in a s gigantic space ship. When he arrived in the space ship he was standing on his feet with a book in front of him. On the front cover it said 'Cooking Humans'. He opened the book and inside it said 'boys are yummyest'. Straight away Alex knew he had to get out of the space ship. Alex was now looking for away out but....

he was caught by an alien. The alien looked like an Octopus with 5 eyes. He tried to run but he couldnot the alien grabed him and would not let go. The alien put him into a wooden cage. In the morning he woke up in the cage. In front of him was a table and on the table was the key to the cage. He tried to reach the key but it was too far away. Then he found a thin stick on the bottom of the cage. He used the stick to help him get the key. He opened the cage and ran in to the next room. On the floor he saw a button. He pushed the grass the button and landed on In a dash he had ran in to his bedroom. Then a strange light hurt his eye. He ran to the window and saw Rex in the air.

[margin notes:]
1 * STOP BARKING * !2* Re,
3.* under his pillow
*4 Then,
(*) Maybe you could give us a bit more here.
*5 put

Figure 6.8

have been through...' in 6.9), figurative language ('I saw the Spanish Armada scatter around us like a bunch of rats being chased by a cat' in 6.9), the passive voice ('he was caught by an alien' in 6.8), dialogue ('"Stop barking!" Alex said...' in 6.8) and use of reversed word order for dramatic effect ('...on the floor he saw a button...' in 6.8).

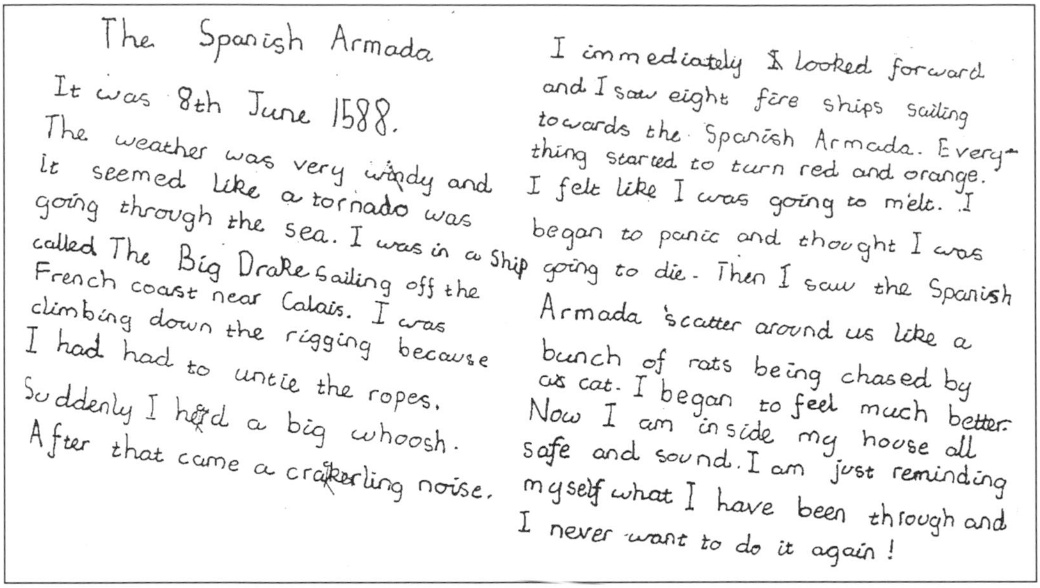

The Spanish Armada

It was 8th June 1588.
The weather was very windy and
it seemed like a tornado was
going through the sea. I was in a Ship
called The Big Drake sailing off the
French coast near Calais. I was
climbing down the rigging because
I had had to untie the ropes.
Suddenly I herd a big whoosh.
After that came a crakerling noise.

I immediately I looked forward
and I saw eight fire ships sailing
towards the Spanish Armada. Everything started to turn red and orange.
I felt like I was going to melt. I
began to panic and thought I was
going to die. Then I saw the Spanish
Armada scatter around us like a
bunch of rats being chased by
as cat. I began to feel much better.
Now I am inside my house all
safe and sound. I am just reminding
myself what I have been through and
I never want to do it again!

Figure 6.9

There is consistent evidence of Jatinder's control of the transcriptional features of writing. His spelling is generally accurate in frequently used words, both monosyllabic and polysyllabic, and he is not afraid to make attempts to spell unfamiliar words. His efforts are consistently sensible phonic attempts, (e.g. 'prervieded', 'inderpendernce', 'ervenchilly', 'cort'). He uses punctuation confidently, including the exclamation mark, and is beginning to use inverted commas for speech. He also makes use of inverted commas for quotations (He opened the book and inside it said "Boys are yummiest"', in 6.8). Only the story contains any use of paragraphing. His handwriting is legible and letters are well formed on the whole; they are joined some of the time, though he often prints when he is writing quickly. Some explicit teaching about the conventions of punctuation, about visual spelling patterns (e.g. for words with 'e' which might sound like 'er' in the child's particular speech patterns, such as 'eventually', 'even', 'parents') might be needed. He might also be given time to practise joined handwriting in order to develop a secure cursive script which will promote speed even in first drafts (see Chapter 5).

Jatinder is in Year 4 and therefore not at the end of a Key Stage, so the use of Level descriptions to make summative statements about his writing is not required. We can say, though, that given the supportive, explicit teaching about writing he is currently receiving, he is well on the way to achieving at least Level 4 by the end of Year 6.

With samples such as these the child and parents, as well as any teacher, are able to review progress. The child can highlight those aspects of writing with which he is pleased and where he feels he has made progress, as well as reflect upon and perhaps set himself targets for areas he needs to work on. The child and his teacher can usefully think about how he feels he might best be helped and a record of such a conference can be made so that the child can look back and see where he has developed. When you first undertake a writing conference with a child, it is useful to have an aide-mémoire of topics for discussion. This might include asking the child to select a piece of writing from any area of the curriculum with which he is particularly pleased. You might then ask why he thinks this is a good piece, what was done well, as well as which kinds of writing he enjoys. Sometimes a child will tell you about writing enjoyed at home; if writing outside school is not mentioned, you could prompt with a comment about your own personal writing (letters, stories, poetry...), or a question. It is quite revealing to ask how the child thinks you could help to improve his writing – you will often find out, from the response to this question, what the child considers to be important in writing.

Many LEAs and individual schools have developed frameworks for annotating samples of children's writing, for noting observations of children at work and for recording discussions with children. One of the most helpful is that provided by the *Primary Language Record* (Barrs *et al.* 1988) or the *Primary Learning Record* (Hester *et al.* 1993), developed by the Centre for Language in Primary Education (CLPE). Many subsequent record-keeping systems draw from the principles of the *PLR* which has recently been revised to provide greater differentiation in the foci at different stages (Foundation Stage, Key Stage One and Key Stage Two).

Another record which has been developed by Croydon LEA, *Writing Development; a Framework* (Graham 1995), focuses on common development patterns and provides a checklist of statements about children working within each *National Curriculum* Level, from 1 to 5. This framework makes a clear distinction between compositional and transcriptional features of writing and teachers highlight statements as they are observed in examples of a child's writing. The compilers point out that the unhighlighted statements provide guidance for teachers about the experiences and teaching which will need to be incorporated into future planning.

TARGET SETTING

Teachers – and children and indeed policy makers who are concerned about raising standards – want to improve children's writing. To this end, negotiating and setting targets which children can aim at, seems quite logical. Talking with children about targets that they can achieve means that we can focus on 'process goals' rather than 'product goals' (see Chapter 2); the research of Black and Wiliam (1998) indicates that process goals give much better results.

In 1999 QCA produced substantial guidance for teachers on *Target Setting and Assessment in the National Literacy Strategy*. This pack explains the different purposes for target setting and provides a booklet of examples of children's work demonstrating evidence of children meeting targets drawn from the *NLS* Framework for Teaching.

Although schools must now agree numerical targets for Year 6 children (quantitative performance targets), for the classroom teacher the main focus needs to be on identifying learning targets 'which can be used with classes, groups or individual pupils and which focus on what children know and can do, their progress and areas for further improvement' (QCA 1999: 5).

Teachers have found it useful to divide targets into those for composition and those for presentation, sometimes using different coloured post-it notes so that the children can actually have the reminders in front of them as they write. There is a problem of children forgetting about an achieved target once they focus on a new target but reminders about this tendency are usually effective.

If targets are set in collaboration with the children, they can 'help children monitor their own learning, reflect on what they have achieved and gain increased control over their own skills and strategies' (QCA 1999: 6). This is precisely the intention of writing conferences and is a far cry from externally imposed targets over which the child has no control. The process links, too, with the whole notion of formative feedback and assessment for learning.

NATIONAL CURRICULUM ASSESSMENTS

At the end of Years 2 and 6 children in primary school sit National Curriculum assessments (originally called SATs and frequently still called this). These national tests provide information which is used to monitor standards and to compare schools' achievements.

Instructions for all of these tests include a note reminding teachers that EAL pupils are not permitted to use bilingual dictionaries and that translations should not be given in any of the English test materials. Many pupils who are at an early stage in developing fluency in English may, therefore, find the test activities rather stressful and you should be aware of the effect of the tests on the confidence of such children.

Key Stage One

The assessment of writing at the end of Key Stage One (Levels 1–3) is carried out by means of writing *tasks*. From 2003 there will be two writing tasks, one long (which will be similar in format to the pre-2003 task) and a shorter task. The example provided of this new task is of writing an invitation to a visitor. 'The two tasks...are expected to be carried out on different days' (QCA June 2002). 'The changes to the assessment of writing aim to gather wider evidence of children's skills by setting two pieces of writing which are different in purpose and form. There will be a choice of content, but the purpose and form will be specified and guideline times suggested' (QCA October 2002). There are also new mark schemes and guidance on marking is provided in a QCA Handbook of sample tests (October 2002).

To prepare for these assessments, teachers will need to ensure that opportunities are provided for children to undertake different kinds of writing with explicit teaching about the texts' purposes, structure and organisation. The writing sessions, apart from the exclusion of the drafting stage, should not be very different from much normal classroom writing. The session is introduced in a similar way to ordinary writing sessions, quite informally, with discussion and guidance from the teacher to help the children think through what they will write, though no specific word lists or models are given. The children must then write independently, using whatever resources they normally use (e.g. wordbooks, dictionaries, general wall displays), but teachers must not give assistance. The assessment of the completed writing is carried out by the teacher, and the *Sample Materials for Key Stages 1 and 2* (QCA October 2002) gives detailed guidance about this, including a set of examples showing evidence of the criteria: these are not level-related.

The only formal test at this stage is spelling. Until 2002, the use of the spelling test for children assessed by teachers as being Level 1 was optional, but from 2003 this will be compulsory for all children. The test will have 20 words which will be marked simply right or wrong. Each child has a copy of the booklet, and the words to be written are dictated by the teacher. Most of the words are those frequently used by children, though there are generally some less usual ones, e.g. 'knife', 'rubbish', 'happened', 'worst' (2001 test).

From 2003, the compulsory spelling test will contribute to the child's overall mark for writing.

Key Stage Two

Writing test

The content of the Key Stage Two assessments changes from year to year, but the basic format and the aspects of writing being tested have remained, with very little variation, over the years. These formal tests must be taken by children throughout the country on the same dates in May and an examination timetable is set in advance. Schools must not open the packs of test papers until the day of the test. There is no doubt that children will need some preparation for these tests, especially if they have been used to working collaboratively and discussing ongoing writing with others. Ideally, there should be no need to change normal working practices in the classroom.

From 2003 Writing at Key Stage 2 will by assessed through two tests; 'children will be allowed 45 minutes to complete the long test, including time for planning, and 20 minutes for the short test. They will be expected to have a break between the two' (QCA June 2002). The example given for the short writing test is to 'write a short description of the activity you have enjoyed most' at an imaginary Activity Holiday Centre. For the long test there will no longer be a choice of different kinds of writing. Children use the planning formats to help them get ideas together so that 'when they write, they can concentrate on the best ways to express them' (QCA October 2002).

There is no invitation or opportunity to redraft, though there might be time for editing. The fact that the test requires 'one-off' pieces of writing does not mean that all of the children's classroom writing should be produced in this way. The routines of planning and drafting will certainly help children in the test situation, though, in the weeks before the assessment, children should also have had some practice in planning and writing to time. The 2002 sample materials describe in some detail the ways in which teachers can prepare children for these tests; the intention is to move away from the heavy focus on completing past papers and training for the test which has happened in some schools. Teachers are reminded that, if Year 6 pupils 'have experienced a varied, exciting and challenging curriculum throughout the year, they are likely to have developed the independent application of their skills needed to approach the test with confidence' (QCA October 2002).

These tests are marked by external markers but teachers are provided, in the 2002 sample materials, with a detailed breakdown, in marked examples, of how the criteria will be applied. The writing, in both Key Stage One and Key Stage Two, will be assessed according to the same focuses.

The aspects of writing to be assessed are children's ability to:

1. write imaginative, interesting and thoughtful texts;
2. produce texts which are appropriate to task, reader and purpose;
3. organise and present whole texts effectively, sequencing and structuring information, ideas and events;
4. construct paragraphs and use cohesion within and between paragraphs;
5. vary sentences for clarity, purpose and effect;
6. write with technical accuracy of syntax and punctuation in phrases, clauses and sentences;
7. select appropriate and effective vocabulary;
8. use correct spelling.

(QCA October 2002)

Spelling is not assessed in the writing test (see separate test) but from 2003 'handwriting will be assessed in the writing tasks rather than in a separate test' (QCA June 2002).

Spelling test

This is a separate test which takes ten minutes to administer. The teacher reads the passage (in 2002, about 'Smokejumpers') and the children write the words into the gaps in their version of the text, in the Spelling booklet. The teacher reads out the text before the children begin to write. These tests are also marked externally.

Concluding points

It is the 'whole writing experience' which is the source of the detailed information needed to monitor each child's development and to plan appropriate teaching. Some of the writing experiences can be incorporated into Literacy Hour activities, but remember that you will need to make provision for more extended writing and for writing in the non-literary genres associated with other curriculum areas. If you look back at the writing samples from Jatinder you will see that some of these arise from science and history and that the characteristics of the different genres needed to be taught in the context of those subjects. The writing element of the English curriculum crosses curriculum boundaries and you will need to be aware of this when you monitor and assess children's writing output. If you have collected samples of writing and have annotated them throughout the year, not only will you be able to focus your planning more precisely, but you will also have all the information you need to make summative Teacher Assessments of the children's progress at the end of the year.

Further reading

Assessment Reform Group (1999) 'Assessment for Learning', in *Assessment for Learning. Beyond the Black Box*. Cambridge: University of Cambridge School of Education.

Bearne, E. (2002) *Making Progress in Writing*. London: Routledge Falmer.

Black, P. and Wiliam, D. (1998) *Inside the Black Box*. London: King's College School of Education.

Barrs, M. and Johnston, G. (1993) *Record-Keeping in the Primary School*. London: Hodder and Stoughton.

Sainsbury, M. (1996) *Tracking Significant Achievement in Primary English*. London: Hodder and Stoughton.

CHAPTER 7

Meeting Individual Needs

Judith Graham

We clearly need a body of research that addresses the writing problems faced by individual learners in today's classrooms. There is scant research focused on the children who struggle in writing classrooms across the grades; on linguistically diverse writers; on children, who despite all efforts, do not grasp sound-symbol relations; on children who are disinterested* in writing; and on special needs children who are mainstreamed into writing classrooms. (Dahl and Farnan 1998: 35–6)

* In the UK, we would use 'uninterested'.

In this chapter, we think about children as individuals who often demonstrate very different achievements in writing, not only in what they choose to write about but also in the levels of attainment that they reach. In most classes, among the children whose progress is sure and steady, there will be some children who write willingly enough but with many errors, some who tend to write about the same topic again and again, some who write at length but with no commitment, some who claim that they hate writing and do the bare minimum or refuse to write at all. In the first set of examples that follow, all these behaviours will be discussed and suggestions for help offered. Then, children who are gifted in writing are considered as undoubtedly teachers want to do their best for these children even though their needs seem less urgent. The 'linguistically diverse' writers of whom Dahl and Farnan speak (see above quotation) are then discussed and then we look at the writing differences between boys and girls. The chapter finishes with a look at the grammatical errors which children make.

CHILDREN WHO WRITE WILLINGLY ENOUGH BUT WITH MANY ERRORS

Eight-year-old Bethany wrote this piece voluntarily and without help. I present it here with transcription aspects tidied up. I suggest you do not look at the original just yet.

Once upon a time, there was a little boy. He was just at the edge of the cliff. He fell. I ran to the phone box and phoned the ambulance. The ambulance came as quick as possible. They took him to the hospital as fast as the ambulance went. He broke his head and he died.

His mum and dad came to the hospital. They were very upset. They was crying all year because he was only four years old. His brothers and sisters were very upset as well.

All of the family came to the funeral. All grandmas and all the grandpas came. They all sang to him.

The next day was his birthday. They all made a cake. It was a chocolate one. And then they put some balloons up. They put lots of seats on the table. All the brothers and sisters sat down. And his mum and dad sat down. And they prayed to him. They had a birthday party.

After that, they went out. They went to the cinema and had a good time and when they came back they thought about brother.

At this point you will probably feel that Bethany has done quite well to sustain a piece of writing of this length and that, on the whole, she has shaped the piece well and remained on topic, albeit swinging rather giddily between death and life. You will be impressed by her hold on family behaviour at crisis times and also by her characters' resilience. You may be wondering to what extent it reflects both fantasy and real elements in her life. On a second reading, you may note some confusion with genres: after a 'once upon a time' opening, we do not expect a disaster account and a first person narrator. You may also think that a child who demonstrates competence with two subordinate clauses, adverbial clauses of reason and of time, could be expected to write with even more complex sentences. But there is lots to commend in this piece and to discuss with its author.

In Figure 7.1 you will see that Bethany's work has been presented with a lot of 'surface noise'. So much in fact, that, in a busy classroom, there would not be time to 'translate' the piece as I have done in order to reveal its characteristics. You can see at a glance that Bethany has transcription problems of every kind. Spelling is phonically logical in some words ('wus a ponr' – once upon a; 'hosbtol' – hospital; 'sisds' – sisters; 'aftdr' – after) but not in others ('hudt' – head; 'ckee' – cake; 'fock' – thought). Her handwriting makes her spelling appear even more alarming: her representation of words such as 'party' and 'after', which appear to be spelled 'pute' and 'uftdr', are probably spelled 'pate' and 'aftdr' but, because she does not close her lower case letter 'a', the words have an apparent arbitrariness about them. Several other letters are wrongly or tentatively formed and re-formed so that we have to work hard to select the correct letter from a graphic arrangement that suggests many. Full stops are mostly in place but they are not followed by capital letters. Capitals, however, appear wrongly in 'MuM' and 'DaD' and 'Ran'. The piece is not paragraphed.

What is a busy teacher to do? In the long run, the most efficient and the most helpful action you can take is to devote time to this one piece and do a full analysis of it. You will then have so much information that you can work on with your pupil that the time will seem a small price to pay for the quality and efficacy of the help which you will then be in a position to offer. You will not of course be able or want to work on more than one or two noted items at any one time; there is ample evidence that children such as Bethany can become quickly discouraged or resistant if you point out too many errors. You will also want to decide an order of priority based on what Bethany can understand and what will make the greatest impact on the writing. Half a term spent working with her on the following should mean that the next piece you sit down to analyse has far fewer transcription errors. Some of Bethany's errors will be shared by others in the class and can be addressed during the Literacy Hour. Indeed the Literacy Hour can be quite supportive for children with difficulties like Bethany as the routines and structure, the 'eyes on print' as the teacher reads aloud, the discussion, the demonstrations and the practice are all most supportive.

Presentation

- Encourage crossing out of a word and re-writing rather than the modifying and over-writing we see throughout this piece.
- Move her into cursive script (signs are there already) and encourage her to keep her pen on the page to form letters correctly.
- Word-process to give her work a professional appearance. Word banks and spell check facilities should interest and support her.

wus a ponr a tum thery was
a little boy he was chiu at
the ech of the chlif. he fel.
I Ran to the foon box and
foond the ablissn the ablissn
cram is thck as posbl. they tock
him to hosbtol is fusd as the
ablissn went. he broock his hudt
and he dud. his mum a Dad chem
to the hosbtol. they wor vere
upset they wos chruin owt yir
becks he was onte for yise old.
they his brufis and sisds wor vere
upset is wel. owl of the fumle
chem to the funeowl. owl gramus
and owl the grenDaDs chem .
they owl sugr to him. the nexs
day was his brday. they owl med
a cree. it was a chokl one.
and then they poot sum bad ons.
up up. they poot lots of sets on the
tebbl. owl the bruss and sidis sat
dan. and his MuM and DaD sat
dan. and they prayd to him. they
had a brfdaypute. ufedr that they
went owt. they went to the senumrs
and had a good turm and wen thay
came back they fock abont brufr.

✗   The End

Figure 7.1

Spelling

- Starting with words like 'was' (which she spells both correctly and incorrectly in this piece) get certain words into her sight vocabulary. Show her how well that works for her with words like 'the' which she always spells correctly.

- Get her to see that 'y' represents the sound at the end of many words ('only', 'very') where she is using an 'e'.
- Help her with the 'ck' digraph, at least at the start of words, where it is never found. Her spellings of 'cliff', 'came', 'crying', 'because', 'took' and 'broke' are all affected by an overgeneralised use of 'ck'.
- Teach her that the inflectional suffix '-ed' is unchanging so it is very easy to get right in words like 'phoned', 'prayed'. Similarly, knowing that the inflectional '-s' is for plurals will help her to avoid mistakes like 'yise' for 'years'. (See Chapters 5 and 6.)
- See if she can detect syllables and, if she can, teach her that every syllable has at least one vowel. She will then have more chance of getting 'brothers', 'sisters' and 'family' right.
- Help her to stretch out words orally so that she can hear their component phonemes. This may be useful in conjunction with seeing the words in print also – notice that her spelling of several words such as 'gramus' (grandmas) and 'funeowl' (funeral) probably indicates good aural ability but no visual fine-tuning.

Punctuation

- Show Bethany how good she is at putting in full stops and tell her you know that she can do it always. Teach her to follow full stops with capitals.

In addition to the above, you will have noticed that Bethany finds it very difficult to represent vowel sounds correctly: 'wor' – were; 'owl' – all; 'yir' – year; 'brufis' – brothers; 'fumle' – family. This is Bethany's biggest challenge. Achieve success in other areas first and then see if work on onset and rime will help her see the regular patterns: 'others, smothers, mothers, brothers'. (See Chapter 5.) All the time, she will need to be reading and/or listening to you reading while she has her eyes on the text, so that her visual strategies develop to complement her aural discrimination.

Before I leave Bethany, it needs to be stressed that her willingness to write readily and at length is at risk unless your approach is sensitive. I have detailed the work that needs to be done on transcription aspects; I am not suggesting that there are no improvements to be made on the compositional side but, in relative terms, she is not doing too badly there so keep her morale high while also making the odd suggestion – such as a bit more pre-planning and revision so that the story-telling opening goes and the 'I' in the story is clarified or excised. Publish her work so that she can see the correct forms of her words and so that she feels her work reaches a wider audience.

In Chapter 8, you will read about two children who have been receiving help for the specific learning difficulty, dyslexia. Many teachers might well think that Bethany should be diagnosed similarly but at this point in her school life she was receiving help from home, from the teacher and from a classroom assistant and she appeared to be making steady if slow progress.

CHILDREN WHO TEND TO WRITE ABOUT THE SAME TOPIC AGAIN AND AGAIN

Week 1 Some tanks can go into the water. They can still have the guns.
Week 2 The tank has two little guns and the little guns fire little bullets.
Week 3 Some tanks have little guns and big guns.
Week 4 The big tank is a 101 Fighter Fox.
(Kevin, aged 6)

There are plenty of explanations for children who tend to write on the same topic over and over again. They may have had success once and be living in hope that the experience will be repeated. They may be extremely interested in the topic and not realise that their rehearsal of content does not enchant everybody. They may feel that their position in the class as authority on a topic may be at risk if they move away from it. Importantly, they may be using the period of writing always about the same things to make progress in some of the transcription sides of writing. Above all, they may be nervous of branching out into new areas. Security in what they know may be important and you will want to respect this.

If you are sure that the writing is not showing any signs of growth for the child, in any area, then consider one or more of the following:

- Increase the amount of time which the child spends writing. We all tend to go round in circles if we do not write frequently enough.
- Get the child to read out work to the class more often in order to elicit peer reaction. The class comments may shift the child into providing more interesting detail and eventually into new areas.
- Publish the child's work so that an end product marks visible achievement and, with luck, a sense of closure.
- Increase the child's exposure to a range of genres and provide new audiences. Kevin could be encouraged to make a picture book for younger children in which a disaster occurs to those guns under water.
- Support moves into new areas: with reading aloud, visits, TV programmes, the offer of taking dictation, writing frames, etc.
- Model (in shared writing sessions) how you move on to new topics when you think it is time.
- Congratulate him when he does branch out. (See further comments on this in Boys and Girls below.)

Some time after Kevin wrote his early pieces about guns he was taken to HMS Belfast on the River Thames. He dictated a long piece, including the following to his teacher:

> Then we went over the bridge and we looked about. There was a 40 mm gun for shooting down aircraft and we put some money in and stood back. Then a voice said, "This gun is for shooting down aircraft and in the background you will hear aircraft flying over you." And then we turned two pedals and made the gun go up and down.

His interests have been respected; his classmates asked him lots of questions; his days of single lines are going to come to an end.

CHILDREN WHO WRITE AT LENGTH BUT WITH NO COMMITMENT

> Once upon a time there were some teddy bears. They went to school. They had the register and then they took out their books. One bear did not listen. He got sent to the corner and had to do sums all the time and then it was home time. When they got home they set off on a boat to go to France and had something to eat (etc.)
> (Lucy aged 8)

Commitment, or lack of it, is difficult to demonstrate simply by presenting an end product. The above child continued this piece for several more pages, adding incidents competently but in an unplanned and disaffected way. There are many such children who settle down immediately to write on given writing tasks and produce the required amount with little fuss and acceptable accuracy but do not seem to care about planning, revising, redrafting, publishing or feedback. It seems as if they are privileging the length of the piece above content; this may be a reflection of teachers' messages about minimum length requirements regardless of genre.

Lucy does not of course keep us awake at night in the way that Bethany does. But there is much that we can do to improve her writing and increase engagement. Try some or all of the following:

- Increase the sense of audience. Children who write only for the teacher are in danger of losing a critical, reflective stance towards their writing. This writer is clearly imitating a young children's book; given the opportunity to read to a real audience of small children, she would probably have planned more carefully, added dialogue and ensured a sense of a significant problem and a final resolution and evaluation.
- Ask the child about the details that are so carefully avoided here. In talk, and when she realised that there was genuine interest in her ideas, this child said that it was because the bear had been so excited about France that he could not concentrate at school and that, because he had been fiddling with the teacher's things, he had had a smack. Many children just do not realise how such detail, far from holding up the story, gives the piece voice and particularity.
- Get writing partnerships going in the classroom (see Chapter 3). Other children will increase Lucy's ambition to improve her writing and getting closer to others' writing will make Lucy care about the community of writers to which she belongs.
- Encourage Lucy to write voluntarily rather than at prescribed times, so that she does not fall into the mechanical writing that she produces so easily on request. Inviting writing areas can be a great incentive (see Chapters 3 and 5).
- Find out what Lucy would really like to write about. Donald Graves' (1983) suggestions for notebooks for individual writing topics are useful.

CHILDREN WHO CLAIM THAT THEY HATE WRITING AND DO THE BARE MINIMUM OR NOTHING AT ALL

Once upon a time there was a dinosaur and
(Neil aged 7)

Most scraps of writing like this end up in the wastepaper basket, thrown there after 30 minutes of a wasted lesson by an angry or despondent child or by the teacher when she retrieves the tightly screwed up ball from under the desk. It is a situation familiar to most teachers and very worrying. Usually these children will add a word or two if you are sitting beside them but once you leave then they will dry up again. The reasons for this behaviour fall into two main categories: anxiety about getting it wrong and a shortage of ideas. The suggestions below deal with both these categories:

- Anxieties about getting it wrong are nearly always to do with transcription elements – letter formation, crossings-out, spelling errors, punctuation omissions. Occasionally they are about content; for instance, if the child is to write a non-fiction piece and you have expressly forbidden copying from information sources and the child does not know how to complete the task in any other way. If you can get the child dictating to you, not only has he the opportunity to witness innumerable lessons on how to form letters, punctuate, paragraph and spell but also more of his story is preserved, so that his morale is raised and at some point he may be willing to take over the writing.

- Reassure the child that many excellent writers leave transcription aspects until after they have got their content down. Have an editing table in your classroom where the piece can go for tidying up by you or appropriate others.
- When the child is stuck on the spelling of a word, suggest that they 'have a go' in a notebook kept for that purpose, find a source for the word in the classroom or write it for them. (See Chapter 5.) It is important that you do not give the impression that writing equals spelling, so keep this bit 'light'.
- Try to give more prior support before you expect writing. Make sure that the topic has been discussed, that a structure is identified and, on some occasions, supplied, that key words are written up to jog memories, that the audience for the piece is identified. (See Chapter 4.)
- Make it quite clear that this is not the final draft, but still ensure that materials which the child is working with are not too scruffy. Many a child will write more readily when they are given your special sharp pencil or a fine felt tip. (See Chapter 5.)
- If children lose heart, suggest that they look at other writers' work to see if they can find inspiration or solutions. Suggest that they go on to some different work and let them return to the piece another day. (Real writers do this.)
- Keep a record of the topics that are of interest to the child so that you can suggest an area when inspiration is short. Remind children of pieces that they have written which you have enjoyed.
- Provide small enticements to write; post-it pads and novelty notebooks may lure the most diffident of writers.
- Allow time away from writing to decorate or illustrate the piece. Time spent on, for instance, illuminating the first letter, is often used fruitfully to muse on how the text could develop.
- Use the word processor both as an incentive and also as a reward for getting on with the work – but do not disrupt the classroom routines you have established for the equipment. (See Chapter 3.)
- Keep a file (with an index) of all writing done, however short, so that the child can see the progress being made.

You will see that there are common themes that keep occurring in these suggestions for children with writing difficulties or reluctance. In truth, what is good practice for all your class is good practice for these children too. Obviously there would be no need, for instance, to scribe for a fluent writer but that child, in her time, may have benefited enormously from such a practice. Regard your inexperienced writer as just that – inexperienced – and do not attribute errors to carelessness nor reluctance to laziness. It is mostly more complicated than that. One of the advantages of a Literacy Hour – in the sense of a predictable classroom routine that will provide structure and regularity – is that it is the less secure children in your classroom who will appreciate the consistency and continuity. Try to provide as much writing time as possible for your children with difficulties, especially of extended pieces. You will also want to encourage writing at home as much as you can (see Chapter 3).

GIFTED WRITERS

You will notice that able children are very quick to experiment with and put into their writing whatever models you have been sharing with them. Their private reading also influences their writing as does evidence of the written word that they see around them in a print-saturated environment. The conventions, tone, vocabulary and style of new genres seem to be effortlessly absorbed by them and no sooner have they mastered a form than they will begin to play with it, perhaps subverting its conventions to amusing effect. At a sentence level too, you may find that a taught session on, for instance, the use of subordinate clauses, will see gifted writers experimenting with how many subordinate clauses they can add to a main clause before the sentence becomes unwieldy. New vocabulary and especially new terminology delights them and will turn up immediately in their writing.

Some able children arrive in school writing accurately, fluently and enthusiastically. It is through the tasks you devise for your gifted writers that you will be able to cater for this deftness. Figure 7.2 is page 9 of a four year old's 'novel', written in a little spiral bound notebook, brought to school on the first day of term. The teacher saw many openings to extend this writing and offered the child the opportunity to write a little bit more about Hadrian's Wall as an entry for an encyclopaedia, to write about a day in the life of a Roman soldier on duty on Hadrian's Wall (she found and read Auden's poem to the child) or to draw a poster reminding rock climbers about safety. After discussion and deliberation, the child chose the last option, concentrating particularly on crash helmets 'so that you don't bump your heads'. Noticing openings of this sort to extend range and depth of thinking is absolutely essential if gifted children (and all children) are not to stand still. It is hard to ensure that the first part of the literacy hour stretches gifted writers, so it is in the guided group work and opportunities for individual and extended writing that you will best be answering your pupils' needs.

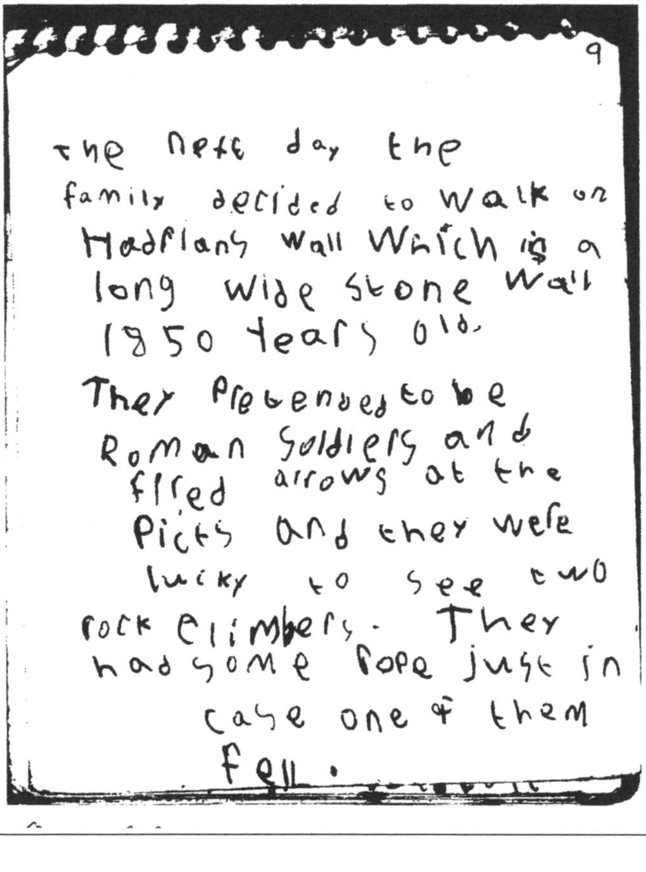

Figure 7.2

Many written activities can be devised that suit the whole class, irrespective of ability. These tasks are of the open-ended type so that a gifted writer can write more, write with more depth and with more originality but essentially on the same subject. Let us suppose a Year 5 class has been reading novels by 'a significant children's author', perhaps Dick King-Smith, and has begun with *Martin's Mice*, which is a story of a cat, Martin, who wishes not to eat mice but to keep them as pets. A written activity that asks children to rewrite an incident as a play scene might lead to opportunities for the gifted writer to write his or her scene with a detailed set of directions to a film director and/or camera crew. You may find the child turns the whole text into a play script, word processes it and insists that the class perform it!

Equally, you may devise a writing frame for most of the class to marshal their thoughts about the serious message of the novel: the rights of animals to be free and not kept as pets. Class discussion will precede this activity but the gifted writer will not need the writing frame and may turn in something that is balanced and logically structured and could stand as an editorial in a newspaper. Few children in the class will go on to read Dick King-Smith's more challenging novels (*The Crowstarver* and *Godhanger* for instance) but able children will, and can then be given tasks tailored to this wider reading. They can bring their reading of the author's novels together, perhaps in answer to a question such as 'You have been asked to recommend a Dick King-Smith novel for a children's radio programme. Say why you would select one title rather than another.'

CHILDREN LEARNING TO WRITE IN ENGLISH AS AN ADDITIONAL LANGUAGE

Before we look at writing with children whose first language is not English, it is important to remind ourselves of what we know in three areas:

1. What do we know about how human beings learn language?
2. What do we know about how human beings learn a second or subsequent language?
3. What do teachers do to give children learning English access to good teaching?

What do we know about how human beings learn language?

We know that we learn language through being surrounded by people using the target language in meaningful circumstances. Because of the nature of children's early lives, some of the language they hear, especially that which is directed at them, is repeated, stressed and simplified. We know that children's language learning involves listening, thinking, playing and adjusting. We know that children experiment with sounds and use intonation 'tunes' to make themselves understood. We know that it is helpful if children are allowed to initiate topics of interest. We know that it is important that people respond to children's approximations and treat them as meaningful. We know that correction of the forms of the language is largely ineffectual in the early stages. Children will go on saying, 'I wented' and 'Mummy goed' and even 'I caughted it' for a long time despite well meaning correction.

What do we know about how human beings learn a second or subsequent language?

Children learning English as an additional language need very similar conditions to those in which they learned their first language. They similarly need models, meaningful circumstances, some stressing, repetition and simplification, time to listen and no pressure to speak until ready, freedom to make mistakes, a chance to choose the topic, a chance to play.

What do teachers do to give children learning English access to good teaching?

In the classroom, the teacher will have to respect the child's early silence and receive responses in non-verbal forms initially. The meaningful classroom which she has created for all children will serve those children learning English well. She will offer planned and structured group work where groups are, ideally, mixed race, gender, ability and language; she will recognise the power and learning potential in narrative, song, drama and story-telling; she will read from fiction and non-fiction texts to her class; she will organise computer time, visits, taped texts in the listening corner and numerous practical activities. She will want to pursue parental involvement and to ensure that the school adheres to its anti-racist policies. In addition, the teacher will check for anglo-centric content in her resources and activities, put up multilingual displays and bring texts in other languages into the classroom.

The teacher will need to make some moves more deliberately and be more focused in her language strategies when she is teaching children learning English and thus she will encourage mother-tongue use, knowing as she does that progress there will be reflected in increased competence in English (see Chapter 2). She will use bilingual helpers to help her make fair assessments, of oral as well as written work, and she will team-teach with them where possible, especially in the Literacy Hour. She will ask for their help or advice in preparing big books and school-made cassettes in two or more languages. As far as writing is concerned, she will encourage children to write in all their languages, use older children to scribe for younger children in their first languages, taking dictation herself and invite parents to participate in writing activities with their children. She will have overlay keyboards and flexible computer software such as *Textease 2000* (a 'click and type' word processing package). Posters around the school and letters home will be in translated form as far as possible, not just to convey contents but also to signal respect for the languages in the community. Software such as Clicker 4's *Wacky Sentences*, designed to support Gujerati children learning English will further reinforce this respect for other languages.

Classroom examples

The following examples illustrate ways of working with children in the writing classroom in which it can be seen that the teachers and schools involved understand the importance of the areas discussed above.

Early Years and Key Stage One

A Year 1 class has been looking at scripts in various languages. All around the room are examples of Chinese, Bengali and Urdu, brought in by the teacher, the children and parents. After a visit to a Chinese restaurant in Soho (where some of the Chinese children were able to show off their reading of the menu), the Chinese script was very high profile for a while. Nil's writing, in Figure 7.3, is in both Bengali and Chinese.

The next piece, Figure 7.4, by Yesmin is interesting as the gap between her competence in Bengali and English is apparent in the tentative copying of her name in the less familiar script used for English (scribed initially by the teacher). Direction and sequence of letters are a problem for her at this stage but her interest in different

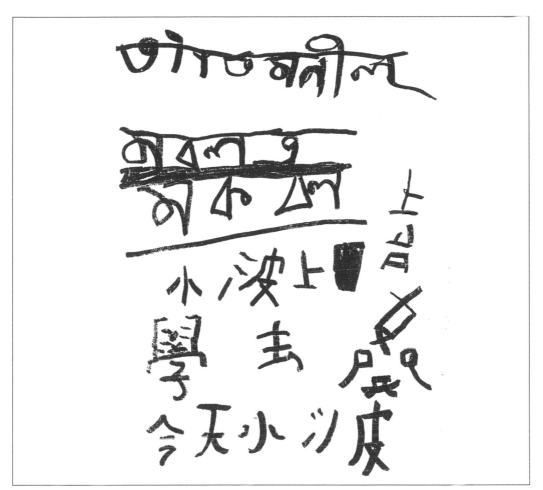

Figure 7.3

Figure 7.4

scripts ensured that she took notice as her teacher scribed for her and for the class.

Shared writing produced a set of instructions and drawings for how to use chopsticks and then captions for a set of photographs of the visit to Soho Chinatown (later made into a spiral-bound class book). All the time, there was lots of emergent writing in several scripts to which the teacher responded positively. The piece by Mahbuba, Figure 7.5, was not 'translated' by the child, who was still at the silent stage, but the teacher pointed out features of various scripts, much to the child's pleasure.

Figure 7.5

In this class, children chose which language they were going to write in and responded to the hospitality their teacher gave to their languages. The teacher dated, glossed and kept all work, even 'unfinished' pieces, and was able at the end of the children's first full year in school to share the progress made, both with them and with their parents. Anxieties, expressed by some parents that progress in English would suffer if first languages were encouraged, were mostly allayed in the light of the children's achievements.

Key Stage Two

In a Year 4 class, the teacher had been sharing traditional tales from several cultures with the class. *Bimwili and the Zimwi* (Aardema and Meddaugh) had been shared several times and a whole-class drama had developed (everybody became the drum, the seagull, the waves of the sea as required). Many of the children could retell the story in story-telling sessions and all the class could sing Bimwili's plaintive ditties. The class was bonded to this story forever it seemed. Many children wrote alternative endings, extra scenes, interior monologues but, for the three children whose work is reproduced in Figure 7.6, the fluency they found came from a retelling. Not reproduced here is the fine picture they drew while they were planning the retelling.

There are errors of course – the one the teacher chose to work on was the '-ed' suffix, which helped sort out 'dropt' and 'ript', where the children have not yet internalised the regular third person past tense and are representing what they can hear. (Bethany (Figure 7.1) has a similar problem.) But remarkable is the control over

> The story of Bimwli and
> The zimwi. one day Bimwli
> went to The seaSide and
> She find a Shell and Then
> When She dropt shell mark
> Zimwli peeded up The Shell
> and Said come here
> Little girl here is your Shell
> and mark Zimwli
> grabed her and thorw. her
> in to a drum with her shell
> when her mother heard
> her Sining and Then They
> ript The drum up and
> took her out and put
> in baes and antes
> and They c heesed
> The moster away
> The END By sy iva
> and Imelda and keeiv

Figure 7.6

the main shape of the story, the introduction of dialogue (albeit without punctuation) and a command over English sentence structure that is closing in on the standard within the class as a whole. Children experimenting with new constructions in writing – such as the sentence beginning 'When her mother' – tend to make errors which they cannot pick up with proofreading (Perera 1984). They need increased familiarity with the constructions and careful teacher support in pointing them out.

Reading and writing connections

This work with traditional tales depends on the teacher being enthusiastic about reading aloud and building up the secondary world which children can then revisit any time in their heads. Re-readings allow deeper meanings to evolve and the texts assume greater and greater importance to children. In addition, with the all-important exposure to the unchanging text, children get some of that same repetition and intonation 'tune' that supported their entry into spoken language. It is very clear that children learning English can hold many of the structures and much of the vocabulary of English when the structures and words are charged with memorable and symbolic meaning. Many a child's writing discloses the rhythms, vocabulary and cadences of an original text, such as 'he begged and begged and begged but no...' or 'Now it was not long before...' or 'Suddenly a voice was heard' or 'Where there is water, there are fish and where there are fish, there are fishermen'. It reminds us how closely tied reading is to children's writing development. All children need to be read to as much as you can manage.

BOYS AND GIRLS

In a chapter on individual needs, the heading 'Boys and girls' may be rather surprising. It probably suggests a mass divided broadly into two roughly equal parts rather than the specialised few whom we have been considering up to this point under the headings of 'children with difficulties', 'gifted writers' or 'children for whom English is an additional language'. But as groups, boys and girls left to their own devices tend to restrict their writing choices and boys in particular depend much on peer approval and what is considered fashionable. It is important to discuss the pertinent issues here, especially as there is ample evidence that a restricted range of writing and extreme brevity are key reasons for boys achieving considerably fewer Level 4s in their end of end of Key Stage Two assessments (52 per cent of boys and 68 per cent of girls in 2002).

Social conditioning

Because subtle and not so subtle assumptions about sex-roles are everywhere in society, including in our classrooms, and because these assumptions affect life experiences, we as teachers have a certain responsibility to try to counteract some of these limiting expectations. The differing social conditioning of boys and girls means that by the time children are in nursery school, a noticeable preference to play outside, to play with large construction toys and to draw and fantasise about large, often destructive, items is evident in the small boys. The girls will more commonly be drawn to activities at tables, be found in elaborate games of domestic play in play corners and be involved in talk with the adults around. In terms of their story reading and television watching and video game playing, noticeable general differences are observable, with girls and boys demonstrating clear gendered differences from an early age.

Classroom action

Teachers have tried to make changes in some of the following ways:

- by monitoring and guiding the activities that children choose in free time. Parents and helpers can be useful allies to get the girls to play with Lego and to get the boys into the role-play area.
- by discussing issues with children, e.g. their toys, colours of clothes for babies, advertisements, suitable presents for relations, etc.;
- by sharing books which foreground some of the issues, e.g. *Piggybook* (Browne), *Jump* (Magorian and Ormerod);
- by helping girls and boys to role-play characters of the opposite sex;
- by checking that all children read fiction and non-fiction;
- by deciding what to do about certain traditional fairy stories and comics;
- by checking that both sexes are represented as central characters in the fiction shared;
- by checking illustrations of roles taken by male and female;
- by checking that authors are men and women;
- by inviting non-stereotypical visitors e.g. female doctors and male nurses into the classroom for children to talk to. A male embroiderer invited into school worked a miracle for boys' needlework. Another class had a visitor (female) who had survived the

Japanese earthquake (two days stuck in a lift) and although her account was not overly heroic, her bravery left a marked impression, particularly on the boys of the class.

Writing and gender

Particularly in writing, teachers have often felt that gender differences are most marked. Boys and girls do very different things in their writing.

Early Years and Key Stage One

Under various action-packed pictures, these captions (transcription aspects are tidied up) appeared in the first school work produced by four-year-old Ben:

> This is a dinosaur and a volcano erupted and some anti-aircraft guns and some people killed the dinosaur.

> This is a sports car and an interceptor was in the sky.

> This is a swimming pool and Aaron went off the diving board and it was the top board.

> This is a golden eagle and it is on the mountains.

> This is a dynamite and a aeroplane fired a long rope and a circle of bombs made the dynamite go off.

> This is a lighthouse and a robber stole a ship and it was tied on a stick and the robber tried to cut the rope but he couldn't.

> This is a lunar module and it is taking off and two space men are climbing into the lunar module.

> This is a submarine and a shark came along.

Here are four-year-old Claire's captions under her drawings:

> I went to the seaside and it wasn't all in sand. It was in stones.

> The princess is mending the giant's socks and she is sitting on a chair.

> My brother Mark when he had a wobbly tooth it went down the plug hole.

> We had a game of getting married and Natalie sprinkled (sbrigcwld!) the poppy petals on my head for confetti.

> Gillian read me a story and then I went to sleep with my knees curled up.

Both sets of captions have imaginative and linguistic strengths but Claire's focus on family, friends, the personal and the domestic (even in the giant's home) is in marked contrast to Ben's inventory of all the most fantastical, violent, powerful and action-packed things he writes about.

Key Stage Two

Do matters change after the children have been in school for three or four years? It will probably not be difficult for you to guess which of the two recounts below was written by a girl and which by a boy. Each child was exactly the same age (7 years, 11 months).

We went to Seven Sisters Rocks to-day and we crossed the Suspension Bridge. We had to walk a long way and we saw an elm tree and it had Dutch elm disease. We climbed a steep rock. Then we got to the first one of the Seven Sisters rocks. We had a look down from the top of the rock and it was a brilliant view. We went to King Arthur's cave and it was full of rubbish. We had a snack. We had an apple and cucumber and raisins. Some people were rolling rocks down the drop. On the way back, we saw an ants nest and someone threw a stone on the nest and all the ants came out to repair it.

On Wednesday, Polly came to stay the night and we played with our little pets, the guinea pigs. We had Snowdrop which was an albino. It was all white with red beady eyes and Joseph, he had all sorts of colours just like a multi-coloured coat. And that's why we called him Joseph. Rachel tied her green bracelet into the cage and the baby guinea pigs jumped through. Polly liked Snowdrop best because it was an albino. Jessica, Polly's sister, was allergic to them so she could not hold them. Then we gave them a lesson to jump through the hoop. It was Snowdrop's turn first. He did it nicely. Then it was Joseph's turn. He did it a bit wrong. At the end of the lesson, we had our tea.

The first text confirms what is generally felt about boys' writing: that it roams further afield than that of girls; that it includes more action; and that it contains more evidence of interest in boyish behaviour. In this case, the boys who threw rocks over the edge and who stone the ants' nest receive no disapproval. (It is possible that the writer joined in with the activities.) It is probable that the audience the writer was hoping to interest in his piece was his own circle of boys who were on the outing and peer approval is no small consideration as we have indicated earlier.

The second piece conforms to a general expectation of a piece from a girl of this age: it is home-focused and concerned with the intimate goings-on of life with family, friends and domestic animals. It is focused throughout on one topic and presents a story which is carefully shaped and cosy in its tone. The audience for this piece was ostensibly the girl's teacher; however, there is some indication that the extra information (how Joseph came by his name, where Jessica fits in) is considerately provided not only for her teacher but also perhaps for some wider, unknown audience.

A better future?

After one has read scores of pieces of writing which appear to confirm these general characteristics of the content and tone of girls' and boys' writing one does doubt whether the efforts teachers make such as those outlined above can make much difference. Certainly we need to investigate and research even more those classrooms where boys and girls are confounding our expectations. There is promising evidence, for instance, that the recent understandings of how to scaffold non-fiction writing with 'writing frames' is giving a boost to girls' writing in that area.

In looking through the notebooks of writing from several boys and girls (from which the above examples have been taken), I am struck by the fact that, although the trend in boys and girls is clearly gender-marked, in all the notebooks there were atypical examples of writing – far fewer in number but clearly there nevertheless. Thus Ben drew a careful picture of his garden, captioned:

Daddy mended the fence and we had a pic-nic

and Claire had a dramatic picture, captioned:

A man and a boy are out in the frost with a dog and the dog fell in some ice and drowned.

At age eight, there was a comparable sprinkling of writing where one would be hard-pressed to guess whether the author was male or female. If teachers notice, commend, share and publish these unrepresentative pieces, children may begin to shift in their understanding of the range they can attempt. The impact of what children have read to them is also significant as is the gender of the reader. What is popular reading in the classroom is influential also. Eve Bearne (1998) knows of Year 6 boys who write romances while Judy Blume is the class cult reading, and girls who are laying out their non-fiction writing with large exploded inserts and pull-out maps.

It is true also that boys are likely to read and write more and differently when they have male examples at school and at home. As most primary school teachers are female and as we cannot arrange for a male in every home, this becomes a tall order, but where schools have, for instance, invited male authors into school, writing's profile has been helpfully increased. Michael Rosen's school visits, where he shares his non-stereotypical poetry with children, have done their part in this long haul towards a widening of what girls and boys see themselves able to write.

It is perhaps important to end this section by reminding ourselves that there are schools where boys' achievements in *National Curriculum* assessments are just as high as those of girls. Research suggests that what these schools are doing right (for all pupils) is capturing the imagination with the choice of books read aloud, revisiting of texts through drama and role and setting engaging writing tasks. These successful schools allow pupils considerable freedom to follow their own interests and children write with a sense of purpose and of audience. Teachers respond positively to compositional aspects so that pupils grow in their beliefs that they have worthwhile things to say. Above all, there is lots of talk – with partners and with the teacher – about all aspects of writing (Frater 2000).

CHILDREN WHOSE WORK SHOWS GRAMMATICAL ERRORS

There have been several instances in the examples of writing that we have used throughout this book of children who import features of their spoken language into their writing. For all children, spoken language acquisition is ahead of written competence as they have obviously not had the same exposure to written language, which is nearly always in standard English. The most obvious errors in this respect are those of non-agreement of subject and verb; thus in Bethany's writing, we find, 'the parents was crying' (Figure 7.1) and in Jatinder's writing, 'there was two ardvarks' (Figure 6.5). Other errors appear in writing in places where we would not notice them in speech. You see an example of this in 'the shop keeper who owned the shop did not know that there was one everyone wanted the christmas tree but it was too expensive' (Figure 5.11). In this section I look at key issues of grammar teaching, part of sentence level work.

What can be taught?

As we saw in Chapter 2 there has been considerable debate about how and what should be taught explicitly as far as grammar is concerned We will not rehearse those arguments here but will remind you that the *NLS* provides a framework for contextualised grammar teaching (sentence level work). The difficulty will be to find ways round the abstractions involved in teaching some aspects. If you cannot explain a rule in straightforward language and in a way that children can take on then it is probably wiser to put your time and effort into lots of examples of the rule in practice, so that children can generate their own understandings and definitions. It is also important to remember that many children have already acquired standard English and use it without error in their writing, so some in your class will bring a great deal of implicit understanding to the teaching you do.

The importance of reading to children and of children reading in the development of their acquisition of written standard English cannot be emphasised enough.

When to deal with grammatical errors that appear in individual writing

If children are well practised in reading their work aloud, either to themselves or a writing partner, then they are more than likely to pick up some of their grammatical errors. When seven-year-old Tony read out his story and came to the sentence 'That night the rabbit's mum comed to the lion's den...' he said straightaway, 'That doesn't sound right' and changed 'comed' to 'came', the past tense of the irregular verb 'to come'. If a child's writing reaches the editing table with grammatical errors still present, individual help will need to be given by the teacher and final marking left in her hands so that no work reaches a wider public with non-standard slips in place. At this final stage the child will be far more interested in the lessons to be learned than if you interrupt the flow of composition at the start of the process. As this book has consistently maintained, it is most important that children know when it is most profitable to give their attention to the various different aspects of writing.

What do you need to know?

Many of the writers of this book were at school at a time when explicit grammar lessons did not happen. Because they are all curious about the language which they speak, write and teach they have given themselves and are still giving themselves lessons about language. The fact that they recognise that there are linguistic niceties that they have yet to master does not mean that they are not 'good enough' users of their language. 'Negatives' and 'passives' do not give most of us many problems but you might have to give yourself lessons to check on 'pronominal reference' and 'fronted constructions'! None of us should be complacent about our knowledge level and it is very important that we all remain curious and go on learning; curiosity about language as well as teacher subject knowledge have been strands throughout this book.

We should not be fearful of teaching children in all the ways that we have been describing even while we are still in the process of developing knowledge of terminology and more difficult linguistic concepts. You need to remember that the subject of this book is teaching about the whole of writing, not just grammar.

Struggling or gifted, writing in English as a first language or as an additional language, girl or boy, the children that this chapter focuses on will all flourish in your classroom when you give evidence of your interest in them and create an atmosphere in which mistakes are seen as moments for learning.

Further reading

Barrs, M. and Pidgeon, S. (2002) *Boys and Writing*. London: CLPE.
Berger, A. and Gross, J. (1999) *Teaching the Literacy Hour in an Inclusive Classroom*. London: David Fulton Publishers.
Bunting, R. (2002) 'How to write really badly: supporting children with writing difficulties', in Williams, M. *Unlocking Writing*. London: David Fulton Publishers.

Eyre, D. (2001) *Able Children in Ordinary Schools.* London: David Fulton Publishers.

Eyres, I. (1995) 'Looking for Pattern: Bilingual Readers Writing', in Bearne, E. *Greater Expectations, Children Reading Writing*, Chapter 7. London: Cassell.

Millard, E. (2001) Chapter 9 in Evans, J. *The Writing Classroom: aspects of writing and the primary child, 3–11.* London: David Fulton Publishers.

QCA (1998) *Can do Better: Raising Boys' Achievement in English.* London: QCA.

Williams, M. (2002) 'Providing a challenge: writing and the able child' in Williams, M. *Unlocking Writing.* London: David Fulton Publishers.

See also *NLS* materials:

Early Literacy Support (2001); *Additional Literacy Support* (1999); *Further Literacy Support* (2002).

CHAPTER 8

Specific Learning Difficulties in Writing

Cathy Svensson

'He joins in discussions enthusiastically but his written work is weak.'
'He still struggles with spelling, even with the words he comes across every single day.'
'I just can't quite put my finger on what the problem is ...'
'I thought he was able until I saw his writing ...'

A SPECIFIC LEARNING DIFFICULTY

There are many specific learning difficulties but the most high profile is called dyslexia; dyspraxia and dyscalculia are other examples. These conditions are considered 'specific' as they always represent a difficulty in one or more *basic* psychological processes. In the case of dyslexia this difficulty relates to understanding and using spoken or written language, while dyspraxia relates to a difficulty in performing familiar or unfamiliar motor skills. Dyscalculia is a specific difficulty in dealing with numbers and calculations. As a condition dyslexia is the most widely documented of the specific learning difficulties. It is recognised internationally across class, language and gender.

The term dyslexia originates from the Greek word 'dys' meaning 'difficulty' or 'malfunction' and 'lexia', taken from the root word 'lexis' meaning language. Use of this term implies that dyslexia is not merely a reading difficulty but encompasses a wide range of language based difficulties, accounting for a delay in aspects of language acquisition, both spoken and written, and compounded by a slow rate of processing and poor memory for words.

THE INCLUSION CONTEXT

The notion of inclusive education highlights equality of opportunity for all. The Special Educational Needs and Disability Act (DfEE 2000) puts individual needs at the heart of inclusion. The Act places the onus on schools to embrace and respond to all pupils' needs, to consider how the school can overcome 'barriers to learning' and make appropriate provision for diverse needs within a mainstream setting.

The SEN Code of Practice (DfE 1994; DfEE 2000) puts Special Educational Needs at the top of every school agenda. It is underpinned by the fundamental principles of inclusion. It categorises four areas of special educational need:

• Communication and Interaction;
• Cognition and Learning;
• Behaviour, Emotional and Social Development;
• Sensory and Physical.

It recognises the language based nature of dyslexia and includes it in the category of Communication and Interaction needs. It rightly reminds us that individual needs may span more that one category. It states that all children with special educational needs should:

- have their needs met;
- normally be provided for in the mainstream classroom;
- have their views taken into account;
- have full access to a broad and balanced curriculum.

It also reminds us that parents have a vital role to play in supporting their children's education.

The fact that dyslexia affects between 5 and 10 per cent of the population means that we can expect one to two children on average, in each class to exhibit symptoms of dyslexia. This, coupled with the philosophy of Inclusion, brings SEN and dyslexia firmly into the classroom domain and is therefore an issue for every class teacher.

Class teachers need to be aware that the range of evidence of dyslexia will vary from pupil to pupil, depending on the child's development and the range and severity of his or her symptoms. Typically, dyslexia is more common among boys but there is no one 'classic' dyslexic type. It can affect children from monolingual or multilingual backgrounds. Not all children with dyslexic symptoms will be on the school special needs register; some should be but are not, some may have mild difficulties, others severe, and many have associated well recognised strengths.

In this chapter we identify the nature and range of the symptoms of dyslexia through a review of two case studies: one a child in a Year 2 class, the other in Year 6. We reflect on their difficulties, through their writing samples and consider some practical support ideas. It is often in a child's independent writing that a class teacher identifies a 'cause for concern' that needs further investigation.

ASSESSING THE WRITTEN EVIDENCE

Immature spelling, handwriting and poorly organised composition are the writing problems most commonly associated with dyslexia. There is often a minimalist approach to the writing task. In order to make an initial assessment of the writing, the class teacher needs to have a well established understanding of normal literacy development. Against this knowledge any unusual deviations or delays can be measured. The teacher can analyse the writing and check for particular patterns of difficulty which can be considered alongside the child's classroom strengths, behaviour, other achievements and learning style. Depending on the outcome of the evidence review, the teacher may, in liaison with the school Special Educational Needs Coordinator (SENCO), decide an appropriate action plan of support.

A CASE STUDY OF CON

Figure 8.1 is a Year 1 writing sample. Without a context for this writing it may look like early developmental writing of a four or five year old in a Reception class. When we discover that the author, Constance (Con) is aged six, in a Year 1 class, is a native English speaker, is considered of above average ability in a high achieving school, our perception of the writing changes. The writer is retelling her news. She has a story to tell but it is without a context and limited to a retelling of one main event. She tells us that she 'bent down to pick up her book.' We do not know that this is a most precious book that had been lost for a long time – given to her by her grandmother for her third birthday. She was so pleased to find her book again that she wrote this 'part' event as her news.

Figure 8.1

What Con knows about writing

When analysing writing it is always important to consider first of all what the child knows and can do. Con's writing shows that she knows:

- writing represents meaning;
- writing follows left to right sequential order;
- sounds are represented by letter shapes;
- spoken words are represented by separate units of letters;
- initial sounds are represented by particular letter shapes.

But ...

- her developmental delay is demonstrated by the immaturity of her writing;
- she has a story to tell but limits it to the bare minimum: it lacks context or awareness of audience;
- she has some knowledge of letter sound mapping. She limits this to first letter sounds in words except in writing the word 'bend' as 'bet'. She shows some early 'fuzzy' representation of other sounds in this word;
- she does not attempt to spell the high frequency words 'to' and 'my';
- she omits to write the first word 'I' of her sentence;
- her handwriting is immature for a child in her second year of schooling. She is learning to write in a cursive script but close inspection of her writing reveals incorrect letter formation (see the 'g', and 'd' particularly) which may further inhibit her motivation to write.

Figure 8.2 is a sample of Con's work one year later.

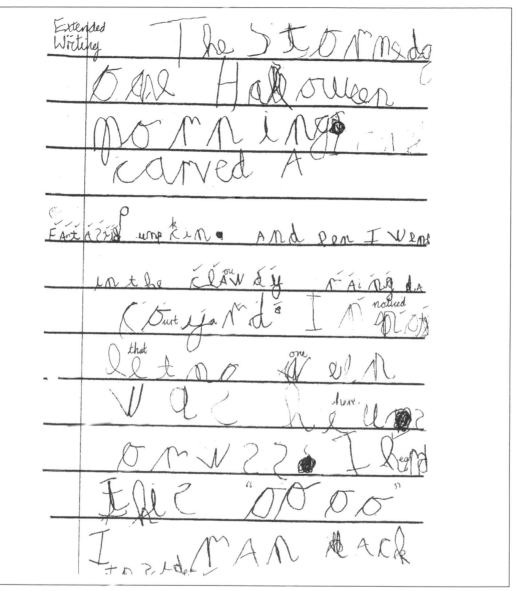

Figure 8.2

This extended piece of writing is a Halloween story titled 'One Stormy Day'. It followed a series of work related to Halloween ghost stories. It was completed with support: the title was copied by the child and key words of 'Halloween', 'morning', 'pumpkin' and 'carved' were all supplied. What is evident is the improvement in Con's ability to tell a story which is facilitated by her improved confidence in spelling.

Figure 8.1 reflects scant knowledge of letter sound mapping of initial sounds only. Figure 8.2 shows a growing knowledge of letter sound mapping to the extent that the pupil notes the most significant sounds in a word e.g. 'courtyard' is represented as 'coyrd', 'heard' is represented as 'hrd'. Some high frequency words are written

Writing Under Control

accurately and no longer represented by an initial sound only ('in', 'the', 'went', 'ran'). Note how Con can maintain more controlled handwriting and spelling at the start of her story. The demands of integrating the skills of handwriting, telling a story and spelling are particularly onerous and reflected in the later loosely controlled handwriting, erratic spacing between words and consistent reversal of 's'. Ongoing difficulties with applying graphic and phonic knowledge to encode words for spelling are reflected in the spelling attempts ('once' spelt as 'orwss' and 'one' as 'ween'). Such difficulties are a common feature of dyslexia.

Con's history

Closer scrutiny of Con's history reveals varied language and organisation difficulties highlighted by the demands made by the writing task. All are closely identified with dyslexia. These following characteristic features of the condition have been well documented by a number of researchers. Children may exhibit few, some, many or all of these indicators.

- Failure to reach the normal developmental goals in language acquisition (Vellutino 1979; Lundberg and Hoien 2001).
- Oral problems in pronunciation and jumbling words (Blacock 1982; Miles 1983).
- Problems in naming everyday objects and in word finding (Miles 1974; Snowling *et al.* 1986; Sheffield 1991).
- Difficulty recognising rhyme and alliteration, counting syllables and recognising and counting phonemes in words (Bradley and Bryant 1983; Liberman and Shankweiler 1985; Treiman 1985; Goswami 1991; Snowling 1995 and 2000).
- Poor auditory memory for words and letters (Chasty 1985; Sheffield 1991; Badian 1995).
- Weakness related to visual discrimination and organisation (Fawcett and Nicholson 1992 & 2001; Stein 2001).

Con had many of the above difficulties but her problems are relatively mild when compared to those of many dyslexic children.

Language acquisition

Con was late to talk. Her mum noticed this when she compared her to her peers but felt that the fact that she was a very contented baby could account for it. She was almost three before she spoke in simple sentences. This is a skill most children achieve by age two (Danwitz 1975).

Oral problems in pronunciation and jumbling words

When Con did start to speak it was difficult to understand her because of mild articulation problems. Following a referral from the local GP she had speech therapy when she was three. The interesting thing was that her difficulties were subtle and barely noted by her family. It was only on school entry that her parents again suspected she had a subtle speech delay when compared to her peers. For example, she said 'puter' for 'computer'; she could not say 'c' accurately, instead she said 't', pronouncing 'car' as 'tar'. Words starting with a cluster were simplified when spoken, for example, 'climb' was pronounced as 'time'. On many occasions she referred to 'Father Christmas' as 'Farmer Christmas' and never seemed to notice her error.

Problems in naming everyday objects and in word finding

Con's difficulty in naming was first noted when she had a new baby sister. It took her some weeks to remember her sister's name, which was surprising as she was obviously so proud of her. The same sort of difficulty was evident in her memory for labels of even very familiar things: animals, characters in favourite stories etc.

Recognition of the syllable, rhyme and the phoneme

On school entry, she was sociable and chatty but her poor phonological awareness was noted. In Reception class, when playing 'I spy', Con could not detect the first phoneme in the word 'sun', suggesting that it might be 'b'. At the end of the Reception class, the teacher noted a welcome breakthrough: Con was beginning to hear initial and significant sounds in words and to recognise rhyme. She could count syllables in words: three syllables for 'croc-o-dile' and two for her full name. She was now at the stage of phonological awareness that many children reach by school entry.

Poor memory for words

Con took a long time to learn the usual nursery rhymes. She took time to learn new vocabulary associated with school such as 'welfare ladies' and 'secretary'. She found it hard to follow two-part classroom instructions, being only able to hold on to one simple instruction at a time. If sent on a classroom errand, she often forgot what to say or do. After she had heard a story she could not easily retell it.

Writing problems

Con was keen to represent meaning with mark making and drawing, but in her case this developmental stage lasted an unusually long time. In stories she always had good ideas about what she wanted to write but she had problems sequencing her ideas into order, deciding what was the relevant part of the story, and where to start. In Reception class Con was a keen writer but took a long time to establish where to start writing on the page. She would happily start writing at the top right hand corner of the page and work downwards, sometimes for long stretches of time, without realising her mistake. The same sort of difficulty was noted in her letter formation. It was very common for her to reverse letters and even words.

She took a long time to progress from writing 'on' as 'no', for example. She was confused by 'b' and 'd' and 'p' and 'q' and, like many children, found it difficult to tell them apart. Her difficulties meant she could not apply letter sound knowledge effectively to her spelling.

By the end of Reception, Con could name five letters and write two from memory. She could write her name, and deviated versions of her name with many reversed letters featuring largely in her writing.

In Year 1 Con learned the other 21 letters of the alphabet. She could write 19 from memory and could map these onto the written letters. She was developing an additional strategy to 'make meaning' in writing, and to 'take meaning' from reading. Despite her above average ability, by Year 2 her writing was similar to the writing of a Year 1 child.

Individual Education Plan

Name: Con
Main areas of concern
Con has been diagnosed dyslexic;
she has delayed literacy skills,
poor memory for words and weak listening skills.
Con's weaknesses are most evident in her writing.

Start date: **January 2003**
Stage: **School Action**
Year: **2**
Review date: **April 2003**
Programme monitored weekly by class teacher and the
Learning Support Assistant (LSA) and half termly by the SENCO.

Objectives	Success Criteria	Support Strategies	Classroom Strategies
Underpinning language target: To be able to name the days of the week in sequence.	Days of the week known. Appropriate labelling of 'today' and 'tomorrow' noted in conversation.	Days of week memory games: 'On Monday I bought a . . .'. Practise using related vocabulary daily: 'tomorrow will be, the day before', etc. Create and draw a simple timetable of activities for each day.	Classroom display of days and activities associated with each day. Discussion on 'today's day'. Display books that include days of the week e.g. 'The Very Hungry Caterpillar'.
Handwriting target: To be able to write 'Constance' in cursive script. To write 's' appropriately.	'Constance' and the letter 's' are written in neat cursive script. Success observed over time.	Write in glitter glue. Trace, finger trace over writing. Experiment with different writing implements. Extend handwriting practice to include daily bead threading and dot to dot activities.	Set up a class office. Provide a wide range of writing implements and accessories. Encourage self monitoring and peer review of writing.
Spelling target: To be able to spell 8 common words: *here, and, that, was, got, play, come* and *have.*	Con can spell 30 Year 1 and 2 common words by Easter break (22 common words already known).	Concentrate on 2 words weekly. Use multisensory strategies. Make the words using wooden letters. Talk about the word. Say the word. Write the word really slowly in 10 seconds. How many times can you write the word in 30 seconds? 'Think and talk' about learning with Con and the method that works best for her. Foster a 'little and often' approach (5 minutes daily practice).	Stick word list onto desk. Use 'look, say, spell, cover, write, check' strategy as routine classroom practice. Encourage and model investigative and multisensory approaches to spelling.

Parent/carers have agreed: to support Con's Home/School Reading nightly. They recognise how sharing texts can improve Con's language/ reading and provide her with models of text to support her story writing. Class teacher to advise parents on recommended texts and approaches to reading.
Support arrangements: Con will have 3 x weekly group support in the Literacy Hour and 1:1 support for 30 minutes with a Learning Support Assistant (LSA). Group support in the Literacy Hour will ensure full curriculum access; individual support will target Con's specific needs.

Figure 8.3

Involving the parents

Parents were surprised when Con's earliest school assessments showed that her progress in reading was slow. Their response was that she loved books, reading and being read to, so therefore this did not seem possible. The class teacher explained to Con's parents that her love of books, her positive home support, and her attitude to reading were all strengths that would help override her early literacy difficulties. She also explained to them the frequent negative impact of delayed speech acquisition and subtle speech problems particularly on spelling and therefore on writing.

She suggested that she continued to monitor Con's progress carefully, and that together they set up an Individual Education Plan (IEP) (Figure 8.3) which would:

- identify a specific short-term target to support her language and writing;
- highlight particular teaching approaches and strategies that would help her achieve these targets;
- involve the classroom assistant in her support programme;
- set a target date to review the success of her programme.

School action

The class teacher collected a range of written evidence in order to build a comprehensive profile of Con's writing across the curriculum. Writing samples included diary writing, extended story writing and cross-curricular samples. She referred to previous end of year reading and spelling assessments and reviewed Con's current spelling support arrangements. In discussion with the SENCO, Con was placed on the 'School Action' SEN register, which meant that her needs were such that the school could adequately support her without involving outside agencies. It was agreed that additional school based support would include group support three times weekly, to ensure access to the curriculum during the Literacy Hour, and in addition individual support once weekly.

With the advice of the SENCO, the class teacher stressed the importance of using a wide range of teaching strategies rather than 'more of the same' which were obviously not working so well.

She explained some of her teaching strategies:

- the importance of making the writing process explicit as a model for Con to relate to;
- the need to engage as many sensory approaches as possible in the writing process;
- the impact of making language experiences 'live' as a stimulus for thought, language learning and writing;
- the need to maintain the excellent habit of reading and sharing varied texts with Con to provide suitable models of writing for her;
- the importance of separating out the skills of handwriting, composition and spelling, to avoid overload and maintain Con's sense of achievement and self-esteem.

MEET SEBASTIAN IN YEAR 6

Sebastian (Seb) is aged ten. He is a Year 6 pupil. As with Con, his poor performance in writing is affected by very subtle language-related difficulties, noted, particularly at this stage, in his problems grappling with new French vocabulary and in learning times tables by rote. The interesting thing is that Seb has particular strengths associated with his difficulties too. Though his handwriting is weak, his drawing, particularly of 3D shapes, is very good. He has advanced ICT skills and is also an able mathematician.

Seb has struggled with the physical act of handwriting and making sense of spelling throughout his schooling. At the end of Year 2, he achieved Level 1 in the English National Curriculum assessments. He achieved Level 2 in Science and Maths as both these topics made fewer demands on writing and spelling proficiency and therefore suited Seb. Currently he works with the above average ability group in maths, the average ability group in science and the below average group for all writing and spelling related activities. Despite producing very untidy, almost illegible maths work he can grapple with very complicated mathematical concepts confidently. His written English is inhibited greatly by his poor spelling. Because of this, he limits what he writes, which means his writing experience is minimal. This exacerbates his difficulties and therefore both transcription and composition skills show developmental delay.

Though his self-esteem is 'fragile', he is well supported by sensitive class grouping. He has opportunity to work with the lower ability group to receive 'nuts and bolts' support, and in the above average group in those tasks that challenge his problem solving and reasoning skills. Seb is on the 'School Action Plus' register as his needs are being reviewed by the local education authority.

In this writing activity (Figure 8.4) Seb was intellectually challenged by the topic of World War Two. The teacher used many rich and stimulating visual aids, pictures, video evidence and artefacts to support her teaching. These approaches were reinforced in a small support group before the writing activity took place. The objective for all the children for this lesson was 'To develop the skills of biographical and autobiographical writing in role' (*NLS*, Y6, T.14).

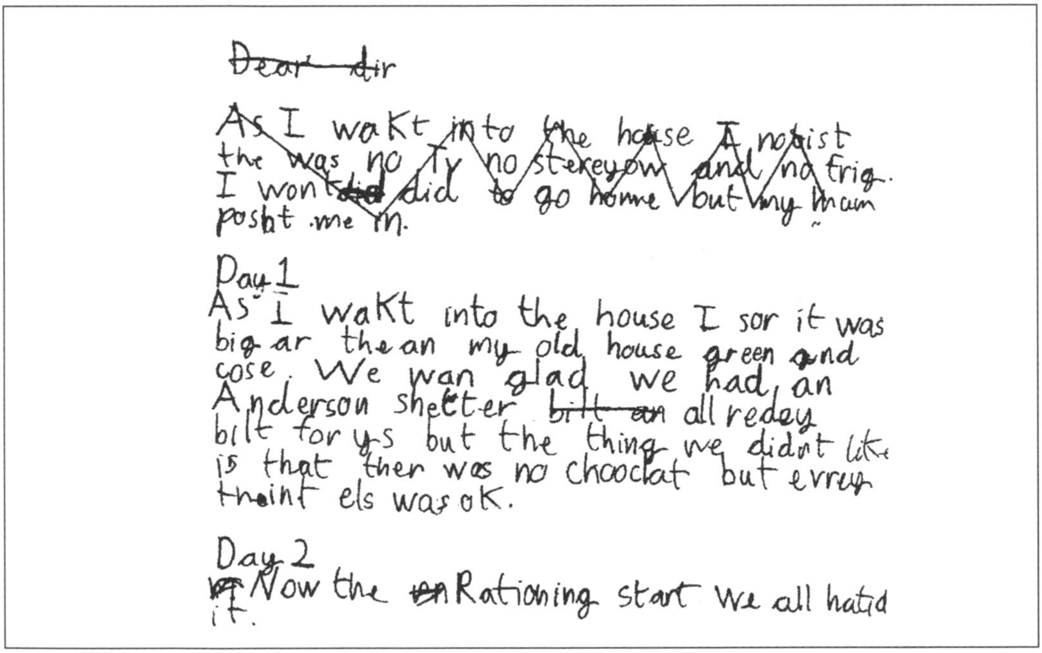
~~Dear dir~~

As I wakt into the house I noist the was no TV no stereyow and no frig. I wont did to go home but my mam posht me in.

Day 1

As I wakt into the house I sor it was bigar then my old house green and cose. We wan glad we had an Anderson shelter ~~bilt an~~ all redey bilt for us but the thing we didnt like is that ther was no chooclat but evrey thing els was ok.

Day 2

Now the Rationing start We all hatid it.

Figure 8.4

Seb gives an account of how he might have felt about the new home he was sent to in order to escape the war. The group support, offered by the LSA (Learning Support Assistant), gave him and others in the group an additional opportunity to handle, review and discuss World War Two artefacts and evidence and gave him access to the writing task. He had a chance to practise using the language associated with this topic, and to think, reason and hypothesise about wartime conditions. Key words were highlighted, read, and their spelling discussed before writing.

We can see that Seb knows about writing first person diary accounts of his experience and is able to sustain the narrative voice. He has understanding of key concepts associated with the war such as Anderson shelters and rationing but the writing lacks descriptive detail.

On the transcriptional side, he uses a sentence break appropriately and follows it with a capital letter. Spelling is mostly alphabetic (see Frith's model in Chapter 5). He spells words as they sound to him, for example 'bigger' is spelt 'bigar', 'cosy' as 'cose', 'already' as 'allredey', 'built' as 'bilt', 'else' as 'els', 'every' as 'evrey'.

Many high frequency words are correctly spelt, e.g. 'into', 'the', 'house', 'it', 'was', 'and', 'we', 'had', 'an', 'for'. However, there are incorrect spellings for other high frequency words such as: 'us' as 'ys' and 'sor' for 'saw'. Seb can certainly read these words accurately but cannot yet spell them when he is faced with the demands of planning and remembering what to write, how to spell, and how to form his letters while controlling the movement of his pencil. It is clear that neither his memory for the visual sequence of letters in the word nor how the phonemes are represented by certain graphemes, is securely established for him. His delay in establishing these skills impacts greatly on the quality and diversity of his writing experience.

His underdeveloped fine motor skills are reflected in his slow, non-fluent handwriting.

Inclusive classroom strategies

The three elements of inclusion (Figure 8.5) highlight the difficulty for the class teacher: to provide support for Seb while challenging him intellectually. She needs to consider her writing objective and whether it can be appropriately adapted or supported to suit his needs, matched to his learning style and made accessible in order to provide an inclusive learning environment.

The class teacher is fully aware of the need to incorporate a range of classroom strategies that will provide Seb with access to the writing curriculum. She uses a wide range of the 'dyslexia-friendly' approaches in the classroom which aim to incorporate high level 'doing and thinking' rather than low level 'copying and colouring'.

She incorporates the following dyslexia-friendly strategies to support his writing.

Teaching to strengths:

- providing activities to extend reasoning, hypothesising and debating;
- using his skill in drawing to complement his writing;
- using strong visual support strategies and suitably uncluttered work sheets to engage Seb, thereby ensuring easy access to text.

Minimising the demand for a written response to each task by:

- using writing frames;
- providing cloze procedure activities;
- choosing from true or false statements to show knowledge of a topic;
- assigning a scribe to each group for oral activities;
- making use of voice recognition, predictive text programmes and tape recording to record a response;
- using drama, hot seating, pair share strategies to explore concepts and responses;

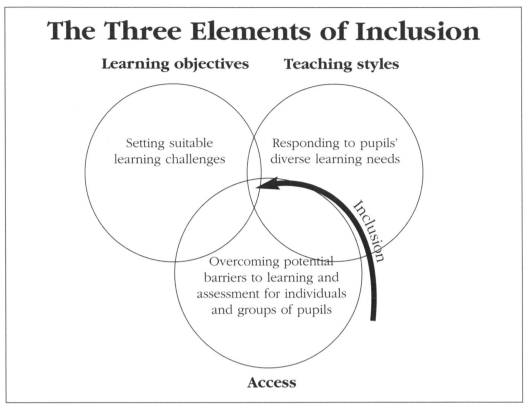

Figure 8.5

- introducing concept mapping, KWL grids, study skills, mind mapping to support prewriting organisation.

Pre-empting Seb's needs:

- backing up writing activities with access to visual and practical aids: lists of topic words, days of the week, alphabet strip, spell checker or dictionary, and appropriate stationery (highlighter pens, markers, sticky notes);
- using innovative grouping arrangements so Seb works within appropriate class groups to match the requirements of the task and his needs;
- breaking writing tasks down into component skills to allow each separate skill to be supported.

Making classroom routines transparent and consistent:

- providing a stimulating, well organised and appropriately resourced classroom.

Specific targets for Seb

Specific SMART (**s**pecific, **m**anageable, **a**chievable, **r**elevant and **t**ime bound) targets are identified on Seb's IEP. The prime objective of these targets is to improve his spelling and phonemic awareness through teaching strategies that he can then apply to other words for learning.

Two different and complementary approaches are needed to support Seb's spelling: one method to support irregular spelling of common everyday words; the other to support learning words in word families.

- The common words 'saw,' 'were', 'us' and 'there' need active teaching in order to commit them to memory. The common words account for the vast majority of words Seb will need to use in his everyday writing. It makes sense therefore to target these words for spelling. They are frequently irregular so a 'sounding out' strategy alone does not work effectively; instead a multisensory approach is needed which will engage as many sensory channels as possible in the learning task. Spelling activities which involve seeing, hearing, feeling or doing, (smelling and tasting are less practicable) will help ensure the best learning conditions. For example, strategies of 'look, say, spell, cover, write, check' and word building with wooden letters should be included as teaching strategies.

The second strategy to use is an investigative approach to spelling, which can be applied when the word to be learnt conforms to a spelling pattern.

- One area of difficulty (noted in the suffix spelling '-ed') can most helpfully be taught through collecting examples of using the '-ed' suffix to represent the past tense. In this way he would learn to generalise use of the rule.
- Rules and uses for 'y' at the end of a word (as in 'cosy' and 'every'); whether 'y' always makes an 'e' sound in this end position could also be investigated. Later the phonemes that the letter 'y' represents could be explored, for example, when does it it make a 'y' sound, an 'e' sound and an 'i' sound?

Specific IEP spelling targets include:

- to secure spelling (this half term) of 18 key common words based on the Year 1 and 2 Literacy Hour words;
- to be able to use the suffixes '–ed' and '–er';
- to improve phonemic awareness;
- to know how the long 'e' sound at the end of a word is spelt.

The way forward

Seb needs both wide ranging and specific support at different levels. He benefits from the stimulation of inclusive practices in a dyslexia-friendly classroom. Here, ideally, he can have his ideas challenged and extended. He has access to the 'big classroom picture' and the stimulation for writing that this provides. Group support for writing reinforces and supports the skills and processes he could not otherwise access independently. Here a wide range of differentiated writing activities and strategies can be explored and supported in a secure group setting. Individual support is ideal for his particular needs: here specific difficulties can be picked apart and dealt with, while the essential opportunity for 'overlearning' writing routines and procedures can also be supported. In these ways the teacher is effectively integrating whole class, guided group and individual support to provide the best learning opportunities for Seb.

Further reading

Augur, J. (1996) *This Book Doesn't Make Sense*. London: Whurr Publishers Ltd.
British Dyslexia Association (2000) *Achieving Dyslexia Friendly Schools*. Reading: BDA.

British Dyslexia Association (2002) *British Dyslexia Handbook*. Reading: BDA.

Crombie, M. A. (1997) *Specific Learning Difficulties: Dyslexia, A Teachers' Guide*. Belford: Ann Arbour Publishers.

Ott, P. (1997) *How to Detect and Manage Dyslexia*. Heinemann: Oxford.

Pumphrey, P. D. and Elliott, C. D. (1990) (eds) *Children's Difficulties in Reading, Spelling and Writing*. Lewes: Falmer Press.

Reid, G. (1998) *Dyslexia: A Practitioners' Handbook*. Chichester: John Wiley.

Riddick B., Wolfe, J. and Lumsdon, D. (2002) *Dyslexia: A Practical Guide for Teachers and Parents*. London: David Fulton Publishers.

Thompson, M. and Watkins, B. (1998) *Dyslexia*. London: Whurr Publishers Ltd.

Tod, J. (1999) *IEPs-Dyslexia*. London: David Fulton Publishers.

Useful websites

British Dyslexia Organisation: www.bda-dyslexia.org.uk
Dyslexia Institute: www.dyslexia.inst.org.uk

References

Adams, M. J. (1990) *Beginning to Read: Thinking and Learning about Print*. Cambridge, MA: MIT Press.

Aldrich, R. (1982) *An Introduction to the History of Education*. London: Hodder and Stoughton.

Badian, N. A. (1995) 'Predicting reading ability over the long term: the changing role of letter naming, phonological awareness and orthographic processing'. *Annals of Dyslexia*, **47**.

Baker, C. (1996) *The Foundations of Bilingualism*. Clevedon: Multilingual Matters.

Bannatyne, A. and Cotterell, G. (1966) 'Spelling for the dyslexic child'. *ICAA Word Blind Bulletin*, Winter.

Barrs, M. (1987) 'Learning to write', in *Language Matters* (**2**) and (**3**). London: CLPE.

Barrs, M. (ed.) (1990) *Shared Reading, Shared Writing*. London: CLPE.

Barrs, M. (1991) *Language Matters: Thinking about Writing*, No. 1. London: CLPE.

Barrs, M. (1994) 'Genre theory: what's it all about?', in Stierer, B. and Maybin, J. (eds) *Language, Literacy and Learning in Educational Practice*. Clevedon: Multilingual Matters/Open University.

Barrs, M. (1996) 'The new primary language record writing scale'. *Language Matters*, **3**. London: CLPE.

Barrs, M. and Cork, V. (2001) *The Reader in the Writer*. London: CLPE.

Barrs, M., Ellis, S., Hester, H. and Thomas, A. (1988) *The Primary Language Record Handbook for Teachers*. London: CLPE.

Barrs, M., Ellis, S., Hester, H. and Thomas, A. (1990) *Patterns of Learning*. London: CLPE.

Barrs, M. and Thomas, A. (eds) (1991) *The Reading Book*. London: CLPE.

Barton, D. and Hamilton, M. (1998) *Local Literacies*. London: Routledge.

Bearne, E. (1998) *Progress in Writing*. London: Routledge.

Bissex, G. (1980) *GNYS AT WRK: A Child Learns to Write and Read*. Cambridge, MA: Harvard University Press.

Black, P. and Wiliam, D. (1998) *Inside the Black Box*. London: King's College School of Education.

Blacock, J. (1982) 'Persistent auditory language deficits in adults with learning disabilities'. *Journal of Learning Disabilities*, **15**.

Bradley, L. L. and Bryant, P. E. (1983) 'Categorising sounds and learning to read: a causal connection'. *Nature*, **301**.

British Dyslexia Association (2000) *Achieving Dyslexia Friendly Schools*. Reading: BDA.

Britton, J. (1982) 'Outline for a case study', in Pradl, G. (ed.) *Prospect and Retrospect: Selected Essays for James Britton*. London: Heinemann.

Brownjohn, S. (1994) *To Rhyme or Not to Rhyme: Teaching Children to Write Poetry*. London: Hodder and Stoughton.

Bryant, P. and Bradley, L. (1985) *Children's Reading Problems*. Oxford: Blackwell.

Calkins, L. McCormick (1983) *Lessons from a Child: on the Teaching and Learning of Writing*. Exeter, New Hampshire: Heinemann.

Cashdan, A. and Grugeon, E. (eds) (1972) *Language in Education*. London: Routledge.

Chasty, H. (1985) 'What is dyslexia?' in Snowling, M. J. (ed.) *Children's Written Language Difficulties: Assessment and Management*. Windsor: NFER-Nelson.

Chomsky, C. (1971) 'Write now, read later'. *Childhood Education*, **47**.

Clark, M. (1976) *Young Fluent Readers*. London: Heinemann.

Clark, U. (1996) *An Introduction to Stylistics*. Cheltenham: Stanley Thornes.

Clay, M. (1975) *What Did I Write?* London: Heinemann.

Clegg, A. (ed.) (1964) *The Excitement of Writing*. London: Chatto.

Committee of Enquiry in Reading and the use of English (1975) *A Language for Life*. London: HMSO (The Bullock Report).

Cotton, P. (1992) 'Let's all join up'. *Child Education*, April.

Cox, B. (1991) *Cox on Cox*. Sevenoaks: Hodder and Stoughton.

Cripps, C. and Peters, M. (1996) *Collins Catchwords Teacher's Guide*. London: Collins.

Crystal, D. (1995) *The Cambridge Encyclopaedia of the English Language*. Cambridge: Cambridge University Press.

Czerniewska, P. (1992) *Learning About Writing*. Oxford: Blackwell.

Dahl, K. and Farnan, N. (1998) *Children's Writing: Perspectives from Research*. Newark, Delaware: International Reading Association.

DES (1967) *Children and Their Primary Schools* (The Plowden Report). London: HMSO.

DES (1975) *A Language for Life* (The Bullock Report). London: HMSO.

DES (1978) *Primary Education in England*. London: HMSO.

DES (1982) *Education 5–9: An Illustrative Survey of 80 First Schools in England*. London: HMSO.

DES (1984) *English 5–16*. London: HMSO.

DES (1988) *Report of the Committee of Inquiry into the Teaching of the English Language* (The Kingman Report). London: HMSO.

DES (1989) *English for Ages 5–16* (The Cox Report). London: HMSO.

DfE (1994) *Code of Practice on the Identification and Assessment of Special Educational Needs*. London: DfE.

DfEE (1995) *English in the National Curriculum*. London: HMSO.

DfEE (1998) *The National Literacy Strategy*. London: DfEE.

DfEE (1999) *The National Curriculum English*. London: DfEE.

DfEE (1999) *Spelling Bank*. London: DfEE

DfEE (2000) *Grammar for Writing*. London: DfEE.

DfEE (2000) *Progression in Phonics*. London DfEE.

DfEE (2000) *SEN and Disability Rights in Education Bill: Consultation Document*. London: DfEE.

DfEE (2001) *Developing Early Writing*. London: DfEE

DfES (2001) *Special Educational Needs – Code of Practice*. London: DfES.

Dixon, J. (1967) *Growth through English*. Oxford: Oxford University Press for NATE.

Dombey, H. and Moustafa, M. (1998) *Whole to Part Phonics: How Children Learn to Read and Spell*. London: CLPE.

Fawcett, A. J. and Nicholson, R. (1992) 'Automatisation deficits in balance for dyslexic children'. *Perceptual and Motor Skills*, **75**.

Fawcett, A. J. and Nicholson, R. (2001) 'Dyslexia and the role of the cerebellum', in Fawcett, A. J. (ed.), *Dyslexia: Theory and Good Practice*. London: Whurr Publishers.

Ferreiro, E. and Teberosky, A. (1979) *Literacy Before Schooling*. London: Heinemann.

Foggin, J. (1992) *Real Writing*. Sevenoaks: Hodder and Stoughton.

Ford, B. (1963) *Young Writers, Young Readers*. London: Hutchinson.

Forrestall, P. (1987) *Look it Up! A Practical Guide for Students of English*. Walton-on-Thames: Nelson.

Fox, C. (1993) *At the Very Edge of the Forest: The Influence of Literature on Storytelling by Children*. London: Cassell.

Frater, G. (2000) *Securing Boys' Literacy: A Survey of Effective Practice in Primary Schools*. London: Basic Skills Agency.

Frith, U. (1985) 'Developmental dyslexia', in Patterson, K. E. *et al.* (eds) *Surface Dyslexia*. New Jersey: Lawrence Erlbaum.

Fulton, D. (1998) *Style and Presentation: Information for Authors*. London: David Fulton Publishers.

Gentry, R. (1982) 'An analysis of developmental spelling in GNYS AT WRK'. *The Reading Teacher,* **36** (2).

Goodman, Y. (1984) 'The development of initial literacy', in Goelman, H., Oberg, A. and Smith, F. (eds) *Awakening to Literacy*. London: Heinemann.

Goswami, U. and Bryant, P. (1991) *Phonological Skills and Learning to Read*. New Jersey: Lawrence Erlbaum.

Goswami, U. (1991) 'Recent work on reading and spelling development', in Snowling, M. J. and Thompson, M. (eds) *Dyslexia: Integrating Theory and Practice*. London: Whurr Publishers.

Goswami, U. (1995) 'Rhyme in children's early reading', in Beard, R. (ed.) *Rhyme, Reading and Writing*. London: Hodder and Stoughton.

Graham, J. (1997) *Cracking Good Books: Teaching Literature at Key Stage Two*. Sheffield: NATE.

Graham, J. and Kelly, A. (1997) *Reading Under Control: Teaching Reading in the Primary School*. London: David Fulton Publishers.

Graham, L. (1995) *Writing Development: A Framework*. Croydon: Schools Advisory Service, London Borough of Croydon.

Graves, D. (1981) 'Renters and owners: Donald Graves on writing', in *English Magazine,* **8**, Autumn.

Graves, D. (1983) *Writing: Teachers and Children at Work*. New Hampshire: Heinemann.

Hackman, S. and Trickett, L. (1996) *Spelling 9–13*. London: Hodder and Stoughton.

Hall, N. and Robinson, A. (eds) (1996) *Learning about Punctuation*. Clevedon: Multilingual Matters.

Harding, D. (1937) 'The role of the onlooker', reprinted in Cashdan and Grugeon (*op. cit.*).

Hardy, B. (1977) 'Narrative as a primary act of mind', in Meek, M., Barton, G. and Warlow, A. (eds) *The Cool Web*. London: The Bodley Head.

Heath, S.B. (1983) *Ways with Words: Language, Life and Work in Communities and Classrooms*. Cambridge: Cambridge University Press.

Hester, H. with Ellis, S. and Barrs, M. (1993) *Guide to the Primary Learning Record*. London: CLPE.

Hoey, M. (1983) *On the Surface of Discourse*. London: Unwin Hyman.

Holbrook, D. (1964) *English for the Rejected*. Cambridge: Cambridge University Press.

Holbrook, D. (1967) *Children's Writing: A Sampler for Student Teachers*. Cambridge: Cambridge University Press.

Holdaway, D. (1979) *The Foundations of Literacy*. Sydney: Ashton Scholastic.

ILEA (1985) *The Volcano: Learning through Drama*. London: ILEA.

Irving, S. (1987) 'Spelling out success'. *Child Education*, May.

Jackson, A. and Lynch, L. (1997) *Using Multimedia to Develop Core Skills in Schools: An International Perspective*. London: Roehampton Institute for AZTEC.

Jarman, C. (1979) *The Development of Handwriting Skills*. Oxford: Blackwell.

Jarman, C. (1982) *Jarman Handwriting Scheme*. Hemel Hempstead: Simon and Schuster.

Johnson, P. (1995) *Children Making Books*. Reading: Reading and Language Information Centre, University of Reading.

Kress, G. (1982) *Learning to Write*. London: Routledge and Kegan Paul.

Kress, G. (1997) *Before Writing: Rethinking the Paths to Literacy*. London: Routledge.

Lane, S. and Kemp, M. (1967) *An Approach to Creative Writing*. London: Blackie.

Langdon, M. (1961) *Let the Children Write*. Harlow: Longman.

Langer, S. (1951) *Philosophy in a New Key*. (2nd edn). Cambridge, MA: Harvard University Press.

Laycock, L. (1996) 'Narrative and writing: young children's dictated stories'. *Early Childhood Development and Care*, **116**.

Lewis, M. and Wray, D. (1995) *Developing Children's Non-Fiction Writing*. Leamington Spa: Scholastic.

Liberman, I. and Shankweiller, D. (1985) 'Phonology and problems of learning to read and write', in *Remedial and Special Education*, **6**.

Lundberg, I. and Hoien, T. (2001) 'Dyslexia and phonology', in Fawcett, A. (ed.) *Dyslexia: Theory and Good Practice*. London: Whurr Publishers.

McKay, D. (ed.) (1970) *Breakthrough to Literacy*. Harlow: Longman.

Marshall, S. (1963) *An Experiment in Education*. Cambridge: Cambridge University Press.

Marshall, S. (1974) *Creative Writing*. Basingstoke: Macmillan.

Martens, P. and Goodman, Y. (1996) 'Invented punctuation', in Hall, N. and Robinson, A. (eds) *op. cit.*

Martin, J. R., Rothery, J. and Christie, F. (1987) 'Social processes in education: a reply to Sawyer and Watson (and others)', in Reid, I. (ed.) *The Place of Genre in Learning: Current Debates*. Deakin: Deakin University.

Maybury, B. (1967) *Creative Writing for Juniors*. London: Batsford.

Meek, M. (2001) 'Introduction', in Barrs, M. and Cork V. (2001) *The Reader in the Writer*. London: CLPE.

Michael, I. (1987) *The Teaching of English*. Cambridge: Cambridge University Press.

Miles, T.R. (1974) *Understanding Dyslexia*. Sevenoaks: Hodder & Stoughton.

Miles, T.R. (1983) *The Bangor Dyslexia Test*. Wisbech: Learning Development Aids.

Minns, H. (1990) *Read It to Me Now!* London: Virago.

Moffett, J. (1968) *Teaching the Universe of Discourse*. Boston: Houghton Mifflin.

Mudd, N. (1997) *The Power of Words*. Royston: UKRA.

National Writing Project (1989) *Responding to and Assessing Writing*. Walton-on-Thames: Nelson.

Ofsted (1993) *The Implementation of the Curricular Requirements of the Education Reform Act: English Key Stages 1, 2, 3, 4. Fourth Year, 1992–3: A Report of Her Majesty's Chief Inspector of Schools*. London: HMSO.

Ofsted (2002) *The National Literacy Strategy: The First Four Years 1998–2002*. London: Ofsted Publications Centre.

O'Reilly, W. and Bostock, A. (eds) (1986) *Ideas for Handwriting*. London: DCLD.

O'Sullivan, O. and Thomas, A. (2000) *Understanding Spelling*. London: CLPE.

Palmer, S. (1998) 'From A–Z', *Times Educational Supplement*, January–July.

Payton, S. (1984) 'Developing awareness of print', *Educational Review*, 2.

Perera, K. (1984) *Children's Writing and Reading: Analysing Classroom Language*. Oxford: Blackwell.

Perera, K. (1989) 'Grammatical differentiation between speech and writing in children aged 8 to 12', in Carter, R. (ed.) *Knowledge about Language and the Curriculum.* London: Hodder and Stoughton.

Peters, M. (1985) *Spelling: Caught or Taught? A New Look* (2nd edn). London: Routledge and Kegan Paul.

Pirrie, J. (1987) *On Common Ground.* London: Hodder & Stoughton.

Pratley, R. (1988) *Spelling it Out.* London: BBC Books.

QCA (1997) *Key Stage One English Tasks Teacher's Handbook.* London: QCA.

QCA (1998) *Can do Better: Raising Boys' Achievement in English.* London: QCA.

QCA (2000) *Curriculum Guidance for the Foundation Stage.* London: QCA.

QCA (2002) *Changes to Assessment 2003: Guidance for Teachers of Key Stages 1 and 2.* London: QCA.

QCA (2002) *Changes to Assessment 2003: Sample Materials for Key Stages 1 and 2.* London: QCA.

Ramsden, M. (1993) *Rescuing Spelling.* Devon: Southgate Publishers.

Read, C. (1971) 'Pre-school children's knowledge of English phonology', *Harvard Educational Review,* **41**.

Richardson, M. (1935) *Writing and Writing Patterns.* London: University of London Press.

Richmond, J. (1990) 'What writers need', in *Making Changes: Resources for Curriculum Development.* London: HMSO.

Rosen, M. (1989) *Did I Hear You Write?* London: Andre Deutsch.

Sassoon, R. (1983) *The Practical Guide to Children's Handwriting.* London: Thames and Hudson.

Sassoon, R. (1990) *Handwriting: The Way to Teach It.* Cheltenham: Stanley Thornes.

SCAA (1995a) *Consistency in Teacher Assessment: Exemplification of Standards in English: Key Stages 1 and 2, Reading and Writing.* London: SCAA.

SCAA (1995b) *Planning in Key Stage One and Two.* London: SCAA.

SCAA (1996a) *Desirable Outcomes for Children's Learning on Entering Compulsory Education.* London: SCAA.

SCAA (1996b) *Teaching English as an Additional Language: A Framework for Policy.* London: SCAA.

Scardamalia, M. and Bereiter, C. (1985) 'Development of dialectical processes in composition', in Olson, D. (ed.) *Literacy, Language and Learning.* Cambridge: Cambridge University Press.

Shayer, D. (1972) *The Teaching of English in Schools.* London: Routledge and Kegan Paul.

Sheffield, B.S. (1991) 'The structured flexibility of Orton-Gillingham'. *Annals of Dyslexia,* **41**.

Smith, F. (1982) *Writing and the Writer.* London: Heinemann.

Smith, F. (1984) 'The creative achievement of literacy', in Goelman, H., Oberg, A. and Smith, F. (eds) *Awakening to Literacy.* London: Heinemann.

Smith, P. and Inglis, A. (1984) *New Nelson Handwriting.* Walton-on-Thames: Nelson.

Snowling, M. J. (1995) 'Phonological Processing and Developmental Dyslexia' in *Journal of Research in Reading,* **18**.

Snowling, M., Stackhouse, J. and Rack, J. (1986) 'Phonological dyslexia and dysgraphia: developmental analysis', in *Cognitive Neuropsychology,* **3**.

Stein, J. (2001) 'The magnocellular theory of dyslexia', in *Dyslexia: An International Journal of Research and Practice,* **7**.

Street, B. (1995) 'Cross-cultural perspectives on literacy', in Maybin, J. (ed.) *Language and Literacy in Social Practice.* Clevedon: Multilingual Matters/Open University.

Styles, M. (1986) *Start-Write*. Cambridge: Cambridge University Press.

Teale, W. and Sulzby, E. (1986) *Emergent Literacy: Writing and Reading*. Norwood, NJ: Ablex.

Temple, C., Nathan, R. and Burris, N. (1982) *The Beginnings of Writing*. MA: Allyn and Bacon.

Torbe, M. (1995) *Teaching and Learning Spelling*, (3rd edn). London: Ward Lock.

Treiman, R. (1985) 'Onsets and rimes are units of spoken syllables': evidence from children', *Journal of Experimental Child Psychology*, **39**.

Treiman, R. (1993) *Beginning to Spell*. Oxford: Oxford University Press.

Tunnicliffe, S. (1984) *Poetry Experience*. London: Methuen.

Vellutino, F. R. (1979) *Dyslexia, Theory and Research*. Cambridge, MA: MIT Press.

Vygotsky, L. (1962) *Thought and Language*. Cambridge, MA: MIT Press.

Vygotsky, L. (1978) *Mind in Society*. Cambridge, MA: Harvard University Press.

Wajnryb, R. (1990) *Grammar Dictation*. Oxford: Oxford University Press.

Wells, G. (1987) *The Meaning Makers*. London: Hodder & Stoughton.

Whitehead, F. (1978) 'What's the use, indeed?'. *Use of English*, **29**(2).

Wilkinson, A. *et al.* (1980) *Assessing Language Development*. Oxford: Oxford University Press.

Wilkinson, A. (1986) *The Quality of Writing*. Milton Keynes: Open University.

Wood, D., Bruner, J. and Ross, G. (1976) 'The role of tutoring in problem solving'. *The Journal of Child Psychology and Psychiatry*, **17**.

Wray, D. and Lewis, M. (1997) *Extending Literacy: Children's Reading and Writing Non-Fiction*. London: Routledge.

Wyse, D. (1998) 'The development of composition', in *Primary Writing*, (Chapter 3). Buckingham: Open University Press.

CHILDREN'S BOOKS

Aardema, V. and Meddaugh, S. (1988) *Bimwili and the Zimwi*. London: Macmillan.

Aesop. *Aesop's Fables*. (trans. Handford, S.) (1993) Harmondsworth: Puffin Books.

Ahlberg, A. and Wright, J. (1980) *Mrs Plug the Plumber*. Harmondsworth: Puffin Books.

Ahlberg, J. and Ahlberg, A. (1986) *The Jolly Postman*. London: Heinemann.

Ahlberg, A. (1987) *The Clothes Horse*. London: Viking.

Aiken, J. (1996) *Cold Shoulder Road*. London: Red Fox Books.

Barber, A. and Bayley, N. (1990) *The Mousehole Cat*. London: Walker Books.

Bawden, N. (1973) *Carrie's War*. London: Gollancz.

Berry, J. and Brierley, L. (1994) *Celebration Song*. Harmondsworth: Puffin Books.

Browne, A. (1986) *Piggybook*. London: Julia MacRae.

Brunhoff, J. De (1934) *The Story of Babar, the Little Elephant*. London: Methuen.

Carle, E. (1970) *The Very Hungry Caterpillar*. London: Hamish Hamilton.

Carroll, L. and Browne, A. (1988) *Alice in Wonderland*. London: Julia MacRae

Cartwright, P. and Campbell, C. (1990) *The Diary of Neil Aitkin*. Leeds: Arncliffe.

Dahl, R. (1982) *The BFG*. London: Jonathan Cape.

Fine, A. (1989) *Bill's New Frock*. London: Methuen.

Hastings, S. and Wijngaard, J. (1985) *Sir Gawain and the Loathly Lady*. London: Walker Books.

Hawkins, C. and J. (1984) *Mig the Pig*. Harmondsworth: Puffin Books.

Hutchins, P. (1970) *Rosie's Walk*. London: The Bodley Head.

King-Smith, D. (1999) *Martin's Mice*. London: Puffin.

Magorian, M. and Ormerod, J. (1992) *Jump*. London: Walker Books.

Moore, I. (1990) *Six Dinner Sid.* Hove: Macdonald Young Books.
Morpurgo, M. (1995) *The Wreck of the Zanzibar.* London: Heinemann.
Murphy, J. (1982) *On the Way Home.* London: Macmillan.
Naughton, B. (1970) 'Spit Nolan', in *The Goalkeeper's Revenge and Other Stories.* Harmondsworth: Penguin.
Pearce, P. (1958) *Tom's Midnight Garden.* Oxford: Oxford University Press.
Pienkowski, J. (1984) *Christmas.* Harmondsworth: Walker Books.
Pullman, P. (2000) *The Amber Spyglass.* London: Scholastic.
Rosen, M. (1989) *The Bakerloo Flea.* London: Heinemann.
Rosen, M. (1995) *Walking the Bridge of Your Nose.* London: Kingfisher.
Rowling, J. K. (1997) *Harry Potter and the Philosopher's Stone.* London: Bloomsbury.
Rowling, J. K. (2000) *Harry Potter and the Prisoner of Azkaban.* London: Bloomsbury.
Scieszka, J. and Smith, L. (1989) *The True Story of the Three Little Pigs.* London: Viking Kestrel.
Story Chest (1980) *The Hungry Giant: The Monsters' Party.* Walton-on-Thames: Nelson.
Thomas, R. (1987) *The Runaways.* London: Hutchinson.
Westall, R. (1992) *Gulf.* London: Methuen.
White, E.B. (1952) *Charlotte's Web.* New York: Harper Collins.

ICT SOURCES

Don Johnston Special Needs, 18 Clarendon Court, Calver Road, Winwick Quay, Warrington, WA2 8QP. Tel: 01925 241642, Fax: 01925 241745; Apple Link: DJSN; Home Page: http://www.donjohnston.com/
Dorling Kindersley, DK Family Library, 1 Horsham Gates, North Street, Horsham, W. Sussex, RH13 5PJ, Tel: 01403 833200, Fax: 01403 274476. Email contact: customerservice@dk.com; website: www.dk.com
Europress: Thomas House, Hampshire International Business Park, Basingstoke, Hampshire, RG24 8WH. Tel: 01256 707727. email: info@europress.co.uk
Hunt, R. (1986) *Talking Stories for Stage 2; More Talking Stories for Stage 2; Talking Stories for Stage 3; More Talking Stories for Stage 3; Wren Stages 2 and 3 Talking Stories.* Oxford: Oxford University Press in conjunction with Sherston Software Ltd, Angel House, Sherston, Malmesbury, Wilts, SN16 0LH.
IT Learning Exchange: School of Education, University of North London, 166–220 Holloway Rd, London N7 8BD. Tel: 020 7753 5092. email: itle@unl.ac.uk
Oxford University Press (1997) *Oxford Compendium.* Oxford University Press: Great Clarendon St, Oxford, OX2 6DP. Tel: 01865 556767. email: enquiry@oup.co.uk
R-E-M, Great Western House, Langport, Somerset, TA10 9YU. Tel: 01458 253636.

Other useful websites:

www2.sherston.com
www.becta.org.uk/technology/software/index.html
www.cricksoftware.com/uk
www.softease.com

Author Index

Subject Index